THE POWER OF TEAMWORK

THE POWER OF TEAMWORK

How We Can All Work Better Together

BRIAN GOLDMAN, M.D.

Collins

Published by Collins, an imprint of HarperCollins Publishers Ltd

First edition

HarperCollins books may be purchased for educational, business,
or sales promotional use through our Special Markets Department.

HarperCollins Publishers Ltd
Bay Adelaide Centre, East Tower
22 Adelaide Street West, 41st Floor
Toronto, Ontario, Canada
M5H 4E3

www.harpercollins.ca

Library and Archives Canada Cataloguing in Publication

Title: The power of teamwork : how we can all work better together / Brian Goldman, M.D.
Names: Goldman, Brian, author. | Description: Includes index.
Identifiers: Canadiana (print) 20220135053 | Canadiana (ebook) 2022013507X
ISBN 9781443463997 (hardcover) | ISBN 9781443464000 (ebook)
Subjects: LCSH: Health care teams. | LCSH: Teams in the workplace.
Classification: LCC R729.5.H4 G65 2022 | DDC 362.1068—dc23

Printed and bound in Canada
FRS 9 8 7 6 5 4 3 2 1

To Elaine Bromiley,
whose tragic story inspired me to write this book

CONTENTS

THE POWER OF TEAMWORK

TEAMWORK

A group of individuals is not a team

D O YOU WORK on a team? For most of us, that's as banal a question as you'll get.

People in all walks of life talk about the importance of teamwork. In sports, it's the difference between winning and losing. At Fortune 500 companies, teamwork builds trust and fosters creativity, collaboration and risk-taking. In journalism, teamwork reduces errors and increases engagement with readers, radio and podcast listeners, and TV viewers.

A team may begin as a group of individuals who have different skills and experience and come from different backgrounds. But a group is not a team. To be a team, these individuals must be interdependent in terms of knowledge, abilities and the materials they work with. And they must work together to achieve a shared goal.

Many of us believe we work in teams because we work in groups. Sports franchises may be stacked with superstars yet never compete for the championship because they are no more than a group of talented individuals bent on pursuing individual awards. Other teams are made up of more mediocre talent yet win titles consistently because they set aside individual achievement in favour of team goals. With professional sports teams, the whole may be much more successful than the sum of its parts.

Team players leverage the talents of individual members. They complement one another. They help each other realize their true potential and create an atmosphere that encourages everyone to do better.

You don't have to play professional sports to know what I'm talking about. At your office, the people you work with constitute a group and not a team if they spend most of their time competing against one another for attention, plum assignments and accolades. It's not a team if only some members are acknowledged at meetings. It's not a team if the leader shuts down discussion when members ask difficult questions about departmental goals and strategies. It's not a team if regular meetings are the place where intriguing ideas go to die.

Once a pattern of anti-teamwork is established, it becomes a vicious cycle. You develop interpersonal habits that inhibit teamwork. You're insecure about the achievements of others because they are not seen as team achievements. Instead of teammates, you see rivals. At meetings, you want to outshine them. If that means criticizing others or snuffing out even helpful suggestions, so be it.

You may be thinking this is just the way things are, but you're wrong. Team-spiritedness can be kindled, but it requires conscious effort and a leap of faith.

Recently, I went to a story meeting for *White Coat, Black Art*, the CBC Radio show I've hosted for fifteen years. The show mixes field pieces with studio interviews that revolve around the experience of patients, their loved ones and health professionals in the context of modern medicine.

Everyone is supposed to come to these weekly meetings with new and fresh ideas for stories. They prep for the meeting by scouring news sources and by working their contacts for ideas, which they then pitch to the group. In a team culture, the other members of the team ask questions that sharpen the focus and help refine the pitch into a decent story idea for the show.

That's the theory. In practice, these meetings may reveal cracks in team cohesion. For one reason or another, story meetings can be showcases for rivalries within the group. There are many reasons for this, but the big one in my opinion is the tendency to fret about mistakes, to single out shortcomings while failing to recognize the unique talents and contributions of everyone on the team. In that sort of culture, everyone gets a meagre ration of praise until one mistake or another knocks them down a peg or two. It makes group members sensitive to criticism and defensive at story meetings. And it's for that reason that they become reluctant to make comments and suggestions. The team begins to fail.

As the only physician in a room full of journalists, my own insecurities have often made me wary of being contradicted on medical facts. I carried that insecurity into a recent story meeting with my team. For some time now, Canada has experienced a severe shortage of acute care nurses who work in emergency rooms (ERs), operating rooms (ORs) and intensive care units (ICUs). The shortage and the reasons for it have attracted lots of news coverage. Our show producer wanted pitches for stories that showed the impact of nurse shortages on the healthcare system.

I had heard about a small hospital in rural Ontario at which a shortage of ER nurses meant the hospital's CEO had to close the ER for most of a holiday weekend. My pitch was to do a field piece in which I visited the hospital to interview the CEO and the people working there.

"You aren't interviewing a nurse," said one of the producers, after hearing my proposal. "This is a story about nursing shortages, and you aren't interviewing a nurse."

The meeting fell silent.

To me, it felt like the moment in the Hans Christian Andersen story *The Emperor's New Clothes* when the child cries out that the emperor is naked. I could feel my face flushing with embarrassment and my thinking frontal lobes being taken offline. I was acutely sensitized to the producer's comment because it was the second time recently that she had raised an objection in a still, small voice that seemed to pack a wallop.

Later in the book, I'll show you a technique used by comedy improv partners to support one another onstage. Intentionally or not, the objection raised by the producer was not constructed to support my idea.

The thing is, up until that meeting, the producer and I had worked quite well together, which made these perceived critical barbs surprising. So surprising that in the first instance, I was unable to respond. But on this second occasion, something very different happened. In addition to feeling embarrassment, I kept my higher centres functioning by being curious.

I remembered the times when the producer and I had worked well together. Recently, the show had changed leaders. Perhaps the barb was less about sending a message to me and more about showing the new leader that she was capable of critical thinking.

"I know that it's important to get the viewpoint of nurses when doing a story about nursing shortages," I replied. "That's a great story idea that I dearly want to do on the show. But the leader asked us to pitch stories not on the nursing shortage and reasons why but on the impact of nursing shortages."

Then I uttered three words that I had never used before in a story meeting.

"Tell me more," I found myself asking. Those three words disarmed the barbs by asking for the critical thinking behind them. The producer began to elaborate on the original criticism. Instead of feeling threatened, I expressed appreciation to her for anticipating criticisms we might get from our listeners and from nurses. We began to support one another. We recognized one another's gifts. We became a team.

As you'll find out later in the book, the words "Tell me more" are part of a team-building technique called Visual Thinking Strategies (VTS), which creates a safe structure that empowers all members of the team to contribute to meetings.

===

I'VE SPENT CLOSE to four decades as a front-line emergency physician. When it comes to teamwork, healthcare is a special case, and I know a fair amount about modern medical culture. Almost every head nurse, dean of medicine or hospital executive I've met uses lofty rhetoric to extol the virtues of teamwork.

"Today's healthcare organizations are filled with skilled, multigenerational, and culturally diverse interdisciplinary team members," wrote Charlotte Davis, a surgical-trauma ICU nurse educator and clinical adjunct faculty member at Clayton State University, in a 2017 article for *Nursing Made Incredibly Easy!* "Although each specialty has a specific focus, we all share a unified goal: We want both the patient care experience and our work environment to be positive. To ensure that patients are satisfied during their healthcare encounter, we must embrace a teamwork approach to care delivery."

People in healthcare constantly talk up the benefits of teamwork while failing to comprehend what that means. This manifests itself in many ways.

For example, ask different health professionals about the team-spiritedness at hospitals and you will get some very different answers. Dr. Martin Makary and colleagues found that out when they surveyed operating room personnel at sixty hospitals across the United States for a study published in the *Journal of the*

American College of Surgeons in 2006. Surgeons rated the quality of collaboration and communication by fellow surgeons as "high" or "very high" 85 percent of the time. Nurses, on the other hand, rated their collaboration with surgeons as "high" or "very high" just 48 percent of the time.

Clearly, there's a disconnect between surgeons and nurses. Some of that may be due to some misconceptions about teamwork that need to be clarified.

In a high-performance cardiovascular operating room, the lead surgeon performs the organ transplant, the first assistant surgeon keeps the field of view free from blood, the anesthesiologist keeps the patient alive and unconscious on a ventilator, and the scrub nurse hands the surgeons instruments and (with other nurses) maintains a strict count of said instruments.

But a shared goal is fundamental. Everyone must feel as if they are joined in a common mission or struggle, or they don't function as a team.

Healthcare isn't about winning championships. It's the business of curing illness, repairing trauma and saving lives. When it's you or a loved one on the table in the OR, the stakes could not be greater.

When I set out to write my fourth non-fiction book, I had no intention of writing about the elemental need for teamwork in healthcare. Then a man named Martin Bromiley told me a story that completely changed my mind.

= = =

MARTIN BROMILEY HAS been a commercial airline pilot for more than a quarter of a century. He's accumulated just over 11,000 hours flying the Airbus A319, A320 and A321 for a major international airline based in the UK. As a training captain, he gets to instruct newly minted pilots in the simulator and in a real cockpit.

As an accomplished aviator and aviation instructor, Martin is steeped in knowledge about the power of teamwork. His interest is not just professional but deeply personal. This is because of his late wife, Elaine Bromiley.

High school sweethearts, the couple met when Elaine was sixteen and Martin three years older.

"She was very different to anybody else I'd met at that stage," says Martin. "She was full of life, very bubbly. She was probably more adventurous and more happy to travel, whereas I was quite reserved, I think."

Opposites attract, and Martin says he and Elaine hit it off straight away. They got married in 1989 in a little church near Aylesbury in Buckinghamshire. Elaine worked in the travel industry and the couple honeymooned in Hawaii. Their daughter, Victoria, was born in 1999 and their son, Adam, in 2001.

In 2004, Elaine caught a bad cold and developed a sinus infection. That led to a severe bout of periorbital cellulitis, an infection of the skin and soft tissues that surround the eyes. It's not a trivial infection. Complications include protrusion of the eyeball and meningitis. Elaine was admitted to hospital for IV antibiotics and recovered. It turns out she had a deviated septum that caused the sinus passages on one side of her face to get blocked.

"She saw a consultant in the hospital," says Martin. "And he said, 'I think we need to sort this out because otherwise you're going to be back in hospital again.' So that was where the plan came from, as it were."

The ear, nose and throat (ENT) surgeon booked Elaine for a functional endoscopic sinus surgery and a septoplasty. The plan was to straighten the cartilage between her nostrils to improve her breathing and the drainage of her sinuses, and thus make her less prone to sinusitis.

Endoscopic surgery is a form of keyhole, or minimally invasive, surgery performed entirely through the nostrils. The surgeon uses an endoscope, which is a thin camera rod with a light at the end, to illuminate, visualize and magnify the sinus tissues. The images are sent to a large video screen in the OR. The surgeon uses specialized instruments to cut and remove tissue blocking the sinuses (such as nasal polyps and scar tissue), to straighten the septum and to reduce the size of the turbinates (projections made of cartilage that sometimes block the nasal passages).

The procedure takes thirty to ninety minutes and can be done at a hospital, a doctor's office or a clinic. Since the operation does not involve cutting through the skin on the face, there is often very little post-operative pain. Most people go home the same day.

The procedure is done under local or general anesthesia.

"It so happened I was going to be off for two weeks at the start of Easter," Martin recalls. "It made sense to have the procedure done at the start of that two weeks off so I could look after the kids."

The surgery was booked for March 29, 2005.

"I don't think I was particularly nervous," he says. "If your partner goes into hospital, it's a bit nerve-wracking. But I didn't expect anything to go wrong."

Martin says they woke up at quarter past six the morning of the operation. Elaine was told to arrive at the hospital by 8:00 a.m. The plan was to take Elaine and their children to the private clinic located next to a publicly funded National Health Service (NHS) hospital.

"The kids would be with Mom prior to the procedure so they could see it wasn't anything scary, and then I'd take them home," Martin says.

The family arrived at the hospital at 7:45 a.m. They were escorted into a private room. Elaine changed into a gown with the children (six and five years old) by her side.

"Victoria was sitting on her mom's bed with Elaine reading a book to her," Martin recalls. "Adam had some toy cars playing on the window ledge."

Over the next thirty minutes, nurses came in to do vital signs. The anesthesiologist also came by.

"He was very jolly and pleasant and just did the usual check on her airway to give her various grades and scores, as it were," says Martin.

Elaine had fused vertebrae in her neck, and the anesthesiologist was concerned that her neck might be so stiff that it could make it more challenging to manage her airway during surgery. After examining her, the anesthesiologist pronounced himself happy with her neck mobility and left the room.

"As bizarre as it sounds, it was a fairly pleasant forty-five minutes," says Martin. "The kids were happy. Elaine was happy, although I'm sure nervous."

A nurse arrived at 8:30 a.m.

"'Right,'" Martin recalls the nurse saying. "'It's time to go off to the operating theatre.'"

The nurse wheeled Elaine's stretcher into the corridor, and the family followed behind.

"As we went down the corridor and her bed was wheeled, we were kind of side on but behind her," he says. "We couldn't see her face, but she put her hand out and just said, 'Bye.' And that was it."

That was the last time Martin Bromiley saw Elaine conscious.

= = =

WHAT HAPPENED NEXT comes from a 2005 report published in England by Professor Michael Harmer, an anesthesiologist and former head of the Department of Anaesthetics at the University of Wales College of Medicine.

There was nothing in Elaine's pre-operative anesthetic assessment that aroused concern. Her vital signs and blood tests were normal.

For the relatively brief procedure, the anesthesiologist chose a standard anesthetic gas called isoflurane carried in a mixture of nitrous oxide and oxygen. Because cutting inside the nose is painful, Elaine was to be given a strong but short-acting synthetic opioid called remifentanil.

For major surgical operations, the anesthesiologist administers a drug that paralyzes the muscles. That makes it easier to ventilate the patient with a mechanical ventilator. From the moment the patient receives a paralytic drug, she is unable to breathe on her own and must be ventilated by a mechanical device or hand-ventilated by the anesthesiologist.

Elaine was not given a paralytic drug. Still, general anesthetics and opioid pain relievers slow the breathing and impair the patient's natural ability to protect their airway and clear secretions. There is always a danger of respiratory distress. For longer procedures, the anesthesiologist usually inserts an endotracheal (or breathing) tube past the vocal cords and into the windpipe or trachea.

Because the procedure was to be brief, the anesthesiologist chose to use a different type of airway device called a laryngeal mask, or LMA. The LMA is inserted inside the mouth along the curve of the tongue as far as it can go and is then inflated. By design, it causes air to pass through the windpipe by blocking it from going into the esophagus.

Anesthesiologists use the LMA as a temporary airway for short procedures such as Elaine's. They also use it as a quick fix when it's difficult to insert a breathing tube and the patient's life is in danger.

At 8:35 a.m. the anesthesiologist gave Elaine remifentanil plus 200 mg of intravenous propofol, a rapid-acting anesthetic drug commonly used to induce anesthesia at the beginning of an operation.

In the ensuing fifty-four minutes, a relatively minor and routine procedure went completely awry.

First, the anesthesiologist tried inserting the LMA but could not because Elaine's jaw muscles were too tight to open her mouth wide enough. The doctor gave another 50 mg of propofol and tried again. He tried two sizes of LMAs and was unable to insert either.

Minutes later, Elaine, heavily sedated and with an unsecured airway, began to deteriorate rapidly. When a patient is under anesthesia, their oxygen level is measured using a pulse oximeter. It's a non-invasive device that tracks oxygen saturation. Oxygen saturation readings usually range between 95 and 100 percent. Values under 90 percent are considered low.

By 8:37 a.m., Elaine's oxygen saturation was 75 percent, and her skin complexion was blue. That indicates she had cyanosis, a medical condition caused by not having enough oxygen saturating the hemoglobin in her bloodstream. Her heartbeat was rapid due to lack of oxygen.

At 8:39 a.m., her oxygen saturation level had dropped to 40 percent, an acute emergency. At that level, vital organs (especially the brain) are at immediate risk of damage.

By 8:41 a.m., the anesthesiologist had put the LMA aside. For two minutes, he tried to increase Elaine's oxygen by inserting an oropharyngeal (or oral) airway—a device that prevents the tongue from blocking the epiglottis—and administering 100 percent oxygen via a facemask. This is basic life support that all first responders use when they find a patient in acute distress.

These techniques also failed, and Elaine's oxygen saturation remained around 40 percent. At this point, Elaine's heart rate dropped to the lower forties, indicating the vital organs were not getting enough oxygen to function. The anesthesiologist then attempted to pass an endotracheal tube into Elaine's windpipe. He administered a dose of a drug called atropine to raise her slow heart rate. He also gave a paralytic drug to relax Elaine's neck and chest muscles to make it easier to pass the breathing tube.

At around 8:45 a.m. a second anesthesiologist came from a nearby operating room to help. After giving the paralytic drug, the first step to intubation is to insert a device called a laryngoscope to shine a light on the vocal cords, and over which the endotracheal tube is passed. But when they inserted the device, they were unable to see the vocal cords. That fact by itself would make it more difficult to secure Elaine's airway and give her oxygen.

About this time, other staff were summoned to help, including Elaine's ENT surgeon. The two anesthesiologists could not see the vocal cords, and they could not ventilate Elaine with the fresh oxygen her vital organs needed.

Doctors call this a "can't intubate, can't ventilate" scenario; it is a recognized emergency in anesthesiology practice for which guidelines are available. Despite this, between 8:47 and 8:50 a.m., both anesthesiologists tried again and again to intubate Elaine. The second anesthesiologist tried inserting a fibre-optic flexible scope, but a pool of blood inside the throat blocked his view. With Elaine's oxygen saturation level perilously low, her heart rate began to slow once again.

At this time, a nurse told the anesthesiologists that an ICU bed had been reserved for Elaine at the NHS hospital next door. As well, a nurse arrived in the room carrying a tracheostomy tray, and advised the doctors of that fact. A tracheostomy, or surgical airway, is a standard procedure to open a hole in a patient's windpipe to provide oxygen directly to the lungs. It is indicated when endotracheal intubation is not an option or fails. It's what you do when you "can't intubate" and "can't ventilate" the patient.

Between 8:51 and 8:55 a.m., the ENT surgeon continued trying to intubate Elaine. He could see the very end of the top part of the vocal cords and tried passing a long, flexible device called a bougie through the vocal cords, over which a breathing tube could be threaded. He too was unsuccessful. Elaine's oxygen saturation remained at 40 percent.

There was yet another attempt with a device called an intubating LMA. Using that technique, the doctors were able, with difficulty, to ventilate Elaine. Finally, her oxygen saturation rose to 90 percent, with an improvement in her heart rate and blood pressure.

The doctors gave Elaine a dose of a corticosteroid drug called dexamethasone to help protect the brain from damage due to low oxygen.

At 9:10 a.m., the doctors decided to abandon the operation and allow Elaine to wake up from the anesthetic. Between 9:13 and 9:29 a.m., the remifentanil infusion that was keeping her sedated was stopped to enable Elaine to breathe on her own. The intubating LMA was removed and an oral airway reinserted. Elaine's oxygen saturations gradually improved to 95 percent, but her blood pressure and heart rate remained markedly elevated.

Elaine began breathing on her own with the oral airway in place, and she was transferred to the recovery room. The anesthesiologist thought Elaine was showing signs of waking up and was breathing in a normal manner.

During the various attempts to establish an airway, Elaine's oxygen saturation remained perilously low for some twenty minutes. That was all it took.

===

MARTIN BROMILEY SAYS the phone rang at around 11:00 a.m. His brother had come to the city to visit the family and was with Martin at home.

"I was so busy with the kids and my brother that I'd forgotten, actually," he says. "It sounds strange to say, but when the phone rang it was a bit of a surprise."

It was Elaine's ENT surgeon on the phone. This was the first conversation between the two men.

"I can't remember the exact words, but he said that she was coming round from the procedure, but she hadn't woken up properly," Martin recalls.

"Do you want me to come in?" he remembers asking the specialist.

"Yes, I think that would be better," came the reply.

"It didn't sound that bad, but obviously I was a bit nervy at that point," says Martin, who left the kids with his brother and made the twenty-five-minute drive to the hospital.

Staff took him to the room that had been Elaine's that morning.

"If you just wait here, the doctors will be with you in a moment," Martin recalls someone telling him. The ENT surgeon and the anesthesiologist arrived shortly after.

"We had some problems with the procedure, but my colleague who knows more about it will tell you all about it," said the surgeon.

"The anesthetist basically said that they had problems with her airway, and they decided that it was probably not working out properly," recalls Martin. "He said they were struggling to get oxygen to her lungs and that they couldn't get a tube down."

Today, Martin Bromiley probably knows as much about the "can't intubate, can't ventilate" scenario as any anesthesiologist. But this was 2005, and he was a commercial pilot, not a doctor.

"I had seen a program a year previously," he says. "It was a short news item about tracheostomies. And I knew that was a way of getting air into the body."

His curious and inquisitive mind was doing frantic cartwheels.

"Did you think about a tracheostomy?" Martin had the presence of mind to ask the doctors.

"No, no," one of them replied. "The oxygen levels were low, but they were fluctuating, so she was never on low oxygen levels for a sustained period. So the safer option was to let her wake up. But unfortunately, she's not waking up as quickly as we thought.

So as a precaution, we've transferred her across to the intensive care unit."

To Martin, this didn't sound so dire. The doctors left the room, and a nurse escorted him down the corridors and out a back door.

"As she led me, the nurse turned to me and said, 'Are you okay?'" Martin recalls. "That seemed a really strange question to ask at the time."

The short walk to the high-security unit felt rushed.

"Press the buzzer, tell them who you are," he recalls the nurse saying. "They'll come and get you. [I] hope everything's okay."

She turned and walked away.

"I pressed the buzzer and a female voice answered and I said who I was, and she said, 'We're just working with your wife,'" Martin remembers. He was told to wait in a nearby room.

Martin says the phrase "working with your wife" gave him a mental image of Elaine sitting up in bed chatting as nurses walked around her plugging things in and doing all that sort of stuff.

He sat there waiting for fifteen minutes in a small, square room just off the entrance to the ICU. Two doctors appeared: one male and one female.

"What do you think has happened?" Martin recalls the male doctor asking him.

"Well, I gather there have been some problems and she's not waking up properly," Martin recalls answering.

"Your wife has been without oxygen for a significant period of time," said the female doctor. "We're looking at significant brain damage."

That was Tuesday, March 29, 2005. A brain scan done five days later confirmed the doctors' suspicions. A day later, one of the consultants looking after Elaine told Martin it was time to start thinking about withdrawing life support.

Martin says he agreed with the consultant immediately because he and Elaine had discussed that very question two years earlier.

"I don't remember what prompted it," says Martin. "It might have been a television program or something like that. It was just one of those in-the-moment conversations. What would you want? Both of us said we wouldn't want to be in a vegetative state."

Elaine Bromiley died at 11:45 p.m. on April 11, 2005.

Martin assumed there would be an investigation, as happens following aviation mishaps. The head of the ICU told him that this seldom happens unless someone sues or complains about the care received. The ENT consultant told him the difficulty intubating and ventilating Elaine was exceptionally rare and could not have been anticipated.

But the ICU doctor was sympathetic to Martin. He was the one who got Professor Michael Harmer to lead an investigation into what happened by interviewing everyone involved. The chronology was released in July 2005, three months after Elaine's death.

In the months and years that followed, Martin Bromiley met with experts in aviation, medicine and human factors engineering—the burgeoning field that focuses on how fallible human beings interact with technology and systems in the real world. Eventually, he founded the Clinical Human Factors Group, a registered charity that works with healthcare professionals, managers and service users partnering with experts in human factors from healthcare and other industries to campaign for improvements in healthcare.

A coroner's inquest confirmed the "can't intubate, can't ventilate" scenario had occurred during those failed attempts at intubation, and also determined that the management of the emergency did not follow then current or any recognized guidance. Too much time was taken trying to intubate the trachea rather than concentrating on ensuring adequate oxygenation.

"It is hard to understand why Dr A, and those with him, persevered in trying to intubate the trachea when standard teaching would be to ensure oxygenation within three minutes of the start of severe hypoxia," wrote Professor Harmer in his report. "The clinicians became oblivious to the passage of time and thus lost opportunities to limit the extent of damage caused by the prolonged period of hypoxia. Not all the clinicians were aware that there was a problem with ventilating Mrs. Bromiley. Surgical airway access should have been considered and carried out."

Those are the hard facts that led to Elaine Bromiley losing her life. Since her death, Martin has worked hard to make doctors aware of the "can't intubate, can't ventilate" scenario. Later in this book, we'll explore how simulation training and crew resource management (CRM)—protocols and approaches borrowed from aviation—can better prepare doctors to face rare situations like what happened to Elaine.

I've placed the story of Elaine Bromiley at the front of this book not only for those lessons but for what it says about healthcare's ambivalence towards teamwork. Although his motivations are more urgent, Martin Bromiley, like me, has spent a lot of time trying to get inside the heads of my colleagues. What he says about healthcare and teamwork is revealing.

"I talk to doctors, nurses and other health professionals about teamwork, or more importantly, they tell me about teamwork," he says. "They describe a situation where a number of people in a team have very set technical roles, whether that be a surgeon, an anesthesiologist, a theatre nurse or whatever it might be. They have certain things to do, and that would probably be defined as good teamwork. To me, that's a very shallow or functional view of teamwork. And then, if we all do it in the right order, everything will be fine. For me, teamwork is much more about the human-to-human connection. It's about how we look out for each other, how we understand each other and how we're able to think through somebody else's eyes, ears or point of view."

When Elaine Bromiley's oxygen saturation lingered at a level incompatible with life, there were three highly trained professionals in the OR with more than sixty combined years of clinical experience. Each, in turn, had a go at trying to secure her airway, but you can argue that the three did not function as a team.

"An airway management crisis, such as the 'can't intubate, can't ventilate' situation, highlights the importance of effective team collaboration for good patient outcomes," says Dr. Johannes Huitink, an anesthesiologist from the Netherlands. Huitink is the founder and director of the Airway Management Academy, a global initiative to increase patient safety during airway management through medical education. "A team is needed because there are multiple tasks to be performed within minutes. The diversity of experience of the team members allows a team to see risks and opportunities from different angles so that it can come up with new solutions and adapt dynamically to changing situations."

That would have included recognizing the "can't intubate, can't ventilate" scenario in time to have saved Elaine Bromiley's life. None of the experienced doctors involved had the situational awareness to bail on "Plan A" and formulate a new plan on the fly—or even to ask for help. There was no leader in the room. And yet there were followers who could have helped. At least two nurses did know about that scenario, and said so, but were ignored. Or perhaps they spoke too quietly because that's what you do when you lack standing in a rigid hierarchy.

"There was a very clear case of teamwork breakdown here, where you had a number of people who knew what was happening, who could see what needed to happen, but were simply unable to influence the outcome," says Martin. "And so teamwork wasn't really a thing in those days. It was just, you do your job and that's good teamwork. But that's not what it is at all."

===

I'VE WRITTEN THIS book because I believe that a lot of us think we work in teams when what we really mean is groups. And that's a problem for several reasons.

Unlike a team, a group is not primed to notice and share information about a problem, like a patient who cannot be intubated or ventilated. Members of a group may not want to look too closely, because if they notice something, they might feel compelled to say something about it. They may not want to call attention to it because they may be wrong. Or they don't want to call it out because they may be right and don't want to deal with the implications. In healthcare, accepting help is sometimes seen as a sign of weakness, and offering help is seen as a veiled accusation of incompetence.

Dr. Huitink doesn't think teamwork is only for sports teams.

"Good teamwork can be compared to baseball champions," he says. "It's not that they hit only home runs; it's that they have more at-bats and can play different positions as needed."

This may surprise you, but even now, in medical culture, teamwork is assumed rather than discussed and taught. One person trying to change that is Dr. Teodor Grantcharov, professor of surgery at the University of Toronto and the Keenan Chair in Surgery at St. Michael's Hospital in Toronto. Dr. Grantcharov is the inaugural director of the International Centre for Surgical Safety—a multidisciplinary group of visionary scientists with expertise in design, human factors, computer and data science, and healthcare research.

"Teamwork makes so much sense intuitively," he says. "It's unbelievable that we have to talk about it today. We don't need to wait for research to understand that the role of the team is critical to success or failure."

Surgeons are often judged by their technical skill. Grantcharov is one of a very few practising surgeons who studies the non-technical skills necessary for teamwork in the OR—things like communication and leadership situational awareness, both of which might have changed the outcome for Elaine Bromiley.

"We found out how important non-technical skills are not only to the surgeon but the entire team, and how significantly the non-technical performance of team members influences the performance of the surgeon," he says. "It supports the theory that our performance is not isolated. It not only depends on our own skills and abilities, but on lots of other factors that can make a difference between life and death."

= = =

OUTSIDE OF HEALTHCARE, most people believe they work in teams. A 2019 Deloitte survey titled "Organizational Performance: It's a Team Sport" found a whopping 96 percent of those asked said at least some of their work is done in teams.

"The shift from hierarchies to cross-functional teams is well underway," the survey's authors wrote. "Our data shows that adopting team structures improves organizational performance for those that have made the journey; organizations that have not risk falling further behind."

Elaine Bromiley died in 2005. In the interim, some doctors have come to understand the value of teamwork.

Dr. Daniela Lamas is a respirologist and critical care physician at Brigham and Women's Hospital in Boston. Lamas leads a team taking care of critically ill patients in the hospital's medical intensive care unit. And she loves it.

"The ICU is an extraordinarily team-based specialty, which is probably one of the reasons that it appealed to me initially," she says. "Being a solo doctor in an outpatient practice is so much less appealing to me, because I enjoy the teamwork nature."

That said, Lamas leads an ICU team at a hospital whose management structure is hierarchical, as it was in the hospital where Elaine

Bromiley met her fate. As an attending physician (a physician who has completed residency and who practises in a hospital or clinic), Lamas is at the pinnacle of her team. Other members include a fellow (undertaking additional training to follow in Lamas's footsteps), senior and junior doctors, and medical students, not to mention nurses, respiratory therapists, pharmacists, social workers and others.

But Lamas also says the hierarchy in which she works is collaborative. "I know a lot about the hierarchical part of medicine because that's the culture in which I trained," she says.

Later in the book, we'll discuss the disastrous consequences for patients who are cared for in a rigid hierarchical system.

When I ask Lamas what she means by collaboration, she tells me a story from early in her ICU training.

"We had this twenty-year-old girl who had overdosed on acetaminophen," Lamas recalls. "She was clearly the sickest patient in our ICU by the time she came in."

Lamas says the acetaminophen had damaged the young woman's liver, which in turn had caused her blood to stop clotting. Other possible adverse effects included brain swelling.

"The fear with an acetaminophen overdose is that it causes liver failure," she says. "You could need a transplant. You could die from this."

The initial management of severe acetaminophen overdose is to give an antidote to try to prevent serious consequences. This particular patient was way past that, however, which is why she was in the ICU fighting for her life. Lamas's goals were to provide supportive care while managing the complications.

"I felt like I was going to be the sole person in charge of her ultimate outcome," she recalls. "I remember rushing into the room and saying, 'All right. I've got to get a central line in. I have to get access so we can give her the blood and stuff she needs.'"

Her take-charge attitude came from a hospital ethos that gave junior residents a lot of autonomy to manage patients, with the expectation that they would sink or swim. She tried but could not put the line in.

Lamas was getting anxious for her patient's welfare when something amazing (to her) happened.

"My attending stepped in," she says. "She started to try to get a line, and then she had trouble. She paged another attending from the other side of the unit, who came in. In the interim, another doctor on the ICU team took care of all the other patients."

People from all around the ICU offered to help without being asked and without complaining. They stabilized the patient, and she got a liver transplant, and the rest of the ICU was run smoothly.

True, there were also people who rushed in from other ORs to offer assistance as Elaine Bromiley's condition deteriorated. But each of these separate ORs worked concurrently and were not interdependent. They weren't a team. By contrast, everyone working alongside Lamas in the ICU that day felt part of a single enterprise.

"I remember thinking, 'Oh, I want to be part of a team like this forever,' which is why I ended up doing a critical care fellowship," says Lamas.

What Lamas experienced in that ICU is not universal, and she's thought a lot about what makes an ICU team more or less good. "I don't think it can be just the whims of personality clicking, though that of course makes for one team being a lot more fun than another," she says. "But I also think it's the structure of the ICU . . . knowing that you are all in this place where people are sick, and nobody's going to get to go home until all the work gets done. Think of it as your weirdest summer camp ever. You can't leave. This is where you are, and these are the people who are there with you, and you're going to make the best of it, and you're going to work hard because everybody's invested in the goal, which is not a hard goal to get behind: let's try to do the best thing we can for these people and make anyone better who can get better."

As you'll find out in the pages that follow, that sense of shared purpose is critical. Every member of the team has a stake in the outcome. More than that, the best teams experience a kind of group ecstasy for a job well done. You'll see more than one example of that too.

Leadership is also important.

"It's something that I think about a lot: trying to command respect, but also to lead in a way that makes it so that the intern isn't scared to talk on rounds when they might be wrong," says Lamas.

These are elements that weren't present the day Elaine Bromiley went in for surgery. And they certainly aren't present in every OR, ICU, ER and clinic around the world. But there are plenty of signals that teamwork is changing healthcare for the better.

Teamwork is making healthcare safer and more effective for patients. It is also making things more inclusive for patients and their families. Teamwork has the potential to reduce burnout and improve job satisfaction for doctors, nurses and others who work inside hospitals, as well as for the paramedics who patrol the streets in ambulances.

Recently, I have felt more like part of the team when I'm on duty in the ER. Nurse practitioners (NPs) and physician assistants (PAs) help foster teamwork. Nurse practitioners have an independent scope of practice somewhere between that of a registered nurse and that of a family doctor. In the ER where I work, they confer with me regarding diagnosis and treatment. Physician assistants do many of the things NPs and MDs do, except they work under the direct supervision of physicians.

When I work alongside PAs and NPs, it feels like I'm working on a team. Diagnoses come easier on teams compared to when I work by myself. It's more fun and more satisfying to work on a team.

Working on a team is a transcendent experience. Once you have it, you don't want to go back to working in a group or alone.

In this book, we will travel alongside health professionals who are making the long and surprising journey from solo artist to team player. From art curators to aviation engineers, we will meet the teamwork experts who are showing health professionals how to suspend their need to shine as individuals and put their trust in the team. And we'll also meet the healthcare people who have taken teamwork to such a rarified level that they now give lessons to people in such diverse fields as entertainment, law enforcement, journalism and automobile repair.

This book was pitched, researched and written during the worst pandemic in a century. There is no question that COVID-19 has been both a catalyst and an accelerant for teamwork in healthcare. But this is not a book about the coronavirus. It's a book about how we can do a better job and become our most transcendent selves through teamwork.

Before we begin to assemble the building blocks of teamwork inside and outside of healthcare, we need to explore some basics. Teamwork is a form of collective consciousness that may be highly developed in humans, but it began much earlier in our evolution.

CHAPTER ONE

JUGGLERS AND NAVY SEALS

*Super-efficiency, the economy of effort
and the science of teams*

Each fall, Canada geese fly south to stay warm, and each spring, they make the return trip north to their breeding sites. They fly in a distinctive V-shaped pattern, with the leader at the apex.

There are several reasons why Canada geese would not get as far if they weren't team players. Each bird flies slightly above the bird in front. This reduces wind resistance and makes flying easier for the birds that bring up the rear. These birds also take turns leading the flock and spelling off their tired colleagues, who get a break by flying at the back. The V pattern also makes it easier to coordinate changes in velocity and direction and to communicate quickly.

Birds that take to the air alone have a harder time of it. "Energy Saving in Flight Formation," a 2001 study published in *Nature*, found that pelicans that fly solo beat their wings more frequently and have faster heart rates than those that fly in formation.

African lions hunt in teams and have success catching antelopes, wildebeest and elephants. One lion spots the prey while the others observe. When their intended prey arrives, the lions encircle it. One lion uses its claws to scratch the rear of the hunted animal, and the others kill through bites to the throat or neck.

"Ant Groups Optimally Amplify the Effect of Transiently Informed Individuals," a 2015 study by researchers at Israel's Weizmann Institute of Science and published in *Nature Communications*, found that longhorn crazy ants coordinate their efforts to pull heavy items of various shapes in one direction.

It's all in the interests of super-efficiency. The term describes the result when the work output of animals in teams is greater than the sum of each contributor.

Dr. Edson Filho doesn't study ants, lions or Canada geese. But the sports psychologist and associate professor of sport psychology and counselling at Boston University's Wheelock College of Education and Human Development knows all about super-efficiency as a driver of teamwork in humans. Filho has authored more than eighty peer-reviewed manuscripts and book chapters, and has given advice to Olympic athletes, a Nobel Peace Prize winner, Cirque du Soleil artists and many other elite performers. He has also studied top performers, including elite surgeons who work alone and in teams.

Filho uses functional MRI and other imaging techniques to measure brain activity. It turns out that the seat of teamwork and the super-efficiency that elite performers demonstrate lurks between the ears. That's why it is also called "neural efficiency."

"For the same level of work, the best brain surgeons are using much less of their brains because they've learned over time to activate only the areas they need to activate," says Filho. "It's the same thing in group work. Once we develop coordination, cohesion and collective efficacy, there is a gain or a surplus in theory. Super-efficiency."

Filho says super-efficiency looks different depending on the type of performance one measures. Filho is a soccer fan, which explains his real-world examples. His favourite players are forward Lionel Messi, who plays as a forward for Ligue 1 club Paris Saint-Germain and captains the Argentinian national team, and Andrés Iniesta Luján, a Spanish professional footballer who plays as a central midfielder and is the captain of the Vissel Kobe club with the J1 League.

"If you were watching Messi and Iniesta playing together back in the day, they shared the tactics, they shared the fundamentals of soccer, but they also complemented each other," says Filho. "If Iniesta passed the ball to Messi, he knew Messi would be able to control it and score. What is interesting is that we can also see that in the brain."

If you were to scan the brains of star athletes who play well together on a team, you'd notice something interesting: the more they are in sync with one another, the more the same areas of the brain light up. Jugglers too, Filho says, but with an intriguing difference.

"We've done research on co-operative jugglers," says Filho. "When they are co-operating, there are shared neural pathways that activate the same areas of the brain, but there are also complementary areas that activate so they can complement one another's actions."

Sports, gymnastics, juggling—it doesn't matter. The aim of peak teamwork is to enter a state in which the quality of the performance is better than what any member of the team can do on their own, and with less effort. It is wired into the human brain.

"Teamwork succeeds because they [teams] divide the labour," he says. "The division of labour aligns with what you call shared knowledge and complementary knowledge or mental models. For a team to work, we need shared as well as complementary ideas, values and skills."

In animals, teamwork is instinctive. Humans, on the other hand, have giant frontal lobes that provide self-awareness, memory language and a capacity to envision and plan for the future. For us, teamwork is part instinct and part conscious choice. Filho says peak performers wage a constant internal battle between teamwork and going it alone.

But how do those frontal lobes factor into the decision to value super-efficiency and the desire and, ultimately, the choice (not instinct) to achieve it?

Filho says the answer likely comes from what's known as the social brain hypothesis. Proposed by British anthropologist and evolutionary psychologist Robin Dunbar, this hypothesis helps explain why humans and other primates developed large frontal lobes to manage complex social systems. Their large brains facilitate teamwork and other social interactions as a matter of survival.

Still, when it comes down to teamwork or going solo, Filho says we need both. But the choice is a matter of trust.

"You might be very confident in your own efficacy, but you don't trust your team's collective efficacy," he says. "Sometimes, you have to improve the performance of the athlete and sometimes you have to improve the performance of the team. Sometimes you fire the coach, sometimes it's the team. Sometimes you need to sign different players. Sometimes it's the team's management. If you want to improve individuals and group performance, you need to know the psychology of the 'I' and the psychology of the 'we.'"

A big part of that psychology has to do with motivation. No matter how virtuous teamwork seems, you cannot assume people (physicians included) will automatically choose teamwork if given the option. Even if they trust their teammates.

Often, the choice comes down to the upfront cost. In a 1992 paper published in the *Quarterly Journal of Economics*, American economists Gary S. Becker and Kevin M. Murphy of the University of Chicago discussed the *coordination costs* of teamwork in an era of increased knowledge specialization. The more people specialize, the narrower their expertise and the greater the need to coordinate one's knowledge with that of others.

Wolves and lions also need to coordinate their actions or fail on the hunt.

In humans, teammates with complementary strengths and abilities must put time and energy into figuring out who does what. This is true of healthcare teams, first responders, special police units, sports teams, circus acrobats and jugglers. For instance, to optimize the overall performance, a superior juggler figures out that they must compensate for the shortcomings of a weaker partner.

"If you throw the ball a little bit off, I can move to compensate," Filho says. To do that, better and weaker jugglers must practise together. These and other factors make up the coordination cost.

Filho and colleagues tallied the coordination cost in an ingenious study. They recruited forty-eight men in their twenties and assembled them into twenty-four pairs. A pair, or dyad, is the smallest possible team. Participants in this study had to have at least thirty hours of experience playing *FIFA* 17—a sports video game in the FIFA (Fédération Internationale de Football Association) series developed by Electronic Arts and released in September 2016.

"We picked *FIFA* 17 because we talked to people who would want to play," he says.

Another reason for choosing a video game to study teamwork is that it enables researchers to collect data from each player with a high degree of reliability.

Participants played *FIFA* 17 while hooked up to a heart rate monitor and an EEG (electroencephalogram), the latter of which measured brainwaves and did thermal brain scans to measure brain activity. Participants played games solo or in teams against a computer or one another.

Compared to when playing alone, when the participants played in teams, their heart rates became more variable and their brainwaves showed more beta activity, which means they had higher arousal or vigilance. The initial cost of collaboration was an increase in stress.

"There was a cost of playing as a dyad," Filho says. "As you play with someone, you have to activate new areas of your brain to meet that coordination cost."

But as the players figured out who was better at tactics and who had better hand-eye coordination, the teamwork part got easier.

"We found that over time, they communicated better," he says. "They listened more and didn't talk over one another. We also saw the development of coordination and shared knowledge."

As dyads, the players' performances got better with less effort.

"As you play together, your brain is starting to automatically adapt to the task, so you only act as needed," he says. "That is called 'economy of effort.' We know from evolution theory that economy of effort is a good thing."

That's one study in one experimental model. But there is plenty of evidence across the board that teamwork makes for better results with less effort.

Edson Filho is a rising star among academic sports psychologists. His 2013 doctoral thesis on team cohesion won the American Psychological Association Dissertation Award in Sport, Exercise & Performance Psychology.

"Essentially, I proposed an integrated framework of team dynamics linking cohesion, team mental models, collective efficacy and team performance," Filho said recently in a faculty spotlight article posted in January 2021 on the Boston University Wheelock website. "It is rewarding to see that my work has generated substantial research from other scholars around the world."

Moreover, he says teamwork has been shown to produce better results across nearly every domain.

"I've looked at it in sports, special forces in the military, and in entertainment," he says. "I look across the board and the science is there."

It's certainly true among successful Fortune 500 companies. One technique that helps ensure strong teamwork is to have employees switch roles on the team to make it easier to mesh. The initial loss of efficiency when employees assume unfamiliar roles is the coordination cost. That it pays off in better teamwork makes the coordination cost an investment.

So if teaming up leads to super-efficiency and, in turn, better workflow, better results and better social cohesion, why do humans often choose not to work in teams? Perhaps it comes down to people being unwilling to pay the coordination cost.

"The short-term versus long-term trade-off is a difficult one that is likely determined by both individual and team factors," says Filho.

He says the task itself is often the deciding factor.

"I think it is all about task difficulty," he says. "Complex tasks require teamwork. We cannot build a skyscraper or send a rocket to the moon on our own."

There is no reason why teamwork can't work in healthcare. Still, the evidence for teamwork in healthcare has been lacking. Filho has identified at least two differences between healthcare and other domains in which teamwork has a proven track record. One of them has to do with goals and objectives.

"In sports, there are outcomes," he says. "You win the team championship. In healthcare, I'm not sure that the outcome is as clear and obvious as that."

As a patient, or the loved one of a patient, you might be troubled to learn that healthcare providers don't feel as if they've won a championship every time they do something good for patients. As a forty-year veteran, I'm not surprised that healthcare teams may only feel like they've captured the big prize when they do something special, like a multi-organ transplant or resuscitating a patient following cardiac arrest.

Filho thinks there's another factor in healthcare that gets in the way of teamwork: lack of a designated leader in most situations.

"In sports there is clear leadership," he says. "There is a clear coach and assistant coaches and a clear manager. There are peer leaders like team captains, starters and substitutes. All these factors are different in healthcare, and that impacts team performance and team dynamics."

Remember Elaine Bromiley? Two experienced anesthesiologists and one skilled ENT surgeon worked feverishly in a solo kind of way and were unable to recognize the "can't intubate, can't ventilate" scenario. There did not appear to be someone acting as the leader during that crisis.

Across healthcare, there is not a lot of talk about leadership, or coordination cost, for that matter.

"To be honest, I'm not sure if people in healthcare appreciate all of these concepts," says Filho.

There could be systemic reasons why healthcare professionals may not want to invest time and energy in coordination costs. They may be prepared to put the effort in once or twice, but if absenteeism and staff turnover are high, they might find themselves having to pay coordination costs monthly.

Dr. Teodor Grantcharov is one of a very few surgeons to say out loud that team and individual performance are inextricably linked. He is the driving force behind the development of the Operating Room Black Box (ORBB). Patterned after cockpit flight data recorders that are mandatory aboard all commercial aircraft, the ORBB is intended to improve patient safety and standardize the training of future surgeons and anesthesiologists. Already, the device, which records terabytes of OR data, has given Grantcharov precious insights on OR teams.

"I'm the same person, but today my performance could be amazing and tomorrow my performance could be terrible," he says. "The difference is the team, the people who are on the team and how we made each other better or worse."

Grantcharov says the impact of teamwork on his own performance is striking.

"There are days when I need to really give 100 percent of my effort to manage the team," he says. "And there are other days when the team picks me up. No matter what happens, I know that I will not be the only person standing between success and failure. No matter how much error and failure and variability we face, we will still ensure good clinical outcomes simply because the team adds that level of resilience that protects all of us."

Part of that resilience is what Edson Filho calls "team cohesion." That's what happens when a team remains united while working to achieve a common goal. For this to happen, everyone on the team needs to believe they have contributed to its overall success.

"Some coaches in soccer are very good at developing cohesion, but they are awful at developing collective efficacy," says Filho. "Others give a lot of confidence to players, but they are not good at creating cohesion, so the team breaks."

It's that hit-and-miss aspect of teamwork in the OR (and the rest of the hospital, for that matter) that should concern all of us.

"In every domain it's the same thing," says Filho. "For every different team, you have to figure out the deep processes that are problematic and how they interact. From there, you develop an intervention."

Sometimes, it takes a sports psychologist to point out the flaws in a would-be high-performance OR team. And sometimes, it takes an ex–Navy SEAL.

= = =

BRIAN FERGUSON HAD a successful career in special operations. Then he made a fascinating segue into healthcare (more on this below). Today, he and his eclectic team of top performers in everything from the military to the Olympics train high-performance surgical teams. The impetus for that unusual career move was a pivotal conversation with a heart surgeon at Cleveland Clinic Heart & Vascular Institute. The famed hospital has a sterling reputation for high-quality care. The surgeon was looking for ways to drive quality even higher.

"He ended up bringing me to his OR," recalls Ferguson.

There are two good reasons Ferguson was instantly intrigued by the offer. One is that his mother's background as a nurse made him familiar with healthcare. The other is that he sees strong similarities between medicine and the military.

"I would say there are three things people in the military and national security want to do," he says. "They want to solve hard problems. They want to impact the world. They want to save lives. And it turns out most people I've met in medicine have those same three beliefs."

Ferguson was born and raised in Cleveland, where the Cleveland Clinic has long been renowned for heart surgery. Its drive to maintain excellence piqued his curiosity, so he decided to watch the surgeon in action.

"On one hand, I was really impressed by the technological advancement," he says. "More broadly, I was astounded at the lack of conversation around performance at the individual or team level."

He was referring to something taught to Navy SEALs, fighter pilots, elite athletes and those in other high-pressure disciplines. But not in medicine.

"You have to have the ability to perform under pressure, which means that you have to understand what fear and anxiety actually feel like for you," he says. "Then, you've got to learn how to mitigate that fear and channel it into effective performance."

As soon as Ferguson said this, I thought of the two anesthesiologists and the ENT surgeon trying (and not succeeding) to intubate and ventilate Elaine Bromiley. If fear of that scenario exists, it could be a powerful factor in failing to deal with it.

"In Navy SEALs, the first thing I had to do was learn what I'm afraid of and how do I get ahead of that self-talk," says Ferguson. "And so here I am in this high-stakes medical environment, and no one is talking about any of this stuff."

Ferguson noticed other things.

"I could just see that there were 'asynergies' in how people were communicating," he says. "There were missed opportunities to communicate before things got crazy, or to debrief afterwards."

Like people in aviation, special ops personnel debrief after every mission or flight, no matter how routine. Ferguson got the surgical team to debrief every day. The very first debrief, which came after one of the unit's smoothest cases, made a critical finding. The nurses noted that heart replacement valves weren't labelled consistently and were located in three different areas of the OR, which led to a routine waste of time looking for the right valve prior to an operation. Addressing that inefficiency by putting the same valves in one spot paid immediate dividends in time saved.

Suggestions like that got the people at Cleveland Clinic to hire Ferguson and his colleagues to help put them on the glidepath to better performance. He may have been about to leave Navy SEALs, but he was taking the tricks he had learned about teamwork over seven years with him.

= = =

"FRANKLY, I STUMBLED into medicine," says Ferguson. "And the idea of high-performance medicine in teams."

It was a stumble nearly twenty years in the making. Ferguson did an undergraduate degree in international relations. In 2002, he got his first job as a White House intern in national security. The period after 9/11 was a very consequential time in American and global history. He was witness to a changing paradigm: from the state of affairs that dominated during the Cold War to one in which non-state actors could leverage technology in networks to have an outsized impact on national and global affairs. He saw the United States amassing huge caches of information via satellite, and then facing the challenge of how to sift nimbly and knowledgeably through that data.

Following his stint at the White House, Ferguson attended graduate school for economics. A career in finance was aborted by the financial meltdown of 2008.

"I really had wanted to serve in uniform, and so I went into special operations and went through basic field training," says Ferguson. "And then I went into the Navy SEAL teams."

As Ferguson explains it, joining the SEALs as a "mature" recruit at the age of twenty-eight meant entering through the Navy Officer Candidate School, a thirteen-week course at Naval Station Newport in Rhode Island.

"Essentially, you go to boot camp, and then you go to what's called basic underwater demolition and SEAL training."

SEAL (an acronym for sea, air and land) training is a six-month program based in Coronado, California. "That's really where they see whether or not you have the chops to be effective," he says. "They find out what's at the bottom of your well. Very few of us have the chance to see how we respond when pushed to the limit."

There are three phases to the training. The first is a seven-week core component in which recruits are challenged to be effective individually and in teams in austere environments that range from cold water to hot sand.

The training culminates in something known as Hell Week.

"In that week, you're awake from Sunday to Friday for around-the-clock training," he says. "You're in the water and it's very gruelling."

Ferguson says the best part of that exercise is finishing it.

"Once you've actually lived through it, it just opens up your aperture about what's possible in the world," says Ferguson. "It's incredibly energizing and liberating."

Getting through Hell Week generally means you've got what it takes to become a SEAL, as happened with Ferguson.

He sees parallels between the gruelling basic training for Navy SEALs and residency, with its eighty-hour weeks and sleepless nights on call. But there is one telling difference. Ferguson says recruits for special operations are put through their paces to find the candidates capable of functioning under duress. But in special forces, deprivation is not an end unto itself.

"We want you to have the confidence that you can effectively operate in that environment," says Ferguson. "But once you've been through it, it's then incumbent on the community to teach you better habits. The rest of the time, we expect you to get as much sleep as possible and to be cognitively at your best. We know you have to be well rested and well fed."

He thinks these are things medicine has yet to grasp.

"I think medicine is very good at getting people exhausted and putting them through gruelling training through residency," he says. "But it doesn't do a good job of reverse engineering those habits to build higher-quality surgeons and physicians."

And if members of the team aren't at their best, Ferguson says, it's likely the team will fail at some point.

Ferguson did two tours of duty in special operations and learned a lot about teamwork. He says that there are roughly a hundred special operators on a team, backed by a much larger team that supports special operators in theatre. There are people who specialize in intelligence, people who keep the operators' unique weapons in good working order, people who specialize in transportation and other logistical arrangements, and people in administration who make sure everyone on the team takes care of personal details that range from dental care to last wills and testaments.

"To put one SEAL in the field, there's six to seven other people involved in getting that person in the field and effectively helping them operate," says Ferguson. "A SEAL team transcends the SEAL operator. That's a really important concept that I think can be valuable in medicine."

By analogy, Ferguson believes front-line physicians, nurses and others are hospital SEALs. Surrounding them are people who work in hospital environmental services and people who sterilize instruments and maintain biomedical equipment, not to mention administrators who make sure the money for clinical programs keeps flowing.

Some things don't quite fit the analogy: for example, self-employed physicians probably aren't told to see a dentist, much less to get their affairs in order.

One thing Ferguson learned as a Navy SEAL is how to function capably outside of his native environment. For humans, that means thriving in the water.

"We're obviously not amphibious creatures," he says. "Much of the training is meant to put you in some heightened state of stress or duress, and then ask you to perform a skill."

Those training exercises range from tying knots in the water at a depth of two or three metres to functioning during a simulated surf hit just as your air supply has been disconnected.

"How do you remain calm and then take that calm and allow yourself to problem-solve in a way that enables you to do a risk analysis to keep yourself alive," he says.

In special operations, trainees learn about using self-talk to keep themselves calm.

"Some people use mantras to stay calm and cool," he says. "The idea is to keep an eye on the present with a sense of urgency that doesn't become overwhelming. That ultimately is a mental game of knowing where you're at and knowing in some cases how to communicate with teammates under water."

Staying calm under duress is not just about being able to keep functioning as an individual but also about functioning as a member of a team.

"Eventually, that skill has to be performed in the context of being a teammate, either in a dyad or sometimes [with] up to ten other teammates," he says.

Until recently, this kind of training has rarely been done in healthcare aside from mock disaster exercises and other simulation training, which we'll explore later in the book.

Following his second deployment, Ferguson decided to leave special operations.

"When you're no longer operational, you're sort of transitioning out," he says.

He was sent to the undersea climate and operation unit in Hawaii. Deployments in Iraq and Afghanistan had given NATO special forces lots of experience operating on land, in the mountains and in the desert.

"We had really let that maritime capability atrophy," he says. His final assignment as a Navy SEAL was to adapt technology used on dry land (everything from smartphones to satellite imaging) for use under the sea.

Ferguson worked with some unlikely partners. They included the Defense Advanced Research Projects Agency, a research and development agency of the US Department of Defense, as well as commercial partners such as Nike and Red Bull.

"It made sense to go to Red Bull, which was known as one of the top institutes in the world," he says. "It's thinking about helping people jumping out of planes and surfing fifty-foot waves. That's human performance on the edge. That is where that collaboration came from, and the real fruit was to look at a similar problem from a totally different angle."

It turns out that experience had a strong bearing on his approach to teamwork, with some huge lessons for healthcare.

During his time in Hawaii, Ferguson says he was given latitude to seek partners outside the norm. That sent him headlong into an entirely new career as a consultant to high-performance medical teams.

=====

IN AUGUST 2016, Ferguson founded Arena Labs. Its mission is "to bring the science of world-class performance, creative mastery, and elite teams to modern medicine . . . not in regulation or policy solutions, but in building high-performing medical teams."

His first client was Cleveland Clinic. Ferguson says he and an associate (who happens to be an F-18 pilot) spent a week watching fifteen heart surgeons do procedures—not as experts in surgery but as experts in teamwork. That led to more work at Cleveland Clinic, followed by other hospitals.

"We got a big contract in Washington, DC, with the surgical services from across all major level-one trauma centres," he says. "That forced us to do this at scale. And that was the start of the business."

As an outsider to healthcare, Ferguson anticipated resistance, and learned how to approach MDs. One way is to frame the message as trying to improve performance incrementally rather than tearing down and starting over. A second is to be humble.

"I've never worked in an emergency room and had to see a patient at 5:00 a.m., but I've done things that are high risk and involve life-and-death decisions," he says. "'Here's something you might try or think about.' That philosophy allowed for a conversation."

Ferguson says he always looks for factors that medicine and special operations have in common. Both get bogged down by bureaucracy and the need to adapt to new technology.

"In national security and in special operations, you see stressed people who have to learn new technology at a fast rate on top of their job," he says. "People are pulled away from their core competency, which is usually a service-driven competency in medicine, in the military and in education. How do you get someone to understand how to get back to that service thing that you love?"

The training he offers to health professionals is almost never about surgery but about the optimal mindset of a surgeon.

"We call it 'neck up' in the military," he says. "It's understanding the power of the mind, how you take care of your body and how you think about fear and anxiety. It has always astounded me that these people who work insanely hard in medicine are not given any of the tools that address human factors."

Such as?

"I have never been in a hospital where an administrator can give me analytics on the overall level of stress and recovery and sleep of their teams," says Ferguson. "We know that physicians and frontline teams are chronically stressed, under-rested and probably not hydrated. These are basic things that would never be acceptable in a military unit or an elite athletic team. And yet, it's just a way of life in medicine, which has always been amazing to me."

When Arena Labs signs on to work with a hospital, they have some non-negotiables.

"Any time we go into a hospital, the two things we require are unequivocal access and the ability to go anywhere we want in the hospital any time," he says.

They use some unconventional methods to monitor hospital personnel, such as sensors to measure heart and respiratory rate and other measures of stress levels.

Each hospital they advise has different needs and wants. But there are common factors.

"The number-one thing we hear is 'no one communicates,'" he says. "People in medicine have emails, two cellphones, text messaging, Ascom phones, pagers and overhead announcements. While people are 'communicating' all the time, they're just talking past each other."

Paradoxically, he says the fix is often to institute regular meetings in which members of the team put down their devices and just talk to one another.

However Ferguson does it, his pitch seems to resonate inside hospital corridors.

"I can't tell you how many times an administrator says, 'Wow, I've never seen this particular physician listen to someone like that,'" he says.

= = =

MEDICAL CULTURE TENDS to be very insular. Ferguson is a big believer in looking for teammates far outside the closed circle of people you work with day to day. He has collaborated with the Santa Fe Institute, an independent non-profit dedicated to conducting research on complex systems science. There, he was influenced by Michael Mauboussin, chairman of the institute's board of trustees. Mauboussin is a finance expert and head of consilient research at Counterpoint Global. He is also the author of three books, including *More Than You Know: Finding Financial Wisdom in Unconventional Places*.

Mauboussin espouses what's known as "consilience." Sometimes referred to as convergence of evidence, consilience speaks to the notion that evidence from independent and unrelated sources strengthens the power of conclusions and decisions. Consilience occurs when you bring people together from very different disciplines but with a shared challenge.

"If you put those people in a room and you frame the question right, you create epiphanies for both of them," says Ferguson.

It was at that pivotal moment in his career that he met up with the heart surgeon from Cleveland Clinic and took his first look at a high-performance cardiovascular surgical team.

Medicine seldom looks for wisdom from outside the group, a behaviour that Ferguson experienced during his time in the navy as well.

"The military is really good at talking to itself," he says. "The solutions we're looking for are probably better explored through new channels of relationships outside of the national security and military establishments."

What do a two-time Olympic gold medallist in the decathlon, an F/A-18 Super Hornet fighter pilot, a former gymnast with Cirque du Soleil, and a former dancer with the American Ballet Theatre have in common? Each is part of the eclectic team of experts at Arena Labs. They're called performance ambassadors.

Erin Cafaro won gold with the US rowing team in the Beijing and London Summer Olympics. She uses cognitive science to help doctors build on individual strengths while nurturing teamwork. John Hiltz spent two decades as a US Navy pilot with more than 3,000 flight hours and more than 450 aircraft carrier landings. He also played basketball at Notre Dame. When he works with medical teams, Hiltz uses his military and athletic experiences to focus on the performance mindset.

Their mission is to bring high-performance wisdom to medicine from outside the world of medicine. It isn't eclecticism for its own sake. It's to share wisdom based on common experiences.

Take bringing test pilots to the hospital. The F-35 strike fighter is a state-of-the-art fighter craft. Ferguson says that a test pilot talked to surgeons about the experience of donning a helmet that fed them lots of data and displayed it on the helmet's visor.

"It became nearly impossible to fly the aircraft because pilots were overloaded with data," says Ferguson. "They grounded it [the helmet] and they took a lot of that stuff away."

That story helped the test pilot advise a team of surgeons trying out a new robotic surgical assistant at the University of Chicago on how to deal with a similar problem.

"There's more and more technology overlaid in the operating room with robot-assisted or minimally invasive surgery," he says. "How do we train humans to evolve in a way that allows that integration and technology so that we're distributing cognitive load while not paralyzing certain members of the team?"

Alexa Miller is also part of the team at Arena Labs. She's an artist who uses a groundbreaking method to teach medical students and practising doctors to work in teams through art appreciation.

"When I first saw the Arena Labs website four years ago, I thought, 'This is exactly what I've been trying to do,'" says Miller. "To work with people in medicine who know there are other worlds out there that have a lot to teach."

Miller says Arena Labs works in part because successful people in everything from special operations to athletic and circus performance have gone through training as rigorous as a cardiothoracic surgeon or a critical care specialist. Yet, she says, they manage to teach while staying out of hospital politics and still achieve a balance of power among all members of the team.

"I think they've done a great job of identifying that medicine is really focused on technical training, but is pretty blind to human performance," she says. "In most high-performance fields, the priority is taking care of both the people and the team so they are able to learn and grow as a unit."

Miller believes the time is right to bring teamwork to medical culture. And she has a powerful tool to help teamwork flourish.

CHAPTER TWO

ART APPRECIATION

*How asking the right questions
can help a team work better*

W HEN AN EIGHTY-EIGHT-YEAR-OLD patient arrives in
the ER with crushing chest pain and has obvious findings of a heart attack on the electrocardiogram (ECG),
the diagnosis is as close to certain as can be. But a single diagnosis is a rarity. The bulk of patients who arrive in the ER are far
more complicated, and the diagnosis more uncertain. Where once
a patient would have had one or two diagnoses, today it's more
like six or seven. Some are diseases and others are complications
of treatment.

When I work in the ER, I've noticed that I make much more
accurate diagnoses and am better at stickhandling those complex-
ities when I work with a team of residents, students, nurse practitioners and physician assistants. Each of us sees the same patient
but notices different things.

I see an older woman who is having trouble breathing and tell
the group I think she has heart failure; I do this because the diagnosis is common and because she looks just like a thousand other

patients I've seen and treated over the years. The NP looks at the same patient and says she thinks she has chronic obstructive pulmonary disease, because she's pursing her lips with each breath (it's an instinctive and sometimes learned behaviour that helps reduce the load on the muscles of the chest and diaphragm). A third-year medical student says he thinks the patient has pulmonary fibrosis, or scarring of the lungs, because her cough sounds too dry to be due to heart failure and because he's read the old chart and has learned that the patient once worked in an asbestos mine and might have an undiagnosed case of lung silicosis.

The diagnosis we come up with as a team is usually richer in detail than the one I come up with by myself. It has the potential to be much more accurate too.

Human factors engineers call that "team cognition."

In a chapter in the 2005 book *Handbook of Human Factors in Web Design*, Preston Kiekel and Nancy Cooke asked why team cognition is an important, even critical component of success.

"A growing number of tasks take place in the context of complex sociotechnical systems," they wrote. "The cognitive requirements associated with emergency response, software development, transportation, factory and power plant operation, military operations, medicine, and a variety of other tasks exceed the limits of individual cognition. Teams are a natural solution to this problem, and so the emphasis on teams in these domains is increasing."

The notion of team diagnosis as a way to reduce diagnostic medical errors intrigues Dr. Pat Croskerry, a retired ER physician and the father of cognitive psychology as it applies to medicine in general and emergency medicine in particular.

"There is an imperative to view the diagnostic process as a team endeavor," wrote Croskerry in his 2020 book *The Cognitive Autopsy: A Root Cause Analysis of Medical Decision Making*.

Croskerry argues that the cognition or thinking that is required to make the most correct diagnosis is a finite resource that may be compromised by human factors such as distraction and fatigue. Under those conditions, he says, doctors can't cope with the cognitive load required to diagnose illnesses. They stop thinking about the diagnosis and start making intuitive guesses that are prone to error. Team diagnosis helps fix that.

As an ER physician, Croskerry says he often asked nurses for their diagnostic impressions of the patients they cared for together.

"I used to talk to some of the older nurses and say, 'What do you think about this?'" Croskerry recalls. "Sometimes they'd be dead wrong. Other times, they'd say things that made me think. I gradually came to a view that if you do start to engage the team, then you are in a stronger position for diagnosis than if you don't."

This notion of team diagnosis is gaining traction. Dr. Mark L. Graber believes strongly in team diagnosis. Graber is a professor emeritus of medicine at Stony Brook University and the founder and president emeritus of the Society to Improve Diagnosis in Medicine.

"Of all the interventions that could possibly help reduce harm from diagnostic errors, I believe teamwork has the greatest potential," says Graber. "Fresh eyes can help catch mistakes, and we know that collective intelligence works in solving complex problems, like diagnosis."

The problem, according to Graber, is that "team diagnosis" is not standard practice.

"It needs to start during training," he says. "Students in every healthcare profession need to understand and gain experience with the teamwork-for-diagnosis process."

There's a way to encourage young doctors to take the first steps down that very path in the early stages of medical school. And it could be the key to teamwork not just in diagnosis but across healthcare.

= = =

GALWAY, IRELAND, IS the home of dotMD, a recurring two-day festival of medical curiosity for doctors and other healthcare practitioners. Five hundred of us from several continents have packed Bailey Allen Hall, a modern, cavernous auditorium at the National University of Ireland.

I'm about to learn a mind-expanding lesson regarding teamwork—a lesson that in many ways set me on the path to writing this book.

Our teacher is Alexa Miller, an artist turned medical educator who co-created a most unusual course for medical students at Harvard Medical School. The course teaches them how to get sharper at medical diagnosis. But Miller doesn't send them to textbooks. Instead, she takes them to the Museum of Fine Arts in Boston to look at works of art.

"What we're going to do is just take a few moments to look together at a work of art and talk about what we see." Miller clicks a remote and the image of a sculpture fills the screen. "You do not need to know anything at all about this work of art to participate. We are just going to practise seeing together."

There are two raised human figures that appear to have been sculpted out of a flat surface of stone. One has visible male genitalia. The other doesn't. Their arms and legs are somewhat intertwined.

"What's happening here?" Miller asks us.

I look at the sculpture, not knowing what I'm supposed to be seeing.

"There are two figures with arms around each other," a woman in the audience offers confidently.

I hadn't noticed that.

"Okay," says Miller. "There appear to be two figures with their arms around one another. What more can we find?"

Others start to chime in.

"The two figures have different moods," says another woman.

"Different moods," repeats Miller. "What do you see that makes you say that?"

"One figure is smiling and the other has a serious look," the woman replies.

"I hear you looking at the expressions on the faces and wondering about what that might imply about their mood and their emotional state," says Miller. "You're noticing that one appears to have a frown and the other appears to be smiling. What more can we find?"

"They're interlocked," says a man in the audience.

"They're leaning on each other," says another woman at the back of the audience.

"They're leaning on each other," repeats Miller. "And what do you see that makes you say that?"

"There are places where the limbs of one figure are touching the torso of the other."

The audience murmurs, as if seeing something in the sculpture for the first time.

"We've really only scratched the surface of the complexity and the ambiguity," Miller says. "The point I want to make to you is to have you notice how much you just opened your eyes."

Throughout the exercise, I find myself reluctant to speak up. I have no training in art appreciation. I'm afraid of suggesting something incorrect or silly. I worry that I'm missing something that I'm supposed to see.

Miller is coming to a point. She starts talking about medical textbooks that are filled with images of X-rays, diseased organs, electrocardiograms and pathology slides.

"A medical textbook *directs* medical learners to learn," she says. "Rather than asking learners to look at the images and make their own judgments, the medical text tells learners exactly what to see."

The piece Miller showed us is *The Wrestlers*, a plaster made in 1914 by Henri Gaudier-Brzeska that hangs in the Museum of Fine Arts in Boston. Even the name, says Miller, is information that biases the viewer, and would have caused us to miss the many observations we made.

By leaving the interpretation ambiguous and uncertain, and by asking clarifying questions, Miller freed us to embrace the uncertainty and pick up on nuances.

As a team.

= = =

THE TECHNIQUE ALEXA Miller used at dotMD is called Visual Thinking Strategies. It is a teaching method that improves critical thinking skills through facilitated discussions of visual images. It uses art to teach thinking, communication skills and visual literacy.

By encouraging participation in a group problem-solving process, VTS helps foster teamwork.

VTS was developed by Philip Yenawine and Abigail Housen. In 1989, Yenawine was the director of education of the Museum of Modern Art (MoMA) in New York City. MoMA was a pioneer in guided art appreciation and received good feedback from visitors on its guided gallery tours. Yenawine wanted to find out whether those gallery talks helped visitors deepen their understanding of art.

It turns out those vaunted tours did little to improve art appreciation among visitors.

I wanted to know how courageous it was for Yenawine, as the museum's director of education, to commission that study.

"Well, I think there were people on my staff who wanted me to put my head in a bucket and go away," he recalls. "They had co-operated with the studies and then they weren't so happy that they did."

The thought that MoMA had an amazing collection of art and a talented staff of exhibit guides and yet might not be enhancing visitors' ability to enjoy art bothered him deeply.

"My life has really been around the whole idea of trying to make art meaningful for people," he says. "I just am not happy when things aren't doing what you intended for them to do. And in education, that's criminal, as it is in medicine."

Yenawine may not have known it, but even back then, he was demonstrating the kind of slow thinking that (much later) would be shown to help develop the team concept in art appreciation. And, much later, in medicine.

Yenawine teamed up with Abigail Housen, a cognitive psychologist whose research had led her to conclude that viewers of art analyze works in one of five predictable stages based on their level of understanding and sophistication.

According to Housen, Stage One viewers (called Accountive Viewers) are relatively unsophisticated when it comes to art. They use their senses, memories and personal associations to make concrete observations. They judge works of art based on what they know and like.

My experience and lack of a working vocabulary for art appreciation tells me I'm a Stage One viewer! Housen's research found that *most* museum visitors are like me.

At the other end of the spectrum are Stage Five viewers (called Re-creative Viewers). They have a long history of viewing and reflecting on works of art and discover something new in every work that they view, even ones they have looked at countless times.

Yenawine realized that MoMA's celebrated gallery talks weren't teaching novice visitors much of anything. What was needed was a framework that would help them make sense of art as they viewed it.

So Yenawine and Housen created VTS. To help untrained observers make sense of art, they developed a set of three questions that a VTS facilitator is trained to ask the observers. The questions are the very same ones Miller posed to the audience at dotMD.

The first question is *What is going on in the picture?* The purpose of that question is to engage members of the group. The second question—*What makes you say that?*—fosters critical thinking by forcing participants to look for evidence to justify what they see. The third question—*What else can we find here?*—encourages participants to think beyond their initial observations.

As the discussion takes place, the facilitator paraphrases each student's observations without judging them. They point at what the student is observing. And they make connections between the students' observations.

"They're called forcing strategies," says Miller of the demonstration at dotMD. "What did they see that made them say what they said when somebody made an interpretation? I asked them to use 'think aloud' techniques to share their thinking and reasoning. I used hypothesizing language so that people could change their mind. That way, we could co-create knowledge together and find a pathway forward."

The three questions provide a structural thinking strategy that participants internalize over time until they can use it independently.

Facilitators like Miller don't tell participants what to notice. Instead, they prompt them to be curious about what they're viewing and to reflect critically on their observations.

A VTS encounter between facilitator and observers stimulates curiosity, critical reflection and something more. Since it takes place in a group in which everyone participates and no one is wrong, the result is an exercise in collective meaning-making.

As I'll explore later in this chapter, that collective aspect of VTS is essential to team building.

Most of the formative research by Housen and Yenawine was conducted not in museums but in American middle and high schools, where the pair discovered that VTS engaged a broad range of students, including those who were interested in art. The students took to the same VTS questions that Miller used at dotMD.

Miller was part of the team that brought VTS to Harvard Medical School.

There are lots of good reasons to believe that Miller's involvement in bringing teamwork to medical students was meant to be.

= = =

ON HER WEBSITE, Arts Practica (www.artspractica.com), Miller describes herself as "a kid who was always drawing." Her subjects were mostly from nature. Playful things. Funny things. Encouraged by her parents, she took a rigorous Advanced Placement drawing program in high school.

"That was all totally observation-based," says Miller. "Everything from still life to working from human models. We'd [also] have all kinds of odd assignments, like [finding and] drawing something you've never seen before, like the inside of a clock."

Years before embracing VTS, Alexa was learning what it's all about.

"I think that experience profoundly changed my brain and changed my whole outlook on the world, because I still look at things with an eye to simplify them," she says.

Miller says that happened during a challenging time in her immediate family, when her older sister was misdiagnosed as a teenager. As a child, she had developmental delay and suffered from anxiety.

"She was diagnosed with a bunch of things that she did not have," says Miller. "She was diagnosed with schizophrenia and obsessive-compulsive disorder. She was medicated so heavily, to the point where she was practically speechless or was so shaky [that] she couldn't even lift a fork to her mouth."

The impact on her sister was profound.

"She had some experiences with doctors that were practically abusive," Miller recalls. "There was certainly some mistreatment that was quite heartbreaking to see and very costly on her development, and her life, and my family's resources."

It was one of the reasons why Miller developed an interest in art.

"It was because her behaviour was so challenging growing up that I got into drawing in the first place, because it was a chaotic, noisy home," she says. "I would just kind of go in my room and draw."

Miller says her sister's life began to turn around in her early twenties, when she was diagnosed correctly with Asperger's syndrome. The developmental disorder is related to autism spectrum disorder and is characterized by above-average intellectual ability, impaired social skills and restrictive, repetitive patterns of interest and activities. Miller says the diagnosis was a huge turning point for her sister and the entire family; she was taken off the psychoactive medicines that were sedating her and she got the right kind of therapeutic support. She also met up with a community of young adults like her.

"I think that was a hugely formative experience for me growing up," Miller says. "I think of how it comes back to the medical pictures and how doctors see. If somebody had simply looked a little longer and said they [didn't] know, before putting false [diagnostic] labels on my sister, she could have potentially had the harm [done to her] minimized."

Miller attended Swarthmore College and got her BA in art history, with extensive course work in education and in African studies. She planned on attending the Wimbledon School of Art (now the Wimbledon College of Arts) in London, England, to continue her development as a landscape artist. Miller arrived in London about a week after 9/11.

"I just felt so thrown," she recalls. "I was just sad and confused. And I had friends who lost friends and family members. I just felt like I didn't want to make the paintings I thought I wanted to make."

The only American in her class, she often felt like a stranger. Emotionally scarred by the experience of 9/11, Miller says she became interested in wounds of the physical kind, beginning with the ones on her own body. Everything from deep cuts to surgical scars.

"I started making little drawings of them [and] turning them into paintings," she recalls. "I was thinking about the shapes of them and how the shapes indicated something about what had actually happened."

A scar, she reasoned, tells the story of the place on the body where some sort of trauma has occurred. Some scars come from minor cuts. Some come from surgical procedures. A fall off a mountain. A shotgun wound from an enemy combatant or a police officer.

"Sometimes, they're part of our mythology, and sometimes we never think about them, or we don't want to," she says.

Miller didn't know it at the time, but she was drawing a direct line between art appreciation and medical diagnosis.

She began working on a photo project (part medical and part personal narrative) in which she would take pictures of people's scars and do oral histories with them about how the lasting mark came to be. Her research took her to the Wellcome Trust, which was founded by medical entrepreneur Sir Henry Wellcome upon his death in 1936. Its £26.8 billion (CAD$45.2 billion) investment portfolio funds academia, philanthropy, businesses, governments and civil society around the world to take on health challenges, including COVID-19.

Wellcome also houses the world's largest archive of medical images, and Miller took it all in.

"I just looked at as many images of scars as I could," she recalls, "to try to learn about scars as an artist."

Many of the photographs and drawings of scars were found inside recent and archived medical textbooks. It was Miller's first encounter with academic writing in medicine, and it was an eye-opener.

"I was really shocked at the way in which the medical learning didactic material *directed* learners to look at images," says Miller. "It was so different from my training as an artist. These didactics just told medical learners what to see."

For instance, the caption on a photograph of a scar on a little girl's face would focus on the illness or injury that gave rise to the scar, and perhaps the girl's age. And it would fail to mention everything else, from the doll the girl carries in her arms to her mother in the background.

"It troubled me that [meaningful] information was ruled out so quickly when it was potentially important humanistically and scientifically," she says. "It made me kind of angry that [it] happened."

Angry, says Miller, because closed-mindedness and the tendency to miss important information often leads to misdiagnosis, which she observed up close in the case of her sister.

Miller completed her MA in studio painting from the Wimbledon School of Art, where her artwork focused on human resilience and medical imagery. She returned to the United States, determined to find a way to train doctors to keep their minds open before making a medical diagnosis.

She first learned of VTS in 2002, when she did a training session with Philip Yenawine.

"I was immediately hooked," she recalls. "It was the first time I'd encountered the art of facilitation of knowledge, rather than its transmission and didactic teaching, and it really resonated."

And that's when she met a like-minded physician at Harvard named Joel Katz.

= = =

DR. JOEL THORP Katz is an infectious disease consultant, director of the internal medicine residency program and vice chair for education at Brigham and Women's Hospital in Boston. Before medicine, Katz was a commercial artist. That unusual background probably made him one of the most likely physicians on the planet to see the potential of VTS as a method to teach medical students.

"Because I was a non-traditional medical student, I was open to the idea of non-traditional teaching methods," says Katz. "It's hard to know, but I think that does give me a flexible way of viewing success and achieving competency."

As Dr. Katz settled into a career as a clinician and teacher at Brigham and Women's Hospital, he noticed some telling patterns among students and residents. They seemed less inclined to observe patients for any length of time and relied too much on MRIs and other technology to make the diagnosis for them.

Katz attended a VTS workshop given by Philip Yenawine, which is how he met Alexa Miller. Katz came to the training workshop with Rachel Dubroff, then a fourth-year medical student at Harvard who was writing a thesis that included a proposal to teach a visual arts–based course to Harvard medical students. The pair approached Miller to serve as the teaching artist for the course pilot.

The curriculum board approved a course for first-year students at Harvard Medical School provided the team conduct research to see if VTS training enabled medical students "to make careful unbiased observation a habit."

The course, dubbed "Training the Eye," debuted on the first-year curriculum in the spring of 2003. Every Friday afternoon for ten weeks, Miller took a small group of students over to the nearby Museum of Fine Arts, just steps from the medical school campus.

"I just remember feeling like a flock of fledglings flying the coop," recalls Dr. Matthew Growdon. Today, he's a young geriatrician at University of California San Francisco. Back then, he was a first-year medical student who signed up for Training the Eye after seeing a pamphlet on a med school bulletin board asking for students who were interested in going to the museum and looking at art.

Growdon is not exactly sure why he signed up.

"Probably more than anything, it was just really nice to get out of the med school because it was such a grind of exams in anatomy, physiology and pathophysiology," he says.

At the museum, Miller and the other art instructors would take the students to look at works of art such as *The Slave Ship* (originally titled *Slavers Throwing overboard the Dead and Dying—Typhon coming on*), a painting by the British artist Joseph Mallord William Turner, and the Seated Bodhisattva, a huge figure carved in ancient China.

The session would start with some sketching.

"I've always had this kind of notion that I'm not a good drawer or sketcher," says Growdon. "It was so much harder and more humbling than I thought it would be. Here I was, taking on the feats of anatomy and physiology and feeling like I'm getting really smart. And then they put me in a museum with a sketchbook, and I'm like, 'Oh my God. What am I going to do here?'"

After sketching, Miller would take the students to a work of art or two, selected for ambiguity of interpretation, and conduct a VTS session.

"You're in front of a work of art," Growdon recalls. "You describe what you see, and then one of your colleagues may say something, and then you're going to be able to respond to them. I think what draws you in about it is just that the method is predictable, it's very non-judgmental, and it feels very safe."

By "safe," Growdon means feeling free to make spontaneous observations without fear of being "wrong," something many medical students feel. In neuroanatomy class back in my own first year as a medical student, I recall attempting to answer a question and getting it wrong. My teacher humiliated me in front of 250 classmates. It took me a few weeks to regain the courage to raise my hand again.

Imagine a student or resident on the wards who is reluctant to suggest a diagnosis that may very well be correct, and you can see the stakes.

VTS trains medical students to speak up, since there are no right or wrong answers and no risk of humiliation.

"I believe that true safety is an environment where everybody feels able to speak and share their truth and say what they see," Miller says.

Safety to share one's truth about a work of art is just the beginning, and an impressive one at that. But the true measure of success is whether medical students feel comfortable enough to apply their newfound observational skills when it comes to patients on hospital wards.

Following the session at the museum, Miller would take the students back to Harvard, where attending physicians would give lectures on things like the visual diagnosis of skin rashes and chest X-ray findings. As with VTS, the aim of these sessions was not to diagnose so much as to describe what they were seeing.

"Sometimes, the attending would bring patients, which was pretty amazing," says Miller.

Then, as now, Dr. Katz and other faculty would also take students to the wards at Brigham and Women's Hospital, where they would use the same VTS method as taught by Miller to get students to make clinical observations on actual patients. He describes a very recent example at Brigham.

A forty-nine-year-old man had been admitted late overnight to the ward where Katz was the attending physician. Weak and confused, the man was unable to speak. A family member had spoken on his behalf to the ER physician, and the resident who saw the patient that night made a presumptive diagnosis of stroke.

To confirm that diagnosis, the resident ordered a computerized tomography (CT) scan of the head. The team was waiting for the results when Katz arrived the next morning.

Katz joined his team—a senior resident, two junior residents and a medical student—on morning rounds to meet the patients who had been admitted the night before by the doctors on call. The team went to the man's bedside for a closer look and introduced themselves, but the patient responded only by nodding stiffly.

"As soon as I walked in the room, I realized that some things didn't fit the description [we'd received] when the patient was handed over to us," Katz recalls.

The most common type of stroke causes weakness and sometimes paralysis of one side of the body, along with difficulty understanding speech. Stiffness is not a typical symptom.

"As we met the patient and looked at him very carefully, it was clear that something didn't quite fit that notion of a stroke," Katz recalls.

Katz wanted his team not to rubber-stamp the diagnosis made by the resident the night before.

"I suggested that we hold off on further history briefly and [instead] simply [and] carefully observe the patient," says Katz.

Instead of telling his team what to look for, he did an impromptu session of VTS.

"After about a minute I asked them, 'What do you notice about this patient?'"

Suddenly, the team began observing things not seen before.

"He's awake and not talking," said one of the junior residents.

"He seems confused, but it's hard to know," said the other junior resident.

"What do you see that makes you say that?" Katz asked the intern.

"He's only responding to the most basic questions with a head nod," the resident replied. "He can blink and nod his head to our request, but he's not moving his extremities."

"What else can you find?" Katz asked the team.

"He's sweating," said the student.

"He has rigid muscle tone," said the senior resident, touching the patient's skin. "And he's warm to the touch."

"He was febrile," added one of the junior residents.

"What do you want to know?" Katz asked the team.

"What are the patient's other diagnoses?" asked the student.

"Anxiety, depression, adequately controlled hypertension and peripheral artery disease," the first-year resident who presented the patient answered. "He has a family history of coronary artery disease and strokes."

"Any recent changes to his medications?" asked the senior resident.

"He was recently started on olanzapine for agitation and poor sleep," the junior resident answered.

Bingo.

It turned out the patient had not had a stroke. He had a much rarer and life-threatening condition called neuroleptic malignant syndrome (NMS). Its symptoms include high fever, stiff muscles, confusion, wide swings of blood pressure and excessive sweating.

The syndrome is a bodily reaction to antipsychotic medications, also known as neuroleptic drugs. These drugs are prescribed commonly for schizophrenia and other types of psychosis. Drugs from this category, like olanzapine and quetiapine, are also prescribed quite commonly these days to sedate older patients with dementia and agitation.

Olanzapine, prescribed to the patient for agitation and poor sleep, was the culprit.

Armed with the correct diagnosis, Katz and his team stopped the olanzapine and treated the symptoms.

"Within a day, he was back to his baseline," says Katz. "He became much more mobile, interactive and conversational."

If you consult textbooks on stroke, you don't see references to NMS. Strokes are caused typically by atherosclerosis and blood clots of the internal carotid and middle cerebral arteries. Katz's decision to use VTS to spur his team to think outside the box may have helped save this patient. Katz believes the experience taught the team some important lessons.

"It taught them the power of looking carefully," he says. "It taught them to recognize and avoid the bias of what the team had been told about the diagnosis of stroke. It emphasized the need to reassess every newly admitted patient."

He also thinks the team learned some humility.

"The ability to question yourself [and] keep your mind open was a great example of the value of VTS in a clinical setting," he says.

===

THE STORY KATZ just told is a powerful example of how VTS can give a team a framework for dealing with the diagnostic uncertainty that is becoming increasingly common in medicine. Katz doesn't like the word *uncertainty* in this context. He calls it diagnostic ambiguity.

"What you're calling uncertainty, or I would call it ambiguity, is such a great aspect of artwork," says Katz. "There's always more interpretation. You can look more deeply and see things in different ways, and that habit of avoiding early closure [is helpful]."

Katz is saying that when it comes to art appreciation, differences of opinion are welcomed, as they enhance the overall interpretation of the meaning behind a work of art. What he's also saying is that there's a place for tolerating ambiguity of medical diagnosis too.

"Multiple truths can be possible at the same time in medicine too," he says. "There are studies showing that the ability to hold on to more than one truth simultaneously corresponds to better diagnostic abilities. Early closure is one of the major sources of misdiagnosis."

One way that VTS addresses that ambiguity or uncertainty is by having participants—be they looking at a work of art in a museum or at a patient on the wards—vocalize their observations.

The technique is called "thinking aloud."

"Sharing your thinking aloud also helps facilitate [and clarify] your thinking," says Miller. "Sharing that pathway is also what can expedite a lot of learning in other people."

According to the Institute of Medicine (IOM), an independent, non-profit organization that works outside of government to provide unbiased and authoritative advice to decision makers and the public, "the diagnostic process ideally involves collaboration among multiple health care professionals, the patient, and the patient's family . . . arriving at accurate and timely diagnoses—even those made by an individual clinician working with a single patient—involves teamwork."

That quote was found in a 2015 report by the IOM entitled *Improving Diagnosis in Health Care*. Team diagnosis may be the future, but solo diagnosis represents a past that is hard to change on hospital wards.

"Somebody still has to take responsibility and accountability [for an incorrect diagnosis]," says ER physician and cognitive psychologist Dr. Pat Croskerry. "It is amazing sometimes when things go wrong how everybody drifts away, and you're the one person that's standing."

Croskerry thinks it will take a substantial change in medical culture to make team diagnosis more widespread. He thinks that VTS may be a tool to do it.

"I believe in it," says Croskerry. "A lot of that can be trained, but to do it, you've got to overcome hurdles in medicine."

VTS is easier to teach early in a doctor's medical training, as is done at Harvard Medical School. At least thirty medical schools across the United States teach it to undergraduates.

Harvard also teaches VTS to practising health professionals at the Integrated Teaching Unit (ITU) at Brigham and Women's Hospital in Boston. The ITU provides medical care to patients while providing lots of practise for young doctors.

Corinne Zimmermann is a veteran museum educator who leads art museum workshops for healthcare organizations, including Brigham and Women's Hospital. Since 2010, she's been taking attending physicians and other health professionals to Boston's Museum of Fine Arts.

Zimmermann's work with clinicians is focused on building teams in a hurry. That's because the residents and students are assigned to the ward for just one month as part of their clinical rotations. And unlike the version of VTS for first-year medical students, the ones set up by Zimmermann include nurses who work in the ITU.

"Every month, a new team of students and residents comes on, but the nurses stay," Zimmermann says. "They're the constants. They're the ones that are on the floor offering care to patients throughout the day. We want all team members to feel respected and listened to."

Zimmermann's approach has been honed by more than a decade of doing this kind of team building in the ITU and elsewhere.

"I work with lots of teams that are very dysfunctional, and I think this work helps," she says. "It doesn't always reach everybody, but I think it does reach a majority of people."

But before taking her students to the museum, Zimmermann takes them to dinner.

"One of my favourite starters is to invite people to tell the story of their name or a story about some aspect of their name," she says. "That's because often, embedded in a story of someone's name, are family and cultural histories, things like that."

The idea behind that is to surprise members of the team with personal details they didn't know about.

"As well as laughing," she says. "I really think it's important to start the team-building sessions with a creative sense of play."

Zimmermann says by the time the group goes to the museum, they've begun to feel psychologically safe to speak up with one another. She explains why that's a good thing.

"One of the things that sometimes surfaces in these sessions is that nurses often have a very different perspective than the attending physicians," she says.

That safety to speak up is paired with the method of VTS, which provides a structure in which members of the team feel free to notice and share different observations about a work of art.

Zimmermann says the magic happens when she creates time and space for participants to reflect on how they interact with one another on the wards.

"There's this really beautiful moment when they are able to stand back and think about how a session in front of a work of art applies to a hospital situation, when people on the team look at things with different lenses," she says. "Are they the person that's moving the conversation forward or the person that's standing back and letting other team members speak up? Are they supporting another team member, or are they just tired and checked out? I'm just inviting them to pay attention to those kinds of things."

Zimmermann is talking about metacognition, which is defined as an awareness and understanding of one's own thought processes and those of others. An everyday example is having an awareness that you possess a lot of medical facts but have trouble recalling answers to questions in high-pressure clinical situations. The fix might be to do a mindfulness exercise that reduces the pressure.

In a 2008 paper published in *Advances in Developing Human Resources,* Alma McCarthy and Thomas Garavan argued that team metacognition is critical to optimizing teamwork.

In plain language, what Zimmermann is trying to do is flatten the hierarchy on the medical team in the ITU by getting them to appreciate how each of them approaches the same patient or situation differently. She says the process has some surprising anecdotal results. She recalls trying to help a team on the ITU led by an attending physician who always needed to be in control and always had to provide the correct answer to every question regarding patients.

"A nice, interesting guy who was really not a leader and who was not doing such a good job at empowering his team," she says.

At the museum, Zimmermann suggested that the attending physician choose a work of art and talk about how it affected him.

"He chose the most delicate, fragile piece of sculpture on a wall," she recalls. "He grew up in a very rough neighbourhood in New York. He talked about how he got bullied and how he had to learn early on what his strengths were. There was something so tender in the way he described his experiences growing up and not fitting in."

She says the team opened up to him.

"There was something very powerful about an attending talking about his own vulnerabilities," she says. "In the ITU, that's such a difficult thing to do. But in the space of the museum, they get to this point where they are willing to be very open."

Dr. Joel Katz says this new approach is transformative to medical culture.

"It breaks down hierarchies, opens lines of communication and addresses assumptions that underlie communication," says Katz. "It's really an amazing program."

And it works because a group of health professionals becomes a team.

"The team approach to diagnosis directly translates to improved medical care, in my opinion," says Katz. "I would say it directly translates to career satisfaction as well."

To some physicians, it may seem like a colossal waste of time to leave a busy hospital ward to head off to the museum.

I met a doctor who brought the museum to the hospital. And that hospital is both literally and figuratively down the road from the dotMD conference where I first met Alexa Miller.

= = =

It's Monday morning in the neonatal intensive care unit (NICU) at Cork University Maternity Hospital in Wilton, Cork, a two-and-a-half-hour drive due south of Galway. The rounded NICU has twelve cots adjoining onto a special care unit with another twenty cots, plus another nursery area with eight cots filled with babies ready for discharge.

Nine thousand babies are born every year in this tertiary care birthing centre. Twelve hundred of them are admitted to NICU; three hundred of them are born premature.

"A twenty-four-weeker was born at 12:30 a.m. last night weighing 650 grams." A senior resident presents the NICU's newest admission. A very thin, pink, premature newborn is bundled up in tiny blankets made of cotton. A thin breathing tube protrudes from her right nostril and is connected to a ventilator that whooshes rhythmically. Thin plastic lines protruding from the baby's belly button connect to an electronic IV pump beside the cot. Adhesive electrodes on the baby's chest connect to a monitor that reads a near constant 170 beats per minute.

The team caring for the premature baby—an attending neonatologist, a fellow, a nurse, a pharmacist and a dietitian—forms a ring around the cot and listens intently. A care assistant replaces supplies on each side of the cot while an orderly disinfects the floors and countertops.

One step back of the team but watching and listening just as intently are two second-year medical students from the School of

Medicine at University College Cork and a thirty-year veteran neonatologist named Dr. Tony Ryan.

"What's going on? What do you notice?" Dr. Ryan asks the students.

"I see a heart and apnea monitor," says one of the students.

"I see a ventilator and an IV pump," says the other student.

"You see a ventilator, an IV pump, a heart and apnea monitor," echoes Dr. Ryan. "You see the technology surrounding the baby. What else do you see?"

"I see soft colours," says one of the students. "It's kind of dark."

"It's soft-coloured and semi-dark?" Dr. Ryan paraphrases the students. "Why do you think that is?"

"To keep from overstimulating the baby," says one of the students.

"Premature babies are often jittery," says the other.

Dr. Ryan is facilitating a session of VTS in the NICU. And the students are looking at a premature newborn instead of a work of art.

"The mother was not given dexamethasone," the resident who admitted the baby continues. "The baby was intubated at birth. She's on a ventilator, twenty over four, thirty with 30 percent oxygen. On the cardiovascular exam, I couldn't hear a murmur. There's no patent ductus."

"What else do you notice?" Dr. Ryan asks his students quietly, so as not to disturb the team.

"There are doctors and nurses," says one of the students.

"I can't see any parents," says the other student.

"Why do you think that is?" Dr. Ryan asks.

"Maybe the baby was transferred from another hospital," one of the students replies.

"What makes you think the baby was transferred from another hospital?" asks Dr. Ryan.

The student looks around the room for something to justify her speculation. She's stumped.

The resident helps her out.

"Dad has gone back home," says the resident. "Mom is still in the labour ward. This is her first baby, conceived through in vitro fertilization."

The resident continues with the lowdown. Meanwhile, the students have participated in a valuable lesson in VTS, thanks to Dr. Ryan.

= = =

SINCE 2012, THE VTS program at University College Cork has been one of the most vibrant. Dr. Tony Ryan trained in neonatology in Canada before returning to Ireland, where he started a neonatal resuscitation program in Cork before helping to create similar programs at every maternity hospital in the country.

"Up to that point, the neonatal resuscitation program was all about skills and knowledge," says Ryan. "But when the teamwork side of things came in, it really changed my mind."

Ryan, who also obtained a master's degree in education, attended one of the early courses in VTS and became a convert. He wrote a paper in 2013 lauding his experiences using VTS to teach medical students.

"I think VTS helps leaders and people to ask questions, to think out loud and to display empathetic listening," he says. "As a result, they're getting multiple perspectives from their peers around them that lead to better decision making, and that leads to better actions. And I think that prevents errors."

= = =

THAT IS MUSIC to the ears of Alexa Miller. One of the reasons she teaches VTS to medical students is to prevent the kinds of errors that led to her sister's misdiagnosis. In 2018, Miller teamed up with the Society to Improve Diagnosis in Medicine as one of its Fellows in Diagnostic Excellence. Not surprisingly, her focus was on how to use art appreciation to manage clinical uncertainty.

She believes that when doctors allow the perspectives of others to help shape what they see in their patients, it expands their knowledge and, in so doing, helps them make fewer errors. It's her background as an artist that tells her so.

"It's in our art habits," she says. "It's just the way artists move through the world differently and how they approach their work."

It's also in the habits of Dr. Joel Katz. That's not surprising, since he was a commercial artist before becoming a physician. He likes and uses VTS. But he's quick to point out it's not the only method that teaches teamwork to medical students.

"I've learned over time that not every arts educator believes in or uses VTS," says Katz. "There are other places that do similar work without it."

I asked him what they use instead.

"They use theatrical improv as a way to improve people's clinical skills," he says. "It sounds like it should be separate from clinical care. In my opinion, it's completely part of clinical care. It's through maintaining our humanity and humility and connections that good doctors are made."

And, as I'm about to find out, it also makes a good team player.

CHAPTER THREE

"YES, AND . . ."

Improv and music as alternatives to competition

I N THEORY, VISUAL Thinking Strategies should get health-care teams to work better together by creating a safe space for each member to share their unique take on any given patient. In that way, the team recognizes that group diagnosis is more accurate than that of any individual team member, no matter how smart they are.

But medical culture has historically been hierarchical, and VTS can't work when ranking members of the team overrule input from those with less seniority.

If the aim is to flatten the hierarchy, the first step is to get each member to recognize one another and understand where each person fits in the existing pecking order. One way to do that is to recruit an expert in theatre improv to apply the same principles to medicine. Call it "medical improv."

Katie Watson invented the term in 2002, when she created a method to improve doctor-patient communication that has since been used to teach hundreds of medical students to better connect with the people under their care and their loved ones. Watson is an associate professor of medical social sciences, medical education, and obstetrics and gynecology at the Feinberg School of Medicine at Northwestern University.

Watson isn't a health professional but a lawyer who clerked in the federal judiciary before coming to Northwestern. She's a celebrated bioethicist who penned the 2018 book *Scarlet A: The Ethics, Law, and Politics of Ordinary Abortion*, which the *New York Times* called "revolutionary."

Did I mention that she is also a playwright and an adjunct faculty member at the training centre of Chicago's Second City theatre?

I wondered just what improv has to do with talking to and listening to patients. Then I read this quote from a provocative paper Watson wrote, entitled "Serious Play: Teaching Medical Skills with Improvisational Theater Techniques," published in 2011 in the journal *Academic Medicine*: "The physician–patient encounter may be structured, but it is never scripted; every physician–patient interaction is to some degree improvised. Both physicians and improvisers must prepare for unpredictability, and the surprising and unrecognized overlap between improvisational theater and medical training and medical practice led the author to develop a seminar that tailors improvisational skills to physician needs . . . an approach she calls 'medical improv.'"

And I thought taking a medical history was highly scripted. It never occurred to me that most of what happens between doctor and patient is improvised.

"All of it," Watson corrected me emphatically.

Watson says the department chair at the Feinberg School of Medicine was likewise nonplussed when she pitched a course on medical improv.

"This is the most obvious thing in the world," she recalls thinking. "Why are they trying to teach them to control the moment like robots rather than swim through the moment like people?"

She gives the example of a patient with diabetes. Physicians should, she says, adopt a somewhat standard approach when asking about symptoms and discussing treatment options.

"But I'm still a human being sitting here," she says. "When we talk about how whatever you're proposing is going to interact with my life, I don't want you to just be reading from a template. That doesn't make any sense to me."

She says the way to break from the template is to pay attention to the patient's facial expressions and tone of voice. A look of bewilderment on the patient's face is your first clue that they're having a hard time assimilating the enormous lifestyle changes needed to control diabetes. That, says Watson, calls for improv.

"We are all improvising every minute of every day," she says. "If I'm not able to respond in the moment, I'm going to have a lot of relationship problems."

When she's not at the Feinberg School of Medicine, Watson runs improv workshops for healthcare workers on hospital wards and departmental retreats.

Among her favourite exercises is one called "Oscar Party." Watson pulls out a deck of playing cards and tapes a different card to the forehead of each participant, from a two to an ace. Everyone but the person wearing the card can see the value of the card.

Watson tells the players to pretend they're mingling at a party celebrating Oscar winners.

"You haven't seen it, but your playing card is your status," she says. "Your goal is to help inform your teammate how high or low they are in our Hollywood pecking order."

There's something about Oscar Party that gets even the stuffiest attending physician to play along. If they get stuck, Watson gives participants tips on how to help each player figure out the value on the card.

"You might say, 'Oh, I loved your movie. I can't believe you didn't win tonight,'" she says.

The trick is for participants to shade their compliments so that the person figures out the subtle difference between winning the Oscar and being the most deserving loser.

Watson has team members mingle like that for a few minutes. Then she does something really clever. She asks participants to take the cards off their foreheads, place them face down on their thighs, and arrange themselves in ascending order of status without looking at their cards.

"It's shocking how close to perfect they line up," she says.

Watson says they accomplish this feat by interpreting subtle clues. For example, the more people who wanted to get the person a drink or just talk to them, the more likely they are to have won the Oscar. Someone who's asked how they managed to score an invitation to the party can deduce that they weren't even close to winning.

For health professionals, the point of Oscar Party is to get them thinking about the existence of a hierarchy in the hospital that is implicit and often unseen. Depending on where you work, surgeons might have higher status than internists, just as specialists hold more sway than family doctors and physicians trump nurses. The next step is to get them thinking about which voices have more influence. That status determines whose voices are disregarded in meetings, even when they have something helpful to suggest.

"When people say, 'I don't do status, I don't see status,' I'm like, 'You're a liar,'" says Watson. "They're human beings. Of course they do!"

Watson steers the conversation from an Oscar party to an academic conference.

"Who wants to talk to who in the hallway?" Watson asks. "If you're a medical student, or you're the intern, you're the resident, you're the attending, we all figure out who is who."

The point of the exercise, says Watson, is that status matters.

This is critical if you're trying to encourage all members of the team to speak up when they notice errors and safety issues in a hospital where status determines whose voices are heard. It's also important even when you work in an explicit hierarchy but don't want to stifle people on the lowest rungs of the ladder.

"Is your goal in attaining high status to lord it over people, or to gather as much social capital as possible so you can distribute it for the greater good?" Watson asks.

She's trying to teach participants to stop thinking of status as good or bad and to recognize that each team member has agency and purpose. And she gives them exercises that provide the flexibility needed to operate at any level on the status ladder, from the first rung to the tenth.

"If you can't play every rung, from one to ten, you have a problem," Watson explains. "Your goal is to be able to play all ten, to know when to deploy that, and to deploy it in a rich and robust way."

Watson says that hospital department heads who are used to wielding power over healthcare teams need to operate quite differently when they're interacting with patients and their family members.

"If you are the brilliant guy who is chief of everything, but you're caring for an eleven-year-old who has come to the ER after being sexually assaulted, I suggest you learn to lower your status," she says. "You may be in charge at the emergency room, but tonight, you're going to be a dad at the daycare picnic, where you're just one more dad. We all have to learn how to play different statuses with different people in different situations and be aware [that] we're doing this within our teams in ways that are constructive or destructive."

Sometimes, you also need to learn how to play up to a higher status. She gave me the hypothetical example of a chief resident in the ER who is short in stature, speaks with a high-pitched voice and in her family of origin is the youngest of six children who never got to pick the movie.

"When the bus crash comes, I suggest that the resident needs to learn how to get big and take charge," she says.

She also says there are important lessons for people who don't have high status on healthcare teams.

"When you see someone abusing status, you take it a lot less personally," she says. "When you understand status, you say, 'Oh, that guy must be insecure. He's always trying to announce that he's a nine. I feel sorry for him. That must be exhausting.'"

=== ===

BEFORE SHE INVENTED medical improv, Watson performed at Chicago spots like the iO Theatre and the Annoyance Theatre & Bar before joining the Second City faculty in 2008. She directed several shows for GayCo Productions, and famously directed the first one-person show by Abby McEnany, star and head writer of the Showtime smash hit TV series *Work in Progress*.

Watson is not the only successful entertainer to teach improv to people like me. For years, Alan Alda, star of *M*A*S*H*, has been using improv to teach scientists and health professionals how to communicate better with one another and with the public.

"Nothing brings you closer to another person than improvisation," Alda told me. "It's the only training I ever had as an actor, and I recommend it to everybody."

In 2009, the Alan Alda Center for Communicating Science was founded at Stony Brook University in New York. The centre uses improvisational techniques that Alda learned during more than fifty years of acting.

"It's not comedy improv," he says. "We don't teach them to be funny. We don't teach them to act. We teach them the basic exercises of improvisation that make them better able to observe the other person. These are observational games. You read what's going on in the other person's head by what you observe in their body, in their speech, and that kind of thing."

Getting partners to mirror one another's movements or getting them to join in a conversation spoken in gibberish are just two of the exercises they teach at Stony Brook.

The aim is to increase trust between health professionals and patients and between members of the health team.

"There's so much more pressure on medical professionals and teams that there may even be less good communication occurring among the members of a team," Alda says. "If it takes a whole team to help one patient, the better they communicate, the better the help will be."

Both the Alda Center for Communicating Science and Katie Watson teach established professionals and trainees. Watson tells me there are varying degrees of success. "The further people get into practice, the more calcified they become and the more threatening it is to try something new, but the more rewarding it is," she says. "With those people, you have to do a totally different workshop. If you don't convince them in the first five minutes [that] this will be a good use of their time, they will just check out."

She says it's much easier with doctors in training.

"Medical students are more plastic and elastic, so the work goes so much faster than [with] my Second City students. You say, 'Jump,' and they say, 'How high?' You say, 'I promise you that this will help. You tell me when we're done if I'm wrong.' They say, 'Okay, let's go for a ride.' They are uniformly thrilled by the end. And I mean uniformly. I've been doing this for a long time."

Amy Zelenski, one of Katie Watson's acolytes, has been teaching medical improv to residents and students in the Department of Medicine at the University of Wisconsin in Madison since 2013. The former actor and current PhD in education designs curricula and teaches communication, empathy, self-awareness and teamwork.

Zelenski studied with Katie Watson and also took training at the Alda Center. Her aim at the University of Wisconsin is to use medical improv to improve interprofessional teamwork. An outsider to medical culture, Zelenski is one of the few people to speak plainly about just how often members of the healthcare team work at cross-purposes.

"What I often see working with physicians and nursing staff and other people—even among different specialties of medicine—[is that] there can sometimes be a lot of ego involved," she says. "They want to be the person who was right about the diagnosis or the treatment, as opposed to treating the patient."

The most rudimentary of improv exercises involve pairs of health professionals. Zelenski says improv exercises build teamwork by getting individuals to shift focus from themselves to their partner.

"The goal of improv is to always make your partner look good and to set them up for success," she says. "If you're trying to make the nurse look good or the caregiver look good, it changes the way that you go about things in ways that are more helpful to the goal of the team."

Zelenski's go-to exercise for making other members of the team look good is a staple of improv called "Yes, and."

The technique is based on the acceptance principle. When each player in an improv scene says something, the partner responds by accepting what the player says as the truth and then by adding a statement of their own. The "and" part of the reply builds on the reality established by the first player.

Without announcing it, Zelenski gives me a demonstration.

"It's so nice to meet you here in the intergalactic space station, and we're here to welcome our new mayor to Mars," she offers.

"Yes, and they've had a problem with the airlock this morning, and I think they fixed it," I reply.

"Thank goodness," Zelenski says. "My goodness, I feel so bad for poor Louise, who got sucked out into the abyss."

"Yes, and she had a hell of a view," I reply as I get into the act.

"Yes, and she went out with a bang," says Zelenski.

Zelenski explains how the "Yes, and" exercise helps foster teamwork from the first offer.

"It's so much about listening," she says. "If you're not listening, you're not going to see the offer or see what they're doing well in order to take that on or highlight it."

Contrast "Yes, and" with a different verbal construction known as "Yes, but," a form Zelenski says is used all the time at team meetings inside and outside of healthcare.

I can confirm that. In the ER, we have an unpredictably high volume of tasks. To free up time, I'd like to be able to delegate. For instance, when a physician calls the ER to refer a patient, I'm supposed to drop whatever I'm doing and speak to the doctor. When I've suggested a nurse take a message, I'm told, "Yes, but" the conversation has to be doctor to doctor. I've suggested that the referring physician send a text; I'm told, "Yes, but" the text doesn't comply with provincial privacy laws.

These replies, correct though they are, effectively shut the door on further discussion. This rigid approach can also have a chilling effect, depending on who is speaking up and for what reason, because it can suggest that even asking a question is a mistake.

At team meetings, "Yes, but" is a conversation inhibitor.

The third type of construction Zelenski teaches at her improv class is a flat "No." In meetings, it's a near-absolute conversation stopper.

Beyond "Yes, and," Zelenski teaches healthcare students to notice the non-verbal behaviour that their partner is offering them—things like undulating digits or pretending to wipe sweat off one's brow. Zelenski teaches them that failing to notice these behaviours can throw off an entire improv scene or a team meeting in a hospital.

Zelenski's six-week course is called Improv for Health Professionals and is offered to freshmen medical students. It begins with getting students comfortable doing scenes in dyads. After that, there are sessions on status and hierarchy, recognizing emotion and acknowledging emotions in other people, and how to think on your feet.

Maya Amjadi recently finished her third year of medical school at the University of Wisconsin. She's in the university's combined MD PhD program. She took the improv course as a first-year student along with senior medical students and trainees in nursing, physiotherapy and social work.

"All the other students were older than me," says Amjadi. "I remember walking into that big open classroom just feeling like I was the most naive person there."

She says Zelenski put her at ease by starting with "Yes, and," "Yes, but" and "No."

"The 'Yes, and' conversation is really easy to keep fuelling," says Amjadi. "You learn a lot from the other person. You get somewhere. You get a lot of information."

During clinical rotations at the hospital, she sees how "Yes, but" and "No" inhibit some healthcare providers.

"A pharmacist, nurse, social worker or clinical manager may have a difficult time speaking up if they're used to being undercut, undermined, disagreed with or shut down," she says. "The more you can agree [with] rather than deny your team members, the more information you're going to get from them and the more you facilitate open communication."

Amjadi recalls putting that training to use when she took care of a patient in his sixties who had cancer with metastases to his lower spine. The metastases compressed the nerves coming off the lower spinal cord, causing paralysis and incontinence.

Amjadi was the youngest member of the team, but she was the first to recognize her patient's complex needs.

"I needed to coordinate his care by contacting his oncologist," she recalls. "To make him comfortable, I needed to call for palliative care. I needed to have an end-of-life discussion with the entire family. That was a lot of coordinating communication with different team members."

She says improv training made her comfortable playing different roles in conversations with a wide range of medical professionals and personality types.

"With improv, you're entering an unknown situation. You can't really plan ahead of time and you don't know what's about to happen. When you go onstage, you have to just sit with that and be present with that and be okay with it. As a medical student on rotations in the hospital, that's a constant."

A paper by Katie Watson and Dr. Belinda Fu published in 2016 in the *Annals of Internal Medicine* suggested "that medical improv deserves further study to determine whether it is an effective training method."

The duo wrote that "medical improv might help clinicians interact with patients and colleagues in a more genuine, humane, and flexible way."

Amy Zelenski believes that patients and their families see the benefits of improv classes.

"If we could train every healthcare provider, we would have a healthier system," she says. "It would be about providing the best care for and with the patient. And I think it would mean individual benefits like feeling better about yourself and more confident in what you have to bring to the table."

===

AS A SEASONED ER physician, I think the biggest challenge in getting health professionals to try medical improv is to get them past their fear of making a fool of themselves in front of their colleagues. It's a challenge a professional musician in Philadelphia relishes. Except he uses a different sort of exercise—one that has a beat.

"Hi, everybody. I'm Josh Robinson. Welcome to the course." Josh Robinson stands in front of a big semicircle of thirty fresh-faced medical students on one side of a large conference room inside the Bluemle Life Sciences Building at Thomas Jefferson University (TJU) in Philadelphia.

Bluemie Life, as they call it, is a state-of-the-art facility for basic biomedical research. During the day, the building hums with the sounds of spinning ultracentrifuges, static-generating scintillation counters and rhythmic shakers.

In the evening, the percussion track is different.

"You're probably wondering what all this stuff is behind you and trying to make sense of it all," says Josh. He points to a table crowded with colourful bucket drums, a djembe, various bells, pots and seeds, an instrument that looks like a cricket and one that looks like a frog.

"I want you to go around and play the different sounds and then write down a word on a flashcard," says Josh. "What's the first word that pops into your mind when you hear this sound? If this sound was a colour, what would it be?"

The medical students have somewhat puzzled looks on their faces.

"Don't think about it too hard, because the goal is to not think," says Josh. "It's to feel."

The course is called Language of Music, and Josh has been teaching it at TJU since 2017. Of all the things intended to make health professionals better team players, a course in drumming is about as off the wall as it gets.

"I'm not trying to turn any doctors into percussionists," Josh tells me.

The course is an eclectic mix of exercises to foster partnerships and teams. The students make maracas, seed drums and other instruments, and then play them solo and as a group.

"They have cues and signals where they have to make eye contact with a certain number of people, or while we're all drumming in a circle," he says. "I have other cues that the direction is to make eye contact with somebody and make a non-verbal agreement to jump up and switch instruments with them while the music is going."

The idea behind that exercise is for group members to keep the rhythm going while switching parts. Robinson says the teamwork part comes from cuing them to pay close attention to one another while drumming.

"I have this rhythm going and then people are jumping up and looking at each other and trying to communicate and agree. Meanwhile, you can't let the rhythm die, so we have to take care of the bigger picture," he says. "I think they're learning to understand themselves and the role they play in the big picture."

That's a core lesson to learn in teamwork. In the big picture, it's less about individual members and more about what the team is trying to do.

Language of Music also tries to get these bright students to put their minds on pause.

"There's not a lot of opportunity [for students] to get out of their thinking space and into the feeling space," he says. "The kind of person who goes into medical school is focused on being exact. There's a lot of tension that goes along with the worry of making mistakes and operating out of a fear of messing things up."

What he's trying to do is coax the students to spend more time just being in the moment. It's a mindset that brought the drummer to this moment in time and this teaching opportunity.

= = =

ROBINSON HAS BEEN a fixture on the Philly music scene for two decades. He was born in 1971 and grew up in Woodstock, New York. His parents were folk musicians who played and recorded as a duo in the 1960s. His dad worked as a sound engineer for the Band for several years following "The Last Waltz," a concert put on by the Band at the Winterland Ballroom in San Francisco in 1976 that at the time was billed as the iconic rock group's farewell concert appearance. The concert was filmed and turned into a successful documentary by director Martin Scorsese.

Robinson's dad was a sound engineer at the Woodstock Recording Studio and was friendly with a lot of famous musicians from the Woodstock scene, like John Sebastian from the Lovin' Spoonful. When Rick Danko and Levon Helm started to get the Band back together (first as an acoustic duo), they hired Robinson's dad as the sound engineer. Josh, then just thirteen years old, got to tag along.

"We would go to Gerde's Folk City or the Lonestar in New York," Robinson recalls. "I remember meeting Levon at one of those shows. My dad brought me to New York City to Gerde's Folk City, introduced me to Rick and Levon, and I got to watch the show. Danko was an amazing guy, so warm to the kids. I was close with his sons. And he would drive us around in his minivan and drop us off at the pinball place. He was always telling us that he loved kids. He's like a big kid."

Other members of the Band, including Garth Hudson and Richard Manuel, rejoined the group, and they went on tour.

"Sometimes my dad would let me sound-check Levon's drums," says Robinson. "So one time I was sound-checking the drums at a nice theatre. And then Rick Danko walks out onstage with his bass to do a sound check."

Danko started playing a song called "The Walk." Robinson knew the song and started playing along.

"I ended up jamming with Rick on Levon's drums while all these people that were working at the facility are looking at me like, 'Holy crap,'" Robinson recalls.

Robinson accompanied his dad and the Band all over the United States and Japan. Along the way, he met many famous musicians, including drummer Bill Kreutzmann of the Grateful Dead.

One night at the Capitol Theater in Passaic, New Jersey, Rick Danko was opening for the Jerry Garcia Band, a side project of the Grateful Dead frontman. Kreutzmann came down to watch Danko's set.

"We're all hanging out backstage," Robinson recalls. "They called us the Band kids. They were like, 'Hey, one of the Band kids is a drummer.'"

Hearing that, Kreutzmann tore a T-shirt, folded it up on a metal table and taught Robinson his first drum rudiment. It's known as a paradiddle, a drum beat that consists of two single strokes followed by a double stroke; for example, right, left, right, right, or left, right, left, left.

"I remember thinking to myself that this guy is wasted," Robinson recalls. "I mean, he seemed kind of wasted to me. But as soon as he started drumming and picking up speed, it was the clearest, most incredible thing. I think he gave me the sticks or the shirt or something. And I was like, 'Wow. I just learned paradiddle from Bill. Cool.'"

Despite those powerful memories, back then Robinson was not planning on a career in music, let alone joining a rock band. In fact, Robinson says his childhood was far from blissful.

"My father was addicted to drugs and an abusive person, so very early on, my mother left him, when I was a baby," he says. "He's just pretty terrible. When you're a little kid, I would say the first emotion to get up the nerve to jump up to help you out is anger. I think emotionally, especially for children, I feel like when you don't know what you're feeling or what's going on and you have no control over it, I feel like anger is always sitting at the front row with its hand up, ready to jump in."

Looking back, Robinson thinks the rage he felt was a smoke-screen for profound sadness and disappointment in his father. Early on, he found some emotional release through drumming. He fashioned a little pot-and-pan drum set-up in the basement. He says he made his first cymbal using the lid to an old salt-and-pepper pot; he tied one end of a rope around the handle and the other end around a nail in the ceiling. It made what he describes as a "crashy, bashy sound."

"I would go down to the basement and pound away on that thing," Robinson recalls. "I was a little kid. But I would come up feeling better. Drumming and football were two ways for me to manage some of the early aggression and anger. I kept drumming throughout my life."

It's a habit he still relies on.

Robinson says his parents weren't planners, and it's a trait he picked up from them.

"I didn't have a lot of inner self-confidence or vision at the time," he says. "It never occurred to me that maybe I should be asking Levon for some pointers. It never occurred to me that this maybe was a career path that I should follow. It was all very in-the-moment kind of stuff."

Robinson acknowledges the fundamental role his dad's connections played in his own career development. And while there were bad moments, some were sublime.

In the summer of 1985, the Band was on tour with Crosby, Stills & Nash. Robinson's dad was the sound engineer, and Robinson was allowed to tag along. He spent part of the summer attending a sports camp for wealthy kids. Robinson says that without a scholarship his parents would not have been able to afford the camp tuition.

"I remember the rich kids' parents would always come in with their fancy Mercedes station wagons," says Robinson.

The Band and Crosby, Stills & Nash were playing a concert at a nearby racetrack and came to pick Robinson up.

"I had my moment when this big old Greyhound bus carrying both bands pulled into the camp, opened up the doors, and the band members came out to help," says Robinson. "I threw my trunk and my duffle bag into the storage compartment and said, 'Let's go.' The whole camp just stood there staring. And I was like, 'Yeah, peace out.'"

===

IN COLLEGE, ROBINSON joined an African Brazilian drum and dance ensemble. A study trip to Cuba schooled him in Afro-Cuban music and convinced him to make music his full-time gig.

Today, he is a member of Alô Brasil, a fourteen-piece Philadelphia-based samba group known as one of the premiere Brazilian bands in the mid-Atlantic region. Robinson also performs with the Spoken Hand Percussion Orchestra, a fusion group with influences from Brazil, Cuba, India and Africa. With his wife, Giovana, Robinson founded Rhythms & Roots, a Latin music ensemble. The couple was selected to the 2003 and 2004 Philadelphia Music Project's Latin Orchestra, led by famed bandleader Johnny Pacheco and Cuban pianist, composer and producer Elio Villafranca. He also performs regularly with Latin music groups, poets and DJs, as well as theatre and dance troupes.

In 2020–21, Robinson was the artist-in-residence in the Humanities & Health program at TJU. The aim of the program is for the artist to work alongside healthcare professionals, patients and their families, researchers, and students to explore how creative practices can help realize a holistic community of care and open new contexts for understanding one another at the university.

His interest in the health professions was sparked when a childhood friend was diagnosed with multiple sclerosis. Robinson made a point of visiting her each time he came home to Woodstock.

"I would play my field drum or my handpan as a way to soothe her," he says. "At a certain point, she lost her ability to speak, and I would just go and play the drum for her. We still were connected, like we could still communicate."

He had a similar experience with a friend who had pneumonia and was in the intensive care unit on a ventilator.

"He was a big fan of a Brazilian band that I played in," says Robinson. "I brought my friend who plays guitar into the hospital, and we played for him what ended up being his last concert. I've always felt like music was this powerful way to connect and express when people couldn't use words."

His father's drug and alcohol abuse and his frequent absences due to work led to Robinson spending more time with his grandfather, a carpenter and a police officer who lived in Philadelphia. Eventually, Robinson moved to the city to be closer to him.

"He had those sandpaper, hard-working man hands," says Robinson. "He was definitely my male role model."

At age ninety-one, Robinson's grandfather had a heart attack and drove himself to Lankenau Heart Institute in west Philadelphia. He lived the last month of his life in the hospital's ICU. Most of the time, he was unconscious. Josh Robinson was with him every day.

"It was my opportunity to take care of him," says Robinson. "I would try to communicate and let him know that I was there. I saw that I was limited by words that I had to choose from to express myself."

Robinson decided to use the language of percussion and brought his steel pan to the ICU.

"I began to play and think about the drum as my voice and my filter for all of the emotions that came out in an improvisational way," Robinson recalls. "For three to five hours a day, I was sitting there, playing next to my grandfather. Hope would pop up and the song would change, and [then] despair and fear and worry, and the song would change. I just used it as this vehicle."

Steel drums emit some of purest and crispest notes of any musical instrument. When played by themselves, their emotional tone ranges from jolly to celestial. The nurses on the ward took notice. They got into the moment and began to compete for the daily assignments closest to the music. The family members of other patients noticed too.

"I would walk into somebody's room and introduce myself and start playing for them," he says. "It was funny because the first guy I went to play for looked like he'd just hopped off a Harley-Davidson motorcycle."

Robinson says the man asked for Deep Purple, Led Zeppelin and Blue Öyster Cult.

"He just closed his eyes and lay back with his big sideburns," says Robinson.

Robinson says he played for patients with advanced cancer. Patients with heart disease like his grandfather. Patients with amyotrophic lateral sclerosis. His steel pan relaxed and soothed them. They needed fewer painkillers. They breathed easier.

Like Robinson's grandfather, they were able to die in peace during their stay in the ICU.

A year and a half after his grandfather died, Robinson dropped his son off at school. The school was situated by the Schuylkill River, and Robinson liked to drum by the water. One day, a jogger approached him. It was his grandfather's heart surgeon.

"We still talk about you, the kid with the drum that looks like a spaceship," the surgeon told Robinson. "You really had an impact on us. I just want you to know that that was an amazing thing you did for him, but ultimately for all of us, because the music transformed the space. People that were working around the music were calmer and it was a de-stressing vibration going through that floor."

Robinson did not seem surprised when I suggested to him that he had become an honorary member of the ICU team.

"I think I gave them some relief," he says. "There are tons of alarms going off and all the sounds are kind of nerve-wracking. I think I ran some interference on those typical frequencies and sounds. I think they probably felt my emotion as I was sitting there sending love to my grandfather through the music."

Robinson took the heart surgeon's words to heart. He started running drum workshops at camps for children with life-limiting illnesses. That led to an invitation to do a presentation for the National Alliance for Grieving Children symposium in Portland, Oregon. He also reached out to Wissahickon Hospice (part of Penn Medicine Hospice Services) and started working there.

His work with grieving families came to the attention of Megan Voeller, TJU's director of humanities. A friend and colleague of VTS expert Alexa Miller, Voeller was the curator and Art in Health program director at the University of South Florida, where she set up a VTS program for students.

Voeller says she recruited Robinson because she wanted to see if improvisational drumming could teach medical students to be more comfortable making mistakes and taking risks. And might that, in turn, spur the development of leadership skills?

As we've seen, VTS encourages health professionals to take risks in voicing their impressions of art. Voeller believes improvisational drumming does the same thing in a more extroverted way. Think of it as a safe place to risk making a fool of yourself.

"They do a lot of group process work that's about creating things together," she says. "And they do so while being vulnerable in the sense that they're often being kind of goofy and experimenting and doing things creatively."

Voeller thinks that nervousness is important to the growth and development of the students. And Josh Robinson says students who take the course soon realize that they're in it together.

"Each student sees that they are not the only one who is terrified of doing this in front of their class," he says. "I see their playful side. I see the ten-year-old in them."

If course testimonials are any indication, the medical students who take the Language of Music love it. Robinson says some students return to musical hobbies they'd long since abandoned on the road to becoming doctors. He told me about one student who picked up a guitar that he had not touched in years and began to play it during a session that was conducted via Zoom because of the COVID-19 pandemic.

"He got inspired to pick up the guitar in the session," says Robinson. "He completely found his connection and his safe haven and everything again through the course. It was mind-boggling and humbling."

Other students have told Robinson that they can see how improvisational drumming can boost teamwork.

"This class also required everyone to be very focused and aware of their surroundings in order to stay with the beat and rhythm of the group," said one of the students.

Robinson says he builds teamwork exercises into the course. In one exercise, the students listen to a track of music and are asked how it makes them feel. After that, they team up with six students and craft a poem made up of each student's answers.

"They come up with these very interesting and creative poems, and then they have to add music to it to accompany the poem, so they're coming up with this performance," he says. "You can see people are embarrassed or worried or silly, but in the end, I think what happens is they always come up with something beautiful and creative, and I think the teams are bonded."

He also builds teamwork by introducing the students to polyrhythms, which are defined as a combination of two or more rhythms played simultaneously while moving at the same linear tempo. Each polyrhythm is named after a formula that lets you know exactly how the different rhythms relate to one another.

Robinson says the exercise teaches students how to hold down a drumming pattern and maintain focus without getting distracted by the patterns played by the other students. It also teaches them that the final product produced by the team is greater than the sum of its parts.

"The pull and tug of everybody trying to lock in is pretty interesting," he observes. "It's powerful. And I think their awareness of themselves in the group and kind of relying on each other and trusting each other seems present, seems like it's translating for them."

Robinson has taught improvisational drumming to established health professionals who work in teams. He says the course helps them value contributions from other people on the team. "They start to build trust with each other that somebody else might have a better idea and it's okay," he says. "It's not a competition."

===

FOR CENTURIES, THE Indigenous Peoples of North America have used songs and drums in healing ceremonies to help with everything from celebrations to facing illness to grieving for loved ones. While percussion has been proven to induce deep relaxation, reduce stress and lower blood pressure, there are, unsurprisingly, few studies on the role of improvisational drumming as it relates to teamwork. A 2018 study published in *Frontiers in Psychology* by Martina Di Mauro and colleagues at the University of Padua and the University of Bath offers some insight.

The team recruited forty-eight volunteers (drummers, other kinds of musicians with no drumming experiences, and non-musicians), showed them audiovisual clips of professional drummers and asked them not to imitate but to improvise each recorded performance based on what they thought or felt the musician was trying to convey. The performances included variations in genre (jazz or heavy metal), tempo, complexity of rhythms, the expressiveness of the drummer (minimal or maximal expressive interpretation of the music) and the drummer's playing style (playing with open or crossed arms).

Each of the participants was able to perceive basic emotions in the drumming such as joy, sadness, fear, anger, disgust and surprise regardless of training or expertise in drumming. The greater the expressiveness of the drummer, the greater the level of happiness that the drumming generated. Drummers and non-musicians found heavy metal drumming more expressive than jazz drumming.

The researchers were surprised that non-musicians perceived positive emotions like joy from heavy metal drumming given the fact that other studies have found that heavy metal music tends to convey aggression and hostility. They concluded that long-term musical percussion training shapes emotional processing, with potential implications for music therapy, clinical practice and the theory of emotions triggered or induced by music.

It would not surprise me if shared emotions were the pathway through which improvisational drumming promotes teamwork.

Mary Jo Hatch, professor emerita at the McIntire School of Commerce at the University of Virginia, is an organizational theorist. Hatch has written extensively about jazz as a metaphor for modern organizational thinking.

This is what she wrote in a paper published in *Organization Science* in 1998: "If you look at the list of characteristics that are associated with 21st century organizations, you find concepts like flexible, adaptable, responsive to the environment, loose boundaries, minimal hierarchy . . . all of those ideas could as easily be associated with a jazz band as a 21st century organization."

The Jazz Experience is an interactive ninety-minute event that explores teamwork, flexibility and creativity through the metaphor of jazz. Following a performance of a familiar song by a live jazz band, participants are given a handheld percussion instrument and invited to join a band of three to six players. Each band gets thirty minutes to create an original piece of music that they will perform for the entire group, followed by an interactive debrief that relates to the corporate environment of the participants.

Many such courses are given to large corporations. Few follow in Josh Robinson's footsteps and serve both health professionals and patients and families. It's what makes Robinson unique.

At medical school, he reminds students that music is good for their well-being. In the ICU, his drumming changes the frequency from the throbbing rhythms of cardiac alarms into something more soothing. He teaches everyone that it's okay to make a percussive fool of yourself.

Katie Watson uses medical improv to teach that one of the most powerful secrets of teamwork is to use "Yes, and" to make the other members of the team look good.

These erstwhile non-medical people bring shared mindfulness and sometimes even shared exhilaration.

When doctors, nurses, paramedics and respiratory therapists on a cardiac or trauma resuscitation team are working to save the life of someone in cardiac arrest, the key to building teamwork is a shared sense of mission.

One of the most effective ways to build that is by getting the team to play games.

CHAPTER FOUR

GAMES

Learning to play for the team

T HE ONLY GOOD thing about the large and dimly lit room is that it's warmer than the chilly January evening in Philadelphia. It takes a moment for one's eyes to adjust. The nine young men and women gathered here are disoriented by the darkness and a bit stressed by a ticking clock on the wall.

Dominating the room is a big table with inscriptions on the surface and hidden drawers around the sides; it is surrounded by pillars, paintings and murals.

"Hey, there's a candelabra," says a young woman.

"This is really stupid," says a young man watching from the sidelines. "Why am I here?"

"Not everybody gets out of here," says a second woman, who sounds like the leader. "We have sixty minutes. Let's divvy up the tasks and see if we can figure this out together."

At each corner of the room, they find clues and bring them back to the big table.

A woman finds a secret compartment hidden behind a framed painting hung on a wall. One of the young men opens one of the drawers.

"I found a key," he says. He takes it to a locked door and opens it.

Most of them seem relieved as they walk through into the next room. But the game is far from over.

===

THE DIG IS one of the most popular first-person experiences in the escape room genre. It's produced by hyperreal adventure company Escape the Room. The Dig is set up as a mystery puzzle, the object of which is to find hidden treasures, figure out the clues and solve the puzzles so you and your team can break free before time runs out.

The young men and women who played the Dig that chilly January night were ER residents taking part in a research study conducted by an ER physician, mechanical engineer and game theorist who thinks escape rooms are an essential step in moulding a group of MDs into a team.

His name is Xiao Chi Zhang, and he did his residency in emergency medicine at the Alpert Medical School of Brown University before coming to Thomas Jefferson University in Philadelphia to do a fellowship in medical education. TJU is also where Josh Robinson teaches medical students improvisational drumming.

Zhang was born in China and moved with his parents to the United States at the age of ten. He's a leading figure in the "gamification" of medical education. Gamification refers to the process of taking common elements of games for amusement and applying them to business, marketing and professional training. It's a hot topic in medical education too.

"Wouldn't it be great to use a 'low stakes' game to emulate something [teamwork] that's really crucial in caring for patients?" says Zhang. "That's how it all started."

Zhang was lead researcher in a 2018 study in which nine ER residents and one senior ER physician and faculty member played the Dig. Participants formed a single group with the goal of escaping the room within sixty minutes. They were given no other instructions and were not told to assign a leader or even if having a leader was helpful. Zhang also went into the room to observe the participants.

After the game concluded, a TJU faculty member surveyed the participants on how they solved problems during the game as well as their impressions of the experience. The data was obtained solely from the post-game survey.

The ER has an unpredictable workflow in which oases of quiet are followed by tsunamis of tumult.

"There's just so many things going on at the same time," says Zhang. "As the attending ER physician trying to orchestrate all of this, I have to know exactly what is going on."

For Zhang, a commercial escape room operates in a similar way.

"Most escape rooms have six puzzles that you have to solve in parallel to each other. And the results of the six puzzles will grant you the answer to unlock this door, which leads to a next set of multiple things. With a time crunch, it really simulates the fact that you can't just do one thing."

With escape rooms, you have no choice but to work collaboratively. It's the same in the ER.

"You don't just sit there and bang your head against the wall for the next twenty-five minutes," says Zhang. "You ask someone else who has a fresh set of eyes to come in and take a look."

The resulting paper's long title, "Trapped as a Group, Escape as a Team: Applying Gamification to Incorporate Team-building Skills Through an 'Escape Room' Experience," explains much.

Zhang says the residents were initially skeptical about the educational value of the experience.

"Because most escape room games are non-medical, the residents felt a little detached from them as specific team-building exercises to improve patient care."

After playing, though, they thought the Dig was like working in the ER. They had to switch tasks quickly, solve puzzles and keep reassessing the situation under time pressure. And they had to create an instant team from a group of individuals to pool knowledge and distribute the puzzle-solving to each participant.

I've been the doctor in charge of many code blue cardiac arrest procedures in the ER. Zhang made me see the similarities between those and escape rooms. Both have a group of people who are thrown together and expected to work together.

Like escape rooms, at the outset some hospital code blue teams may seem chaotic.

"The first room [in an escape room game] is always the hardest because that is where you're put into this new environment," he says. "You don't know who's going to be the leader."

A hospital's code blue team usually has a designated leader. But in the ER, where I work, there may be four or five staff ER physicians capable of leading. The doctor who first saw the patient usually takes charge. But sometimes, that doctor is near the end of their shift and tired. A fresher colleague may make a better leader at that point. In those cases, a leader may emerge in much the same way that they do in an escape room.

"What I find to be very interesting is that it really reflects a social hierarchy," Zhang says. "From the moment the door opens, you're going to have or identify the likely leader in the first three seconds."

The best leader is calm, has good situational awareness, delegates tasks and can switch tasks for people who are getting frustrated.

"In a poorly managed code, it's often loud, hectic and scary," he says. "But in a very well-run code, it's quiet. In fact, most people don't even say anything because you removed all that tension."

Zhang believes the quiet in code blue resuscitations and escape rooms demonstrates cohesion among group members, and that there's an implicit (if not stated) shared responsibility, with each member of the group contributing to solving the puzzle or saving a life.

"Regardless of what challenges they faced, they knew exactly what to do. And then they gained confidence and trust in each other."

Zhang says games are also becoming part of the medical curriculum because they're more fun and less stressful and because they remove the high stakes of failure. When it comes to teaching teamwork, he says games might be better than didactic methods.

"Much of teamwork is through experience. Much of it is through in-situ simulations like this, where you didn't know you had these skills until I put you in these situations."

Escape rooms teach budding ER doctors teamwork. But there's another kind of game that teaches ER managers how to work with managers of other departments in a big-city hospital. And you don't need an escape room to try this one out.

===

IT'S THE DAY before the 2019 QSEN (Quality and Safety Education for Nurses) International Forum, in Cleveland, Ohio. The annual forum gathers nurses and allied health professionals, managers and researchers to share knowledge and best practices on how to improve the quality of healthcare.

Thirty-two nursing students and professionals sit four per table at eight round tables in a breakout room. Instead of viewing a PowerPoint, they're about to play a board game. Not Monopoly or Snakes and Ladders; this one is called Friday Night at the ER (FNER).

Jill Steiner Sanko, an assistant professor at the University of Miami School of Nursing and Health Studies, gives players the rules of the game.

"You will each play the role of a department manager at a community hospital," says Steiner Sanko in a clear voice. "We have compressed the hospital into four departments."

All of the players are paying close attention.

"And one more instruction before you go and play on your own," she says. "You will at times see an event card when you flip the arrivals cards. When you do, just turn over the top event card in each department and do what it says on the card during the next hour of gameplay. Go ahead now and continue to play the game on your own."

The players have fun at first, but by the end of the game, there's some tension. The situations depicted in FNER feel quite real to the players.

"I can humbly say that I didn't play it well," says Mary Dolansky, director of the QSEN Institute and an associate professor at the Frances Payne Bolton School of Nursing at Case Western Reserve University in Cleveland. "I wasn't a systems thinker."

I was eager to learn more about FNER. Jeff Heil gave me a virtual tour. Heil is the CEO of Breakthrough Learning, the company that makes and sells FNER.

"This is a top-down view of the game set up on a table," says Heil. "Typically, there are multiple tables set up in a room, but for the purpose of the demo, we're just going to look at the one. It's four people, each tasked with managing one department. This is a simplified hospital, of course."

Though I'm an ER physician, Jeff isn't letting me manage the ER.

"We don't allow healthcare workers to play at their usual department," Heil explains.

I tell him I'll run critical care.

"It won't take very long into the game before you blame the ER for all your staffing and bed problems in critical care," he says.

There's a point to this. Hospital managers have trouble thinking beyond their own department. FNER forces you to consider how your department in the game dovetails with the three other departments.

Each department has rooms represented by white squares. Within those rooms, there are blue beads (patients) paired with white beads (hospital staff). The players must maintain a one-to-one ratio between patients and staff.

Heil tells me to think of those staff beads as optimal proportions of doctors, nurses, technicians and administrators for each patient.

"Players need to keep adequate staff with patients at all times as represented by that one-to-one ratio," says Heil.

FNER runs over a simulated twenty-four-hour period condensed into a single hour of actual playing time. There are five steps in each simulated hour on the clock that teams must complete before moving to the next hour.

"The first step is patient arrivals," he says. "You can see there are inflow arrows leading into each of the four departments. This is how patients enter the hospital from the community, which is represented by the two jars of blue beads on the table. That's the community."

In the game's ER, patients arrive as walk-ins or by ambulance. Patients leave the hospital via the ER or the step down unit.

At the start of the game, players in each department have room for additional patients. Over time, random factors eat up that additional capacity.

In each simulated hour, players managing surgery, critical care or step down may decide not to receive more patients. The player managing the ER can divert ambulances to surrounding hospitals. What the ER player can't do is block incoming patients who walk in, though they can be directed to wait in a separate area in which there are no staff to watch over them.

Staffing the department is the fourth step, and it is another critical decision players must make every hour. Since one of the key rules of the game is to maintain a balance between patients and staff, players can call in extra personnel.

"Think of the additional staff as agency, contract or overtime workers," says Heil. "They come at a premium, but they can help managers accept more patients."

At the end of each simulated hour, managers record things like the number of patients waiting to enter and any extra staff that they brought in. When they complete the five steps, they move on to the next hour by flipping to the next arrivals card, which shows a new set of arriving patients.

As the game progresses, things start looking different on the game board. Green dots appear on some of the blue patient beads. They signify patients who are ready to transfer from one department to another but haven't moved yet.

"In the real world, it can take hours from the time a patient is ready to transfer to the time they actually move," says Heil. "In the game, we simulate that delay. The other thing is that the receiving department might not be willing or able to accept the patient at that time. Thus, it takes two co-operating managers to complete a patient transfer."

Heil says players have told him the scenarios seem real.

FNER also has curveballs, like a nearby hospital diverting ambulances. That increases the influx of patients in the ER. A staff member in critical care gets sick and goes home, forcing that department to reduce the number of patients.

"Arrivals keep pouring in and there's mounting pressure to prevent new patients," he says.

Diverting ambulance arrivals may seem like a smart way to block new patients, but FNER shows the impact on other departments—and opens players' eyes to a more effective solution.

"Players avoid calling in extra staff because that's a cost they're trying to manage," says Heil. "In fact, adding extra staff is relatively inexpensive compared to the impact on financial performance of serving fewer customers."

FNER shows players the extra cost in a way that gives them an apples-to-apples comparison. In the game, extra staff costs forty points per unit. But diverting ambulances costs 5,000 points per vehicle. Any tactic that benefits one department at the expense of the others means points lost.

"You come to realize how interconnected the different departments are and how much managers depend on one another," says Heil. "You watch your decisions play out in front of you. In this simulation environment, you develop an intuitive understanding of systems that's otherwise lost in the real world."

A sixty-to-ninety-minute game (twenty-four to thirty-six hours of elapsed hospital time) is followed by a two-hour debrief. Heil says FNER teaches three lessons on teamwork. The first is collaboration. The second is innovation, which is code for creative thinking. For example, the game shows players that bringing on enough extra staff effectively doubles the number of patients they can admit to their department.

The third lesson is decision making driven by data. During the game, a facilitator walks around with a stack of data cards that contain answers to critical questions, such as the cost of bringing in extra staff. But you only get to see the cards if you ask the facilitator the right questions.

"Many people don't ask for data," Heil says. "They make assumptions with limited information, which leads to decisions that are well-intended but have adverse consequences on the system."

Players take valuable lessons on teamwork back to their hospitals. I wanted to find out whether teamwork is a by-product of the game or the core goal.

"It depends on how you define teamwork," he says. "We define high-performance teams as those that are able to apply systems thinking to the work that they do. We distill that into the core strategies of collaboration, innovation and data-driven decisions [in a way] that they can apply without picking up a textbook or getting a degree in system dynamics."

Jeff Heil has updated FNER and is growing the business in North America and around the world. Games like Monopoly have staying power. So does FNER, which has been around for nearly thirty years.

FNER was invented by a hospital consultant named Bette Gardner who was trying to figure out how to stop one ER from filling up with more patients than the doctors and nurses could handle.

Gardner also just happens to be Jeff Heil's mum.

===

IT'S THE MID-1980s, and Bette Gardner observes the chaos extending from the ER of San Jose Medical Center (SJMC) to nearby streets. She can see an ambulance tantalizingly close to the hospital. But there's a life-altering hitch. The hospital is redirecting ambulances to other facilities because it has more patients than it can handle. At a time when every second counts for the patient in the back of the ambulance, the paramedics in front need to find another hospital ER that is accepting new arrivals. And fast.

Since the 1980s, American hospitals have dealt with crowded ERs by diverting ambulances. Canadian hospitals have tended not to do that, after several high-profile deaths caused by delays in treatment.

Gardner, a healthcare management consultant in San Jose, was seeing the effects from inside the ER. Friday nights were especially bad. She describes waiting rooms filled with patients waiting for hours for treatment. She says they coped by placing two gurneys in a treatment cubicle and putting gurneys in hallways.

"It looked like they were bursting at the seams with patients and kind of running out of space," she says.

In 1986, ambulances were diverted from SJMC 5 percent of the time. By 1990, Gardner says, it was 35 percent. She says local hospitals and the city did studies and found that ER overcrowding was a symptom of a bigger problem.

"We learned that the most effective actions were not local to the emergency department but downstream from [the ER], where other departments' actions or inactions were creating backlogs."

They came up with unique solutions, like creating a pool of staff that could be deployed where they were needed most urgently. There was also a budding movement to bring systems thinking from academia to front-line workers.

At a conference in Boston, Gardner played a tabletop simulation game designed for the manufacturing industry. She had an "aha" moment on the flight home.

"It just came to me that I needed a tabletop game," Gardner recalls. "I could see it instantly. Everything fell into place. I knew it could work."

Gardner sketched out the FNER game board on a four-by-four napkin. On the other side, she wrote bullet points of some of the key dynamics of the game.

Back home, Gardner drew a prototype of the game onto brown butcher paper; she set it on a kitchen table and used dried garbanzo beans and macaroni as game pieces.

She invited three hospital managers and a nurse to give it a try. To them it seemed hokey at first, but as the game progressed and the hospital ER got overcrowded, something clicked.

"They started reaching across department boundaries to share resources," she recalls of that first dry run. "They were coming up with ideas. They were moving from siloed thinking to systems thinking. It was happening before my eyes."

Gardner named the board game Friday Night at the ER to create a sense of fun mixed with real stakes.

===

TODAY, FNER IS one of the most successful board games for people who work in hospitals. But a funny thing happened on the way to that milestone. Successful companies like FedEx, Intel and L.L.Bean have their employees play the game, as do not-for-profits like Habitat for Humanity. Today, close to half of FNER players work outside medicine and become more successful by learning about hospital teamwork. Other satisfied clients include the CIA and the Federal Emergency Management Agency.

Phil Cady is a systems thinking consultant and academic in Canada who uses FNER with public- and private-sector clients.

"I've used it with groups ranging from Engineers Without Borders Canada to the public service convention in the government of Nova Scotia to the World Cup and Supreme Committee for Delivery and Legacy in Qatar. Companies all over the world," he says.

There are some substantial differences between the Canadian and US healthcare systems. Canada's is funded through the provinces, unlike the for-profit healthcare delivered in the United States. I asked Cady, who is on the faculty of the Physician Leadership Institute, if the matter has come up at the institute's leadership training events.

"It's been a non-issue," he says. Cady finds that people outside of healthcare have an open mind about FNER's applicability to the systems in their line of work.

"No matter where we are, there are processes that go from acute care to needing services, to being monitored, to being discharged that everyone can empathize with," he says.

Cady says people outside of healthcare who play FNER feel the same pressure to co-operate that hospital managers feel as the game clock gets closer to midnight.

"There's this great sense of interdependency that comes with it," he says.

"At the executive level, we use the game, and it is followed by a discussion and a whole afternoon on polarity management," he says. "That is like the Caramilk bar secret. It unlocks it because they have fun and it's engaging."

But Cady says the debrief sessions following the game take it beyond "edutainment."

"I walk them through a process of how to apply it to their 'real world' issues," he says. Take the tension between environmental exploitation and environmental stewardship, for example. In FNER, players learn that diverting ambulances helps the ER but harms critical care. In the same way, what facilitates the exploitation of natural resources may be bad for stewardship.

"A nice polarity, similar to cost and quality," he says. "You pay attention to one, but you can't neglect the other. You overfish and there's going to be a net drop, right?"

The key, says Cady, is linking the fun learning experience with a practical application in the workplace.

= = =

FNER IS A tabletop game that was created for hospital managers. Other games are for health professionals. RETAIN is a tabletop board game that complements training in neonatology, the specialty that provides medical care to newborn infants. Ten percent of newborns require help with breathing from birth, and one percent need ventilators and other high-tech help plus skilled personnel.

It's that one percent of sick infants that Dr. Georg Schmölzer wants to train doctors and nurses to save. Schmölzer is a neonatologist in the Alberta Neonatal Program, a clinician scientist with the University of Alberta, the founder and director of the Centre for the Studies of Asphyxia and Resuscitation, and the holder of a PhD in neonatal resuscitation medicine.

Schmölzer says term babies seldom need his expertise. It's the preemies, some of whom weigh as little as 500 grams, who need it most.

"It's quite a stressful situation," he says.

Often, they need to be resuscitated at birth. For the babies, their parents and their caregivers, the stakes couldn't be higher. Schmölzer wondered if a game could improve training.

"RETAIN started off as an idea I had many years ago," he says. "Your med school doesn't really prepare you for anything. You start your residency and your first night on call and you are scared."

In 2015, to address that fear, he created a video game that helps get learners through that first night on call. It covered scenarios involving resuscitation at a NICU.

"We used real delivery room recordings to create those scenarios so that no one can say 'That never happens,'" says Schmölzer.

Two hundred and seventy real cases were used as source material for RETAIN. Schmölzer recruited a team from an undergraduate computer game class to design the digital prototype. They used a template from *Neverwinter Nights*—a role-playing game that takes place in one of the environments of Dungeons & Dragons.

Schmölzer says that version felt too much like an amusement game for doctors. Still, the team won an award at a university gaming conference and were joined by expert game designers. Together, they wrote the algorithm for RETAIN, complete with medical treatments and other orders, on computer cards. In addition to the computer game, they created a tabletop board game.

At one session, a nurse playfully dropped a card with the word *towel* written on it onto a baby being resuscitated, and said she was drying off the newborn. That got a laugh and a brainwave.

"We switched some of the cards to action items," says Schmölzer.

RETAIN had evolved into a game NICU doctors and nurses play alone or with up to four players as an interdisciplinary team. Players assign themselves to roles from printed identity cards, with actions and objectives dependent on the role. The scenarios range from easy to challenging. The game concludes with a debrief of what the players did and what they might do differently.

"By intention, there's no rush," says Schmölzer. "You can always pause the game and discuss it."

The digital version of RETAIN carries an element of time pressure. Four mistakes on that version means the players have lost the game and the simulated newborn dies. The point is not fear but better communication and teamwork.

Some studies have suggested that breakdowns in communication lead to many newborn deaths. Schmölzer says simulation training reduces errors by encouraging participants to speak up when they see a way to improve care.

Simulation training has gained traction as educators like Schmölzer recognize the value of learning through doing and practising as a team. And he's not the only one.

Dr. Teresa Chan is an emergency physician and a leading teacher in the emergency medicine residency program at McMaster University in Hamilton, Ontario, and has collaborated with Dr. Xiao Chi Zhang at TJU in Philadelphia.

Chan co-developed GridlockED with emergency medicine faculty and medical students. GridlockED is a six-player board game that, like FNER, enables learners to practise running the

ER. But this game is distinctly Canadian. Unlike in FNER, ambulances may not be turned away. Gridlock occurs when there are no more hospital beds. GridlockED teaches co-operation to help patients move in and out of the ER. You win if you get enough points, keep your patients safe, reduce errors and make it through an eight-hour shift. Communication and teamwork are the lifeblood of the game.

As Dr. Zhang said, serious tabletop games like GridlockED, RETAIN and others enhance training and teamwork. Compared to simulations, they're cheaper and a lot less labour-intensive. But simulations plunge you into a more realistic scenario.

An unexpected one makes the experience even more compelling and nerve-wracking.

= = =

"ANN, THIS WILL make you a bit sleepy." The young gynecologist pushes the plunger in a 5 ml syringe filled with midazolam, a sedative that works in two minutes.

"I'm feeling drowsy," says Ann, her voice muffled by a high-flow oxygen device, a breathing mask and a beeping heart monitor.

Dr. Glenn Posner looks on impatiently. The experienced gynecologist is about to perform a hysteroscopy, a minor procedure for diagnosing and treating abnormal vaginal bleeding. Ann is sedated so Posner can dilate the cervix and insert a thin telescope that enables him to look inside the uterus for abnormalities. He's showing his young colleague how to do it.

From the procedure tray, Posner takes a 10 ml syringe filled with local anesthetic to numb Ann's cervix.

"Sorry, this will sting a bit," says Posner.

"I'm not feeling well," Ann says unexpectedly.

The rhythmic beeping of the heart monitor slows to a stop, and the smooth, regular tracing turns into a jagged sawtooth.

"Call a code blue," Posner says as he starts chest compressions. His young colleague makes the call, and then starts fumbling with an oral airway and oxygen tubing.

At this small community hospital, there is no dedicated cardiac arrest team. When the code blue call sounds across the hospital communication system, people pour into the procedure room from everywhere.

Posner never knows in advance who is available to attend. He spots a respiratory therapist (RT).

"Al, can you help with the airway?" Posner asks the RT, who tries to connect a plastic tube into a suction unit on the wall. But he can't get it working.

"I've got the crash cart," says a nurse, wheeling in a cart with drawers that contain resuscitation drugs and other supplies. The nurse opens a sealed pack of cardiac leads and connects them to the defibrillator on the crash cart. But when the nurse turns on the defibrillator, no electrical tracing appears on the monitor. The patient is in distress, and the monitor is dead. Two gynecologists try in vain to help the nurse.

"One amp of epinephrine," orders Posner.

"I can't find any," says a second nurse, sounding alarmed. "Someone call the emergency department and tell them to bring three amps."

The wall suction and the defibrillator don't work, and one of the most essential medications used during a code blue isn't on the crash cart. Ten minutes have elapsed since Ann went into cardiac arrest.

Posner's gaze pans the room, making eye contact with everyone.

"Everybody take a deep breath," he says. "Nobody died."

If it isn't obvious to you yet, Ann is a mannequin. But that doesn't matter to the health professionals assembled here. When the code blue sounded on the hospital communication system, only Posner and his young colleague knew it was a simulation.

The whole point is to help teams work better together and to figure out latent safety threats. Now, everyone in that room wonders what would have happened had this been a real patient.

= = =

"MY JOB IS to sneak mannequins into the hospital," says Dr. Posner, medical director of the Simulation Patient Safety Program at the University of Ottawa's Skills and Simulation Centre. He's also a gynecologist.

"When I'm not wearing scrubs but nice clothes and I walk onto the ward, the nurses think, 'Oh shit, Glenn's here. Where's the mannequin?'"

Smuggling a mannequin onto an actual ward is known as an in-situ simulation. When you run simulations at a fancy centre away from the wards, team members say things go wrong because of the unfamiliarity of the environment and equipment. Running a scenario on their own ward eliminates that factor.

The other advantage of in-situ simulations is that they catch people who would normally skip these exercises.

"Instead of people taking the afternoon off, I can sneak into the hospital with my mannequin and scream, 'My uncle's having a heart attack. Somebody do something!'"

How do colleagues feel when they're called to an emergency only to find that the patient is a mannequin?

"I've made their heart race," he says. "They're pissed off because they've just been punked, but that quickly changes to appreciation because they have ideas about how this crisis could be managed better."

Posner has been pro-simulation since he was a resident in obstetrics and gynecology in 2005. He took postgraduate training in medical education and simulations from the University of Cincinnati. He thinks they're critical to the education of young physicians.

"When a fourth- or a fifth-year resident has to make the decisions themselves, it's a safe learning environment to make mistakes."

Posner says the second most important thing about simulations is the scheduled debrief that follows.

"It's the forty-five minutes afterwards when you beat this case to death with what went well and what could have gone better," he says.

There's a whole branch of research on debriefing. Experts from Canada and the United States have developed a technique that replaces the traditional Socratic method of questioning with more gentle suggestions on better management of the case.

"It's a much nicer and safer way of exploring a knowledge gap or a performance gap," he says.

During the debrief they also break down how the team communicated; for instance, did the leader identify themselves clearly, or was that assumed but not stated clearly?

"Hopefully the next time they lead an [actual] emergency, they'll remember my teaching and they'll say, 'Okay, Joanne, you're the most senior person here. You be the leader, and we'll be the followers,'" says Posner. "Followership is also hard in medicine. The hierarchy in medicine is so rigid sometimes."

One of his most formative experiences with simulations came early on, when a mentor ran a scenario that brought residents in ob-gyn and anesthesiology together for a simulated code blue set inside an OR.

"What was most interesting in the simulated environment was to work on teamwork skills and communication skills," says Posner.

Posner was one of the first to bring health professionals from different specialties and their residents together in one simulation. One reason is to address latent and actual biases that hospital personnel have about one another. To an emergency physician like me, general surgeons sometimes appear sullen and obstetricians tired.

"If you don't have the real specialist playing themselves, then all you get is a caricature of that specialty," says Posner.

He says they also bring nurses and other allied health professionals into each scenario so that they function in their usual roles during the simulation. During an actual resuscitation, nurses make helpful suggestions based on their experience. It's unrealistic to expect doctors to go through code blue simulations without nurses to prompt them.

Ultimately, Posner says, multidisciplinary simulations serve two main goals.

"Number one is to get everybody together in the same room, learning the same thing with the same objectives," he says. "That is really rare in medicine."

The second goal is to identify and address hidden dangers. Remember Ann, the mannequin who had the code blue during a hysteroscopy? Posner says that scenario happened to an actual patient.

Posner has done this for two decades. He works with Dr. Vicki LeBlanc. In addition to being the director of the University of Ottawa Skills and Simulation Centre, LeBlanc is also chair of the Department of Innovation in Medical Education at the University of Ottawa. She has a PhD in experimental psychology and has studied the effects of stress and emotion on performance and how to prepare people for that.

As a junior faculty member in the early 2000s, she remembers simulations not getting much respect. She says some colleagues thought working with mannequins was like playing with dolls.

Twenty years on, she says learners must do simulations before trying a procedure for the first time on an actual patient.

LeBlanc became interested in how simulations might mitigate stress while working with Ornge (Ontario's air ambulance service) more than ten years ago.

"We had a patient simulator in a trailer that went around

the province doing education for paramedics," recalls LeBlanc. "Sometimes, they would get stressed because they knew that they were being observed."

She'd seen the same paramedics perform those duties admirably in the field. She says some paramedics said they weren't feeling stress even though their heart rate and blood cortisol levels (a stress hormone) went up during the simulation. Her findings were published in 2005 in the journal *Prehospital Emergency Care*; she concluded by recommending systems and training to support and prepare emergency workers "who face acute stressors as part of their everyday work."

Simulations helped researchers recognize poor performance caused by stress in paramedics. LeBlanc says stress in one paramedic can spread to other members of the team. Even leaders are vulnerable to its impact.

She says simulations hold the key to bringing teams together in low-stakes scenarios while waiting for an experience that's real. Because you never know when that is going to happen.

===

AT 3:50 P.M. on January 11, 2019, a double-decker bus operated by OC Transpo, the public transit agency for Ottawa, crashed into the Westboro station. The bus entered the station, jumped the curb and slammed into the steel overhang of the bus shelter awning, which sliced through the vehicle and struck the passenger platform.

Part of the bus's upper deck sheared off on impact. The collision killed Bruce Thomlinson, Judy Booth and Anja Van Beek. Twenty-three people were injured, some gravely. Dozens of ambulances, fire trucks and police vehicles were dispatched to the scene. Their pulsing lights coloured the snow red as darkness fell on the wintry scene. Paramedics and firefighters worked hard to remove and attend to survivors from the mangled upper deck, where survivors' legs and seats were crushed up against one another.

Dr. Andrew Willmore is the medical director for emergency management at the Ottawa Hospital, and associate medical director of the Regional Paramedic Program for Eastern Ontario.

"Unfortunately, for the Westboro crash, there were people that were very hurt, and many were entrapped within the bus," says Willmore.

Paramedics alerted the Ottawa Hospital that they would be dispatching five to seven patients with severe injuries to the hospital's Civic Campus, a 569-bed facility that is one of the hospital's three sites. The ER there was teeming with other patients, but the crash site was just minutes away.

Hung Tan is the manager of emergency management at the Ottawa Hospital.

"I was driving home from a meeting with public health, and I got a phone call from my friend who is the director of the ED, saying, 'Hung, there's been a bus accident. It's the real deal,'" Tan recalls.

Tan drove straight to the hospital to direct operations from a command centre. He says they were in close contact with paramedics at the scene and with ambulance dispatchers to get a clear sense of the number of casualties.

"In parallel, we started mobilizing," he says.

Dr. Guy Hébert, head of the department of emergency medicine, called a code orange—the hospital code for the activation of a disaster plan designed to free up beds and operating rooms to cope with the onslaught of patients.

"We knew we wouldn't have that much time to prepare," Hébert told the *Ottawa Citizen*. "When I was told there would be at least five severely injured patients, and there was the possibility of more, that's when I made the decision to call the code orange."

Calling a code orange creates a cascade of events and actions; all of the departments that have been trained in the protocol jump into action.

"Any surgery that could be stopped was stopped to free up OR space," Willmore explains. "We cleared up the hospital and got ready."

Hospital personnel quickly cleared one hundred patients from the emergency department. Those who could be discharged safely were sent home, while others were moved to medical units, the post-anesthetic care unit, and the Ottawa Heart Institute. The ER's waiting area was packed with patients and had to be cleared; some were transported by ambulance to nearby hospitals.

By 4:20 p.m., just half an hour after the crash, staff had cleared the entire emergency department of patients, and freed up eight trauma bays for casualties. Meanwhile, off-duty medical staff arrived on the scene and assembled into eight trauma teams (one for each bed in the trauma bay). They included a trauma team leader, an orthopedic surgeon, a vascular surgeon, an emergency physician, several nurses, a respiratory therapist, an anesthetist and a resident in trauma surgery.

Extra surgical equipment was brought in, and housekeeping personnel were mobilized to clean trauma bays and rooms so that casualties would not have to wait. Extra staff were summoned to care for any other patient who walked into the ER that night.

Paramedics began arriving with casualties. Each time rescue crews managed to extricate someone from the wreckage, the paramedics on scene gave staff at the ER a five-minute warning of imminent arrival.

"The patient would come with medics, go through a very quick triage process and then be brought into a resuscitation bay, where they would be handed over to the hospital team," Willmore recalls. "They'd be under the care of an emergency physician or a trauma surgeon. Sometimes an anesthesiologist was in the room."

The trauma team assessed each patient quickly and whisked those with injuries to the OR for surgery. Multiple teams operated in concert to save the life of every person who was rescued from the bus.

This took place on a frigid winter evening, and many of the casualties had hypothermia or low core body temperature. Additional equipment was needed to warm those affected.

"The really sick ones got sent pretty quickly to the operating room," says Willmore.

In the OR, they received damage control surgery, which means stopping any internal bleeding and setting broken bones that require urgent attention. Following surgery, patients were transferred to the ICU. Some needed additional surgery afterwards.

Dr. Sudhir Nagpal, chief of vascular surgery, was called in to repair blood vessels in a patient who had broken both of his legs. At various times that night, as many as five vascular surgeons were in the OR.

"That hasn't happened before," Nagpal told the *Ottawa Citizen*. "This is, hopefully, a once-in-a-lifetime event."

In addition to addressing the patients' physical needs, the hospital called in a team of social workers to tend to the emotional needs of patients who were conscious, as well as their relatives.

The disaster plan worked to perfection.

"No one who made it to the hospital alive died," says Dr. Glenn Posner. "The code orange and the trauma team ran like an absolutely well-oiled machine. You wouldn't have known that there was a mass casualty event going on in that emergency department because it was so smooth."

And just what made that ER run so smoothly following the Westboro bus crash? Good outcomes often arrive on the backs of mistakes and lessons learned. And that's just what happened at the Ottawa Hospital.

Six years earlier, in September 2013, a code orange was declared after a VIA Rail train collided with a different OC Transpo bus.

The train, bound for Toronto, entered the transitway crossing at Smiths Falls as the double-decker bus turned left on express route 76. As the driver negotiated a left turn, cries of "Look out!" "Stop, stop!" emanated from the bus. Seconds later, the bus collided with the left side of the train. Four passengers seated on the upper deck were ejected from the bus and died at the scene. A passenger on the lower deck was thrown forward and died later on. Nine others were seriously injured.

The Ottawa Hospital declared a code orange, but in 2013, just two patients were brought there for treatment.

"We redeployed everything to the Emergency Department, waiting for hundreds of patients that we were expecting, given the social media information that was going on," says Dr. Andrew Willmore. "It was all hearsay. It ended up being two patients."

He says the repercussions were felt from the ER all the way up to the hospital C-suite.

"Our hospital CEO came downstairs and said, 'What the heck happened? How can we paralyze a tertiary care academic centre?'" Willmore recalls. "'How could we not have gotten this information from the field?'"

Willmore and his colleagues looked for answers, and concluded they'd relied too heavily on social media reports of casualties while not communicating effectively with first responders and dispatchers. He says the hospital lacked an incident management structure that included designated communication lines with first responders and other partners.

"We uncovered this big gap, and it was really something we could sink our teeth into," says Willmore.

Hung Tan agrees.

"We went down that road with a clear mandate to identify how we're going to respond to mass casualty events and ensure that there's a structure in place so that the key individuals and stakeholders are aware of what they need to do," Tan says. "A key item was making sure that a proper governance structure and leadership group was established to start that journey."

Instead of having a disaster plan collecting dust in a closet, the hospital created one that could be refreshed as often and as quickly as needed. They embraced the idea that first responders at the scene of a disaster were their teammates. They also teamed up with the hospital administration.

"We established the Department of Emergency Management as a standalone, not something that was attached to other things," says Willmore. "We ensured that we had dedicated staff to do this work."

The hospital used mock disaster exercises (think simulation on a very large scale) to stress-test different code orange scenarios. One simulation that took place just two months prior to the Westboro bus crash was eerily similar.

"That was literally the entire hospital," Willmore recalls. "We worked with housekeeping. We worked with logistics. We worked with different clinical areas. We established command posts. We reached out to partners in the military and paramedics. We had representatives from different departments observing, and we ran a limited exercise within the trauma bay."

Dr. Glenn Posner, the guy who sneaks mannequins into the hospital, was there when the mock disaster was staged. He saw professionals from different parts of the hospital work as a giant team. Like the people who learn about systems by playing FNER, they saw how actions at one level affected those at other levels.

"You had individual teams taking care of individual patients at one level, and then the next level up, you had the trauma team leader keeping situational awareness of all of those patients who were being looked after by individual teams," says Posner. "You had the hospital leadership as a whole coordinating between the operating room and the emergency room. Each group of paramedics had their own debriefing and talked about what went well and what could have gone better."

As a result, they developed new disaster guidelines. Just two months later, the real thing ran like clockwork.

"It all happened the way it should because we had just talked about it," says Posner. "If only we had infinite funds, we should do these exercises every single year, right?"

When you think of the lessons learned and the lives saved, the cost of disaster exercises and simulations seems a lot cheaper.

CHAPTER FIVE

EYES AND EARS

Trust is at the core of every good team

I T'S ONE THING to learn teamwork theory by running clinical simulations, playing an elaborate board game, doing "Yes, and" improv exercises with a partner onstage or drumming single paradiddles. Sooner or later, though, health professionals need to put those lessons to the test in a real clinical setting.

Especially one as austere as Renfrew County, a 7,500-square-kilometre land mass that's been called the heart of the Ottawa Valley. "Renfrew County is a unique place. I consider it an incubator." Michael Nolan peers out through the windshield of a 2015 Ford Expedition Emergency Response Vehicle. The chief of the Paramedic Service and director of Emergency Services in the County of Renfrew knows every square metre of road, river, field, farm and hiking trail in the region.

Nolan is a powerfully built man with dark, penetrating eyes and a mind full of ideas on how to deliver modern healthcare. He uses the word *incubator* a lot as he points out what makes Renfrew County such a fascinating place to practise paramedicine.

"It's got the largest military base in Canada with Garrison Petawawa," he says. "It's the home of nuclear energy at Deep River and Chalk River, which is an incubator of ideas and thought, with some of the smartest people in the world having immigrated to Renfrew County. We've got a very interesting mix of agriculture, forestry and a poor population."

A paramedic by training, Nolan thinks well beyond the role of first responder. He's a student of population health.

"We've got all of the elements of the socio-economic determinants of health and the challenges related to access to care," he says. "There's a lack of primary care physicians and no acute care hospitals in the county. We've got challenges related to age and poverty. We also cover Algonquin Provincial Park on our doorstep. We've got ski hills, racetracks and white-water rafting. And we've got little old ladies sitting on the farm years after their husbands have died, wondering how they're going to pass their time."

Nolan has overseen emergency services in Renfrew since 2004. Before that, he was the manager of Emergency Management and the deputy chief of the Ottawa Paramedic Service.

In Renfrew, he supervises 160 paramedics who cover all 7,500 square kilometres of the county. And they don't all work at the same time.

"Right now, one paramedic ambulance is covering 1,000 square kilometres," says Nolan. "You think about that. It brings many natural challenges of distance versus time. Where you live should not have a bearing on whether you live. That's a really nice way to sum up the challenges of disparity with respect to access to health services."

Nolan is building a team to tackle those disparities while delivering urban-style healthcare on the long and winding roads of Renfrew.

Those roads can be bumpy, in every sense of the word.

= = =

ON AN EARLY morning in August, I'm riding shotgun in an all-wheel-drive truck loaded with medical equipment. The bumpy, one-lane dirt road kicks up a cloud of dust that partly obscures my view.

"Aren't you glad I made sure you put on your seatbelt?" Matt Cruchet cocks a sideways glance at me while he watches the dusty road ahead.

"You have a gift for understatement," I reply. My knuckles have been drained of blood as they grip the dashboard. The crinkles in the creases around Cruchet's eyes offer the only clue that he's smiling. I try to stay in the moment.

With COVID-19 an ever-present threat, Cruchet is decked out in an N95 mask and disposable gloves, as am I.

The bumpy dirt road we're on leads to a cottage on the shore of Kamaniskeg Lake. The closest town, Barry's Bay, has a population of just over 1,300. Barry's Bay, Combermere and Wilno are the three towns found within the Township of Madawaska Valley in Renfrew County.

Renfrew is home to roughly 100,000 people, most of whom come from families that have lived here for generations. They are farmers and foresters who live off the land. They tend to be older and have healthcare needs that are often hard to meet in rural parts of the country. One in five people in Renfrew does not have a family doctor or nurse practitioner. Urgent care centres and walk-in clinics are almost non-existent.

And when either is an option, just getting there is a road many are unable to traverse if they don't own or are unable to drive a car. There is no public transportation in Renfrew. For many older people here, the only way to get any sort of medical care is by getting to the closest ER by ambulance.

I practise emergency medicine in a big-city hospital that has all the tools of medical diagnosis and resuscitation. Ottawa, the closest major healthcare hub to Barry's Bay, is two hours away by car.

Still, as I'm finding out, Renfrew County is an incubator for some of the most innovative healthcare ideas for teamwork in Canada, if not the world. It's the only place I know of where a frail senior can get virtual long-term care in the comfort and privacy of her own home, and where a white-water rafter who suffers a cardiac arrest on the Petawawa River gets his heart restarted by a defibrillator delivered just in time by a drone.

Teamwork is the glue that makes it all work.

Our destination is the home of Mary Lou Turner. She's seventy-seven years old and lives by herself in a single-storey log cabin at a hunting lodge that she and her husband, Jack, ran together until 2014, when Jack died. It's located by a lake about nine kilometres south of Algonquin Park.

"This goes back fifty-three or so years as a destination for Americans to fish and hunt in and around the Algonquin Park area," Cruchet tells me. "Mary Lou has got some health issues that need close monitoring, so today I need to do some blood work for her, just to see where she's at so that we can report back to her oncologist."

We pull up on a patch of dirt just outside a door to Mary Lou's house, which backs onto a lake. Cruchet hauls a couple of cases of equipment out of the hatchback. He's a tall, fit man in his forties with a full head of salt-and-pepper hair. In addition to his mask, gloves and other personal protective equipment (PPE), Cruchet is decked out in typical paramedic garb: a blue shirt with insignia crest on the right arm, a matching pair of blue trousers and a stethoscope draped around his neck.

"I've been seeing Mary Lou for a couple of years now," he says as he collects his medical gear at the back of his truck. "She came to our attention when she was discharged from hospital after a new diagnosis of multiple myeloma. We've been involved with her care ever since."

Cruchet has been a paramedic since 2012. He's well trained in the familiar role of emergency first responder. But we're not in an ambulance, and this is not a 9-1-1 emergency call. It's more like those good old-fashioned house calls your grandmother's GP used to do.

"Come on in." A tiny voice answers Matt's strong first responder–type knock at the door. Matt enters first. I follow a physically distanced two metres behind as Matt leads me to a wood-panelled dining room whose walls are decorated with mounted plates that feature local wildlife.

Mary Lou Turner sits beside a small dining room table covered by a hand-embroidered linen tablecloth. She's wearing a navy-blue blouse and grey slacks.

"How've you been?" the paramedic asks Mary Lou as he unpacks a portable automated blood pressure monitor and pulse oximeter on the dining room table.

"Pretty good except for the humidity," Mary Lou replies. "I had the air conditioner on because I couldn't take it anymore."

He takes her vital signs.

"No falls or close calls or anything like that?" he asks while wrapping a blood pressure cuff around her arm.

Mary Lou shakes her head.

"Have you been out and about at all?"

"Just with my daughter," Mary Lou replies. "I don't do any shopping by myself. She takes me out and I stay in the car as she does the shopping. I enjoy that."

"Anybody visiting these days?" he asks.

"Other than you, the other paramedics and my daughter, no one else comes in," she says.

Beyond illness and death, for seniors the coronavirus has brought a pandemic of isolation and loneliness.

"Your blood pressure is 146 over 73," says Cruchet. "Your heart rate is 108. I don't remember you having a fast heart rate. Are you feeling okay otherwise?"

"I feel fine," says Mary Lou. "Honestly, I do."

"No chills or night sweats?" Cruchet asks.

"No, no," replies Mary Lou.

"No difficulty breathing, shortness of breath, cough or chest pain?" he asks.

"No," she says. "Maybe I'm a bit excited."

The paramedic isn't satisfied.

"I'm just going to go get my heart monitor and I'll have a quick look at what's going on there," says Cruchet.

Mary Lou was diagnosed with multiple myeloma three years ago. Symptoms include bone pain, loss of appetite, nausea, constipation, fatigue, weakness or numbness in the legs and mental confusion.

When multiple myeloma is well-localized and has not spread beyond the bone marrow, the five-year survival rate is nearly 75 percent. The odds of survival drop when the disease has spread well beyond the bone marrow.

Mary Lou takes an oral chemotherapy drug called lenalidomide. It works by boosting the immune system. She takes six pills at a time once a week on Thursdays. Her oncologist is in Ottawa. Mary Lou's only contact with her during COVID-19 is via phone calls.

Like a lot of seniors who live in Renfrew, Mary Lou does not have a family doctor. That makes Matt Cruchet's regular home visits even more important to her well-being.

"You have no idea how much I appreciate it," she says. "I don't want to go to the hospital, where I might be around people who got infected."

Cruchet returns, lugging a portable heart monitor. He attaches heart monitor leads to Mary Lou's exposed wrists and ankles and pulls out a pulse oximeter from a gadget bag attached to the monitor.

"Just pop that on your finger, and we'll double-check that it matches with your heart rate," he says. "I'm going to have a quick listen to your lungs too. Take a couple of deeper breaths. Your chest sounds nice and clear."

The paramedic fixes an eye on Mary Lou. The diagnostic wheels turn inside his curious mind. Cruchet has good reason to be concerned. Dehydration is the most common cause of a fast heart rate on a hot summer day like this. But multiple myeloma puts Mary Lou at risk of infections that can cause fever and raise her pulse.

"I think your heart rate is up because you're excited," he says, finally.

Still, the paramedic decides to do some blood tests. He spots a promising vein on the back of Mary Lou's hand. She winces as the needle enters the vein. Enough blood trickles out to fill two blood tubes.

"You just like to hold my hand," says Mary Lou.

"It's the best part of my job," he says. "We'll send this blood work to your oncologist and hopefully everything will be fine."

He labels the blood tubes and puts the used needle in a portable container for disposable sharps.

"You let me know if anything changes," says Cruchet. "If all of a sudden you're feeling more tired than usual or if you feel like you're fighting something. Any hint of a fever, chills or anything like that."

"Honestly, if I wasn't feeling good, I'd let you know," she says.

"I'll just give you a phone call tomorrow to follow up and make sure everything's cool," he says as we walk out the door.

As we drive away, I ask why he reached for the cardiac monitor.

"My guess is that she was probably a little bit nervous," he says. "But I just wanted to make sure that she was in a regular sinus rhythm and not in atrial fibrillation."

That's an irregular rhythm that puts patients Mary Lou's age at increased risk of stroke. Cruchet says he gets lots of intuitive hunches like that.

Emergency physicians like me provide episodic care. It's a luxury for me to see a patient often enough to recognize a subtle change in heart rate or other vital signs.

But this paramedic knows Mary Lou and dozens of patients like her because he does house calls on a regular basis. He figures this is the twenty-fifth time in two years he's paid her a visit.

Cruchet and fellow community paramedics here work in a system that takes extraordinarily good care of patients young and old while preventing unnecessary trips to the ER and admissions to hospital.

Cruchet is not Mary Lou's doctor, and he's by no means the sole reason why she's alive and well and still living independently. But he plays a critical role in an innovative healthcare team that cares for patients like Mary Lou in one of the most remote parts of Canada.

===

THE TEAM WORKS in a program called Health Links. It's a mobile network that focuses on the 5 percent of patients who, like Mary Lou Turner, have the most intense healthcare needs. They also account for a whopping two-thirds of healthcare costs in the province of Ontario.

Health Links provides patients with seamless access to healthcare services. At its core is a tight-knit team of doctors, nurses and allied health professionals and community agencies.

Dr. Jonathan Fitzsimon is a family physician in Arnprior, a town in Renfrew County at the confluence of the Madawaska River and the Ottawa River. He's also the chief of medicine at Arnprior Regional Health. He says that when community paramedics like Matt Cruchet do house calls on patients like Mary Lou Turner, they are "the physician's eyes and ears."

"I trust his judgment," says Fitzsimon.

That trust comes from experience working with paramedics like Cruchet, although Fitzsimon recalls that it took a while to establish.

"I'd go out and do the house call myself," Fitzsimon recalls. "Then I'd realize that he was right. I don't need to go and check things for myself."

I want to know how often Fitzsimon realizes he's part of a healthcare team instead of flying solo.

"Every single day without fail," he says. "If I tried to do my day on my own, every single day, there would be an element that would not function as well because without the team I wouldn't have the input of somebody else."

He means the eyes and ears of all the other members of the team. That might mean a community paramedic like Cruchet, a nurse practitioner, registered dietitian, physiotherapist or occupational therapist, speech and language pathologist, the director of clinical care at a long-term care home or a home care coordinator.

Sarah Junkin is another member of Dr. Fitzsimon's team. She's a nurse practitioner doing primary care alongside Dr. Fitzsimon. Before that, she was a public health nurse for three years. She also did bedside nursing and worked in hospice care.

"I wanted opportunities to consult and work together as a team," she says.

Junkin also sees patients as part of the Health Links program.

"I would do a lot of face-to-face meetings with those nurses and the paramedics when they come in," she says. "Prior to COVID-19, they would come to our office frequently. It's easy to grab them and check in on a mutual patient. You'd get a knock on the clinic door, and there's the paramedic, who was hoping to run something by anyone if they're available."

Often, says Junkin, a phone or in-person conversation with a patient gives her cause for concern. A hallway consultation with a paramedic like Matt is both convenient and good for the patient.

"They can check in on the client and can contact us afterwards," she says. "Then we're able to brainstorm together what we think needs to be done."

Those hallway consultations are one method of exchanging ideas. Another is a single electronic medical record to which each member of the team has access.

Whatever the mode of communication, being able to brainstorm as a team is particularly useful in Renfrew County. Junkin remembers one of her first clients—a woman I'll call Ethel. She called the clinic in distress, and it was the NP's turn to answer the phones.

"It was really hard to get a good history from her in terms of how she was doing," recalls Junkin.

What Junkin needed was a set of vital signs and eyes on Ethel.

"She's way out there and I'm here in the office," says Junkin. "I don't think she needs to be seen in the emergency room, but we do need to get an idea of what's happening to her."

Junkin located a community paramedic close to where Ethel lives and asked her to do a house call.

"Turns out she had pneumonia," says Junkin.

The paramedic got the family doctor to call in a prescription for antibiotics. Almost anywhere else, Ethel would have ended up in an ER, which for her is hard to access.

"That's the beautiful thing [about] having the paramedics being able to go see her, assess her clinically and get an oxygen saturation," says Junkin.

The NP says she's shocked by the number of patients in Renfrew who don't have a family doctor and who go to the ER to have prescriptions renewed and receive other routine care.

"If they don't have access to care, their health is going to deteriorate," she says. "They can feel safe and at home. It's amazing to be able to offer that service to patients who don't have a family doctor."

The teamwork model in Renfrew County should be applied in every region and province in Canada, and elsewhere. Almost everywhere, it's the exception and not the rule. Even converts like Dr. Fitzsimon are amazed at how well it works.

"I think the difference was COVID," he says. "It was the crisis that got us to make this work. We'd started forming these relationships, and we'd had a bit of primary care and paramedic interaction through Health Links. When the crisis came and the funding and the permission came, then we really did just form a team."

COVID-19 provided the final spark that put Renfrew's model of teamwork on steroids. But the foundation had already been laid. And the person who was arguably most responsible for that is Chief Michael Nolan.

= = =

NOLAN, WHO HAS spent a good chunk of his early career working in the high Arctic and in remote parts of Northern Ontario, wants to even up the odds of survival by bringing to Renfrew the kind of paramedicine practised in places like Toronto and Ottawa.

One way to do that is to train paramedics like Matt Cruchet to be adaptive generalists.

"Our paramedics have truly become the Swiss Army knives of the healthcare system," he tells me during one of several drives through Renfrew.

For Nolan, that means inspiring them to do much more than respond to emergencies. It means training them to do house calls, run flu shot clinics, pick up prescriptions, stitch cuts, treat dehydration and do advanced pain management and palliative care.

It also means acquiring some noteworthy gadgets to support them.

Nolan pulls over on a road in a town he doesn't want me to name. He points to a nondescript office building.

"We have a drone parked on the roof." Nolan peers through aviator sunglasses as he looks up.

The drone is at the centre of Renfrew County's Remotely Piloted Aircraft System. It's one of several pilotless aircraft pre-positioned in Renfrew that enable paramedics and other emergency responders to deliver defibrillators, medications and even donor blood right to a patient who is gravely ill or injured.

To do that is a challenging exercise in team building. Nolan says he had to create safety protocols for paramedics that overlap seamlessly with similar systems in aviation.

"We're the first to use drones to deliver automated external defibrillators, medications, flotation devices and so on," he says.

Nolan's intriguing background includes a 2002 master's degree of Arts, Leadership and Training in the Division of Organizational Leadership and Learning at Royal Roads University, Victoria, British Columbia. His training in organizational theory made him see that paramedics, doctors and nurses often do not see themselves as members of the same team.

"I think that that's probably the greatest disservice we could do both to the paramedicine and to the patients that we're intending to serve," he says.

A second issue is an implied hierarchical system in which doctors are always the bosses.

"The fallacy is that teams need to be hierarchical," Nolan says. "I think teams need to be horizontal by design and equal by design."

A flattened hierarchy is what enables a paramedic like Matt Cruchet or a nurse practitioner like Sarah Junkin to call a family physician like Dr. Jonathan Fitzsimon to discuss a patient.

"I've done everything I can to build relationships and build trust so that those conversations can happen amongst my peer group with primary care physicians, with hospital CEOs and with policy-makers to make sure that it is truly a level playing field," Nolan says.

Nolan thinks paramedics must respect physicians, and vice versa. And that means being able to appreciate how the decisions he makes affect doctors and other professionals not under his jurisdiction.

"I think taking a collaborative approach to leadership nets out better results for everyone," says Nolan. "It enables everyone to contribute and to come to a consensus for the best outcome for all."

But how, exactly, does Nolan flatten the hierarchy between, say, doctors and paramedics or between nurses and paramedics? Who makes the first move?

The first requirement, says Nolan, is that he recruits and trains paramedics to push their scope of practice higher and higher.

"We're intubating, doing blood work and inserting intraosseous needles," he says. "We're doing all of the 'whiz-bang' medicine doctors do without anybody ever looking over our shoulders. We've been able to ride that 'kid-nephew' relationship with physicians, especially ER physicians."

That skill comes in mighty handy to people like me in the ER. Take, for instance, the moment when paramedics bring a patient in full cardiac arrest to the emergency department.

When the paramedics are trained in the latest techniques in advanced cardiac life support, it becomes natural to just let them continue to run the resuscitation.

"If they've already intubated the patient, started IVs, given emergency cardiac medications and even done a bedside ultrasound, the doctor has invited us to maintain our place at the head of the bed and work this cardiac arrest together."

Lately, Nolan has also noticed that the doctors and nurses in the ER are asking instead of telling paramedics when to stop resuscitative efforts.

"Whether that has evolved out of necessity or whether it's something that we've learned in our leadership techniques, it is now part of the job for all of us."

That is a logical extension of the first responder role for which paramedics are known and respected. They've made their most extraordinary gains in responsibility by pushing their way into community paramedicine, where they help patients prevent and self-manage disease in their own homes.

It's a huge shift in the relationship between paramedics and patients.

"We're no longer just barging into homes, dirtying up carpets, getting into tiffs in the living room and searching through the underwear drawer looking for their health cards and their meds," says Nolan. "We're actually taking the time and sitting down with people and truly understanding the power of the trusting relationship that they have with our profession."

Chief Nolan has done more than almost anyone else to push them in that direction. For nearly twenty years, he has been both the face and the voice of community paramedicine. He has built a durable legacy by co-authoring and supporting peer-reviewed papers. Colleagues from around the world have come to Renfrew County to study Nolan's model of community paramedicine. Nolan chaired the first international standard on community paramedicine by the CSA Group, a recognized leader in the development of safety standards.

Nolan is working with the Ontario government to set up Canada's first virtual long-term care program. More than 36,000 Ontarians are waiting for a bed in a long-term care home. Nolan's proposal would enable community paramedics to team up with family doctors and home care agencies to provide nursing home–type care for frail seniors in their own homes.

Nolan is a paramedic whose management training and experience have given him a systems approach to intractable problems in healthcare. He is nothing if not quick in noticing gaps and using paramedics to fill them.

"I talk about paramedics being nimble and I talk about them

being present," he says. "There are paramedics in every community in Canada. In many of those communities, we are the only healthcare providers. . . . Some have hospitals, some don't. Some have family doctors, and some don't."

Nolan believes it's easier and far less expensive to equip and train paramedics to raise their scope of practice than it is to evacuate the patient or bring in a more expensive provider.

The other essential part of Nolan's approach is that he teams up with doctors and other healthcare providers. He recruits other providers without making them feel as if he wants paramedics to replace them.

In the boardroom, he fosters teamwork rather than competition with leaders of medicine, nursing, and hospital CEOs. Nolan says being part of a team also means seeing things from the point of view of each of the players around the table.

"I think being a good listener is first and foremost," he says. "It's about understanding others' needs and priorities before imposing your own. Sometimes it's about being able to articulate a vision that resonates with others' needs first."

If he wants to sell his vision to family doctors, he shows them how community paramedics enable GPs to take better care of their patients. When he talks to hospital CEOs, he says his vision cuts down on unnecessary admissions. When he talks to municipal politicians, he emphasizes the cost savings from fewer 9-1-1 calls.

"It's about me understanding what the others that I'm speaking to care about at any given point in time," he says. "And then it's me reflecting on how our objectives coincide."

And Nolan keeps adding tools to that Swiss Army knife of paramedicine. This time, it's about assembling a team on a mission to keep patients as comfortable as possible during their final days.

= = =

"BILLIE, HOW ARE you?" Matt Rousselle nearly shouts over the noise of an air humidifier as he greets Billie Hobbs. She has end-stage congestive heart failure. Rousselle is an advanced care community paramedic with special training in palliative care. Between the din and the mask he wears, he knows it's hard for Billie to hear him.

"I hope you left all the COVID-19 germs there," says Billie, a frail woman in her nineties who is propped up in a hospital bed that dominates the main-floor living room of a modest home in Arnprior, the same town where Jonathan Fitzsimon practises family medicine.

"You're just in time," says Billie's daughter, Susan, who moved in to take care of her mother. "The occupational therapist says we should get that quilted mattress pad out from under her. She says the bed is going to do all the work and we don't need it. But different visiting nurses have said my mum needs the pad. It's very confusing."

"You mean the lifter pad?" Rousselle asks. "I can take that out without having to move your mum too much. I'll just roll her a bit."

Standing on Billie's left side, Rousselle carefully rolls her onto her right buttock and pulls out the pad in one fluid motion. Billie is quite frail and easy to lift. Susan winces despite the gentle manoeuvre.

"Her skin is exquisitely sensitive now," says Susan.

"I know, it's pretty thin," the paramedic agrees.

Billie's deterioration has been precipitous.

"Mom's only been like this since Saturday morning," Susan says. "The day before, she was mobile and interactive and walking, eating, drinking and everything."

"I'm exhausted," says Billie.

"Well, if you want to sleep, don't fight it," says Rousselle. "We're going to give you a bit of morphine now, okay?"

"After you moved me," says Billie, who winces.

"Susan, why don't you give the morphine and I'll watch to make sure you do it correctly," says the paramedic.

Susan draws up a dose of morphine into a 2 ml syringe. She uses an alcohol pad to carefully clean the IV port she's about to inject with the powerful opioid pain reliever.

"I'm putting this in now, Mum." Susan never takes her eye off the syringe.

"You're doing this every four hours or as needed?" asks Rousselle.

"It works out to [once] every three hours," she says.

Rousselle makes sure Susan has enough supplies and gives her tips on everything from nutrition to preventing pressure sores.

"I'm going to see who's in tomorrow and the weekend, and I will get someone to check in with you guys," he says as he packs up his equipment. "Billie, you take care of yourself, okay?"

"You too," says Billie. "Nice to see you again."

"You're doing a good job," Rousselle says to Susan. "She's lucky to have you."

"We're good together." Susan looks anxiously over at Billie, who has fallen asleep.

As we drive off, Rousselle says he is worried about Billie.

"She's quite wet with congested lungs," he says. "I'm worried her laboured breathing and hypoxia will cause agitation, and I don't know if Susan is ready to deal with that."

He plans on chatting with Billie's doctor about sedating medications and on filling in his paramedic colleague who is on call.

"We'll do check-ins every day," he says. "She's got a good team. It's not just us. She has quite a few people working for her."

"If Billie didn't have a community paramedic like you, what would her chances be of ending up in hospital?" I ask Rousselle.

"She would probably be in there now," he says.

During the first wave of COVID-19, Matt Rousselle and other paramedics in Renfrew County got trained to provide palliative care for patients like Billie. Renfrew is one of the first regions in Canada to have community paramedics do end-of-life care.

"Right now, we're assisting the palliative care teams, but ultimately we're going to be getting the calls . . . for someone that's not feeling well," he tells me. "I don't want to have to wait for a day to get a doctor to come to the house, or have to take the person to a hospital. I want to be able to look after it."

The patients and families Rousselle and colleagues are trying to help don't call 9-1-1 for minor problems. Like Billie Hobbs, they're at the end stages of congestive heart failure or chronic obstructive pulmonary disease. Many have incurable cancer. Some are an hour away from death.

He says they call emergency services because they have trouble coping with end-of-life care. Most of the patients and families he sees do not want to be taken to the hospital. But they don't know how to manage at home.

"It would be nice to be able to deal with these situations rather than having to call a doctor," he says. That includes relieving pain and breathing trouble. It might mean bringing a hospital bed to the home when the patient is too weak to walk upstairs to the bedroom.

In setting up the palliative care training program for paramedics, Chief Nolan says he made sure every member of the team was on board, from patients to practitioners.

"We've had no pushback," says Nolan. "The physicians have been incredible in embracing not only the skills of the paramedics but also the relationship and the trust that goes along with that. Families have been overwhelmingly accepting of the role of paramedics in palliative care. The patients themselves have been very welcoming to have a paramedic check in on them."

To achieve the main objective of avoiding a transfer to the hospital, Rousselle spends five or even ten hours at a patient's house.

"We fix the issues that people don't know how to fix," he says. "To keep people relatively calm, relatively pain-free and able to cope at home is hugely satisfying. I've seen too many bad deaths in my career to ignore this. This, to me, is the way we should be going."

Billie Hobbs died of heart failure on August 3, 2020, just days after I met her.

Trust is the key thing that enables a mobile network like Health Links to flourish. These paramedics know their stuff. Patients like Billie Hobbs and Mary Lou Turner trust paramedics because they know them. Physicians like Jonathan Fitzsimon trust paramedics because the paramedics have proven themselves. Various agencies trust one another because they communicate. Trust is what enables them to come together as a team in a flattened hierarchy.

Matt Cruchet, Matt Rousselle and Chief Mike Nolan know that this is the way healthcare should be going. It's going that way in a rural and remote part of Ontario, thanks to a team. And every well-oiled team can use a Swiss Army knife.

CHAPTER SIX

PUSHBACK

*Embracing a "see it, say it" approach
in the face of disaster*

A S WE'VE SEEN, people in healthcare can learn a lot about teamwork by learning to be less serious. Games, improv, simulations and even drumming can help them learn how to play together while also planning for medical crises. These activities help build trust in the field between members of the team—which is crucial when disaster strikes. Interestingly, there are domains outside of healthcare that have even higher stakes. And the lessons they can offer about applying teamwork to avoid catastrophe are just as important to master.

= = =

"NICKI, ARE YOU ready for a brief?" Captain Niall Downey makes quick eye contact with his first officer as he keeps his attention on the complex instrument panel in front of him.

"Yeah, I'm ready. Here's the current ATIS," Nicki Reynolds replies crisply. The automatic terminal information service, or

ATIS, is a continuous broadcast of recorded aeronautical information for busy terminals like Dublin Airport. Transcripts—like the
printout Nikki now passes across the flight deck—are available
from the aircraft's ACARS communication system.

Downey and Reynolds are seated in an Airbus A321neo
that can ferry 184 passengers. Flight EI 127 is scheduled to
depart Dublin Airport at 13:30 Irish time and arrive at Pearson
International Airport in Toronto at 16:15 local time, assuming the
meteorologists have got the headwinds pegged correctly.

"Niall, the ATIS shows Runway 28 Left as the departure runway," Nicki continues. "There's a strong crosswind from the left
coming over the Dublin mountains, so we'll maybe need to use the
crosswind takeoff technique, full forward stick till one hundred
knots and setting the power first to fifty knots, then seventy before
selecting takeoff thrust and expect a few bumps once airborne."

"Good idea. Departure on 28L looks good too," replies
Downey. "There are thunderstorms in the area, though. I can see
one off to the west in the direction we're heading, which we may
have to dodge on the way out, so we need to let ATC [air traffic
control] know that we may not be able to follow the SID [standard
instrument departure]."

"Copy that," Reynolds replies. "NOTAMs [notices to airmen]
show a couple of taxiway closures, which might mean we go the
long way and burn a little more fuel than usual."

This is the mundane yang to the glamorous yin of transatlantic piloting. Downey is a twenty-year veteran; Reynolds has
four years' experience. Both are completely absorbed in a pre-
departure procedure that begins in the operations area, printing
the flight plans and reviewing weather or NOTAMS (things like
information on airports and airspace on departure and usability of
alternate airports).

As captain, it's Downey's prerogative to choose who is PF
(Pilot Flying) and who is PM (Pilot Monitoring). With a strong

crosswind and the need to make a sharp right turn on takeoff, Downey chooses the more challenging first leg. That means Reynolds flies the plane back to Dublin.

The two aviators are getting ready for pushback, the standard procedure that pushes the aircraft's nose from the gate using a ground vehicle attached to or supporting the nose landing gear.

Now, Downey and Reynold rehearse "what if" scenarios.

"In the event of a failure before V1, I'll call 'STOP' or 'GO,'" says Downey. "For 'STOP,' I'll close the thrust levers and select max reverse thrust."

"You'll call 'Spoilers, Reverse Green, Decel, one hundred knots, seventy knots' and advise ATC," says Reynolds.

"Take no further actions except to silence any warnings till the aircraft has stopped, reverse is cancelled, and I've set the parking brake," says Downey.

"We'll then take a big breath and assess the situation," Reynolds answers.

Additional emergency scenarios including engine failure, windshear and others are covered next, followed by a detailed review of the flight management programming.

"Nicki, are you happy and in agreement with all we've covered?" Downey's tone is devoid of tension.

"I'm in agreement," Reynolds replies.

"Have we missed anything?" asks the captain.

"No, not a thing," says the first officer.

The distinction between the flying and monitoring pilots is important, since both have clearly defined responsibilities throughout the flight and during the pre-flight preparations. For instance, Reynolds goes outside to conduct a "walk-round"—a visual inspection of the exterior of the aircraft—while Downey stays on board to do a security sweep of all stowage areas; he also checks safety equipment such as lifejackets, fire extinguishers and fire axes.

Downey checks switches in the cockpit, ensuring everything is working correctly, and programs the flight management computers, inputting the flight plan and forecast winds (essential in transatlantic flights to ensure accurate time predictions and fuel burns). Meanwhile, Reynolds collects up-to-date weather and airport information, such as which runways are operating. She also programs a tablet with crew names and assignments, fuel data and takeoff performance calculations, and performs various other duties.

Downey and his first officer have been on board for less than thirty minutes. They met for the first time in the operations area less than ninety minutes ago. The uncanny thing is that the structure of their back-and-forth conversation makes it feel as if they've known one another for years.

There's a method going on here. Downey and Reynolds are part of a team. Downey's the captain, but First Officer Reynolds isn't shy about speaking up. Neither are the cabin or maintenance crew, or the air traffic controllers in the tower.

Together, as they prepare for pushback, they're working hard to discover errors, to spell out the worst-case scenarios and to plan what they might need at any stage should they declare an emergency.

For Downey, it's a team approach he's spent the past ten years trying to teach doctors while dealing with pushback and turbulence of a very different kind. But if anyone is up to the task, it's Downey. Commercial airline pilot is his second career. Before that, Dr. Niall Downey piloted the OR as a cardiothoracic surgeon.

= = =

DOWNEY EARNED HIS medical degree at Trinity College in Dublin in 1993. He was born and raised in Derry, Northern Ireland, in 1969, and grew up amidst the violent political clashes of the seventies and eighties. He's the youngest of five boys, and the only one to pursue a career in the sciences.

After his medical degree and postgraduate residency, he did cardiothoracic surgery at the Mater Misericordiae University Hospital, the national centre for cardiothoracic surgery and heart and lung transplantation in Ireland, before returning to Belfast.

Nearing the end of his sixth year of residency, Downey was functioning at the level of a specialist surgeon.

"In Belfast, they let me do a lot of stuff that they wouldn't normally permit at my level back then," says Downey. "The main one was coronary artery bypass grafting. I did about three hundred of those. I opened and closed the chest by myself and was starting to do the stenting of the top end of the Dacron graft onto the aorta."

Surgical residencies are among the most all-consuming and gruelling postgraduate programs. To all concerned, it's a huge investment in time, effort and sacrifice.

"I loved what I was doing," he says. "We were doing 120-hour weeks. I was coming in on my nights off to do research papers, and to do transplants and things. I would still love to be back doing it."

Though he adored it, Downey could see problems in the operating room.

"It wasn't teams," he says. "It was groups of individuals who were vying for jobs. It was dog eat dog and there was no working together. If you made a mistake in theatre, by the time you came out, the entire ward knew about it. Everyone was constantly looking towards their next post."

To get a position as a heart surgeon on staff, you first had to obtain a position in what's called a consultants' training program.

"I think twenty-four of us applied for the consultant course," he says. "I was third-best-qualified, but I didn't make the short list of six. They gave the job to one of their friends' sons. Nepotism is alive and well in Irish society generally and no less so in healthcare."

I became a GP emergency physician after just two years of residency because it afforded me the time to become an author and a broadcaster. The thing is, I was permitted to practise medicine. It must have been very hard for Downey, then thirty years old, to abandon a career in cardiothoracic surgery after so many years of training.

"I couldn't stay there knowing that I was not going to get a long-term job," he recalls. "The longer I stayed there, the harder it was going to be to try and find an escape route."

That escape route came not long after, when Downey saw a half-page recruitment ad for pilots by Aer Lingus (the flag-carrier airline of Ireland) in one of the Sunday papers.

"Four and a half thousand applied to Aer Lingus that week, and they took on thirty-eight of us," he recalls. "I was number eleven."

Downey says he and nine other student pilots went to aviation classes in Oxford, England, followed by hands-on training just outside Phoenix, Arizona. The course takes people off the street and trains them from scratch to fly two-hundred-seater jets in just eighteen months.

At thirty, Downey and two others were the oldest members of the group. The three youngest students were just eighteen years of age and fresh out of high school. Downey wasn't just older; as a cardiothoracic surgeon, he brought gravitas to the training.

"I realized it wasn't a game, and that there were real consequences to what we were doing," he says. "The first time I stepped up into an Airbus 321, I probably had more of an idea that this is real, whereas at ages seventeen or eighteen, that doesn't really sink in quite as much."

Like Downey, I have feet in two very different yet linked worlds. For me, it's medicine and broadcast journalism. For Downey, it's surgery and aviation. The heart surgeon's one-eighty into commercial piloting gave him an utterly unique opportunity to view two very different worlds and cultures from an objective perspective.

As you'll see, that has a critical bearing on his wisdom regarding teamwork.

Beyond the training itself, Downey noticed right away several big differences between the two domains. In surgery, he felt as if his twelve years of training were disposable. At Aer Lingus, he was told from the outset that the airline regarded the £120,000 worth of training he underwent as an investment.

"They give you a job, and they move you straight onto an Airbus 321," he says. "They do everything they can to hold on to you for the next forty years. It's a completely different mindset."

A big part of holding on to pilots for that long is continuous training and upgrading of skills. But those weren't the only things that demonstrated to Downey a completely different mindset.

= = =

THE DETAILED VERBAL show-and-tell that Downey and Nicki Reynolds engaged in prior to pushback is just part of a set of training procedures known as crew resource management. CRM is defined as the effective use of all available resources for flight crew personnel to assure a safe and efficient operation, reduce error, avoid stress and improve efficiency.

One form or another of CRM exists in many if not most dangerous areas of endeavour, including at nuclear power plants and for mission control in space exploration. The big idea behind CRM is to reduce human error.

David Beaty was one of CRM's first advocates. In 1969, the former Royal Air Force and later British Overseas Airways Corporation pilot wrote a book called *The Human Factor in Aircraft Accidents*; it was an early bible of CRM.

In aviation, the period from the fifties to the nineties was marked by larger and more powerful aircraft and more sophisticated cockpit instrumentation. Until people started talking about

CRM, little had been done to make sure humans were capable of piloting those planes. It took a string of air crashes (especially during the seventies) to demonstrate that something needed to be done to restore the faith of passengers.

For example, on December 28, 1978, United Airlines Flight 173 was scheduled to fly from John F. Kennedy International Airport in New York to Portland International Airport in Oregon. As the plane neared Portland, things went awry. As the National Transportation Safety Board (NTSB) determined, corrosion of the right landing gear caused a malfunction when the gear was extended, and the pilot burned too much fuel before attempting to land the plane on the damaged gear. Out of fuel, the plane crashed in the suburbs of Portland after all four engines flamed out. Eight passengers and two crew members died, and many more were injured seriously.

The NTSB determined that the probable cause of the crash was mostly human error, noting in its report "[t]he failure of the captain to monitor properly the aircraft's fuel state and to properly respond to the low fuel state and the crewmember's advisories regarding fuel state. This resulted in fuel exhaustion to all engines."

The NTSB also faulted the cockpit crew, noting "[t]he failure of the other two flight crewmembers either to fully comprehend the criticality of the fuel state or to successfully communicate their concern to the captain."

The seventies brought other flight disasters. In 1972, Eastern Air Lines Flight 401 crashed into the Florida Everglades after an inadvertent disengagement of the autopilot by cockpit crew caused the plane to lose altitude unnoticed. Ninety-six of 163 passengers were killed, along with some members of the crew. And, in 1977, KLM Flight 4805 and Pan Am Flight 1736 collided on the runway at the airport on the Spanish island of Tenerife, the largest and most populous of the Canary Islands. Spanish authorities determined that the primary cause of the accident was the

KLM captain's decision to take off, believing (through miscommunication possibly related to a language barrier) that air traffic controllers had given him clearance. Five hundred and eighty-three people died, making it the deadliest airline mishap in aviation history.

Some trace the origins of CRM to "Resource Management on the Flightdeck," a 1979 workshop sponsored by NASA. That workshop and others found that between 70 and 80 percent of aviation disasters could be chalked up to human frailties such as weak leadership and poor teamwork. And the roots of both can be found in the all-too-human failure to communicate.

At one time, CRM stood for "cockpit resource management," a term coined by John Lauber, a psychologist with NASA. The idea was to address the command hierarchy in the cockpit by encouraging the co-pilot and other crew members to speak up if they thought the pilot was making serious mistakes.

CRM has gone through several evolutions. Early iterations focused on interpersonal skills, crew psychological testing and leadership, situational awareness, stress management and teamwork intended to interrupt a serious chain of errors. Third-generation CRM was the first to expand the team to include cabin crew, aircraft maintenance personnel and others with a stake in aviation safety. Fourth-generation CRM integrated the training with all kinds of flight instruction, and specific behaviours were added to airline safety checklists so that the basics of CRM are observed in all normal and abnormal situations. Fifth-generation CRM stated that errors are inevitable, and that the system needs to "trap" errors and mitigate the damage. Non-punitive incident reporting was added.

Sixth-generation CRM was adopted in the early 2000s and is considered the best version because it acknowledges that crashes are the result of human errors both inside and outside the cockpit—for example, through bad communication by air traffic controllers. The way to address those risks is to widen the team to include air traffic controllers and other significant players.

Sixth-generation CRM also introduced the concept of threat and error management (TEM), which improves the margins of safety in aviation through the practical use of human factors engineering. The late psychologist Robert Helmreich developed TEM and other advances in human performance.

===

ALL OF THESE developments in the history of CRM were news to Niall Downey on the day he began training to be a pilot.

"I'd never heard of CRM before," Downey recalls. "There was no concept of that at all in healthcare back then."

Long before he knew about CRM, he longed for its precepts as a way to build teamwork in healthcare. When he worked at the Royal Victoria Hospital in Belfast, Downey suggested that residents do rotations in cardiology and anesthesiology as part of their training in cardiothoracic surgery.

"And the response from the head of the department was, 'If you don't like our training program, you know where the door is.'"

Downey's first exposure to CRM as a trainee pilot made him feel he had found his people and his guiding principles.

"We see crew as basically involving almost anyone who's got any skin in the game, or any input at all," he says. "So we have access to an awful lot of people."

That awful lot of people includes the pilot, the co-pilot, the cabin crew, the engineers on the ground, the people that push the plane back and give the pilot clearance to start the engines, and the air traffic controllers (by radio and across oceans by satellite phone).

It also includes passengers.

"When I'm flying, I can't see my engines from where I sit," Downey explains. "A passenger might be able to report to me that there's something dripping out the bottom of the engine before I'm aware that there's a problem, so they can pass that on to the cabin crew."

Hearing Downey talk about the role passengers play in CRM reminded me that far too often, patients and their families are excluded from similar conversations in healthcare.

From a doctor's perspective, I might have imagined a pilot or chief purser gaslighting the passenger who reports seeing something dripping from the bottom of an engine. Downey says that does not happen, thanks to CRM.

"Someone still has to be in charge," he says. "But the idea is that the information flows a lot more easily. The most junior cabin crew member can call me to the back of the airplane, and if necessary bypass the senior cabin crew member, and come directly to me if there's something they're concerned about."

A flatter hierarchy enables the pilot to get more pertinent information. In theory, that reduces errors by making decisions more accurate.

"And when we're actually making decisions, we troubleshoot with the other crew members and say, 'Well, this is what I'm thinking, what are you thinking?'" Downey acts out the script. "Ideally, you ask them first what they're thinking, so that I don't lead them to agree with me."

The crucial importance of this lesson was made clear by the 1997 crash of Korean Air Flight 801 on approach to Antonio B. Won Pat International Airport in the US territory of Guam. The crash killed 229 of 254 people on board.

The Boeing 747-300 was en route from Korea in heavy rain and poor visibility conditions. The crew attempted to land the plane using instruments only, though the NTSB found that the instrument landing system (ILS) was not functioning that night. The pilot believed that the ILS was working, while the flight engineer disagreed. The cockpit voice recording revealed that the crew noticed that the airplane was descending steeply, and that the airport was not in sight.

The aircraft slammed into Nimitz Hill, three nautical miles short of the runway, at an altitude of two hundred metres. The NTSB said the accident's probable causes were the captain's poor execution of a non-precision approach, pilot fatigue, poor communication between the flight crew and Korean Air's lack of CRM training.

Here's the thing. The NTSB also criticized the first officer and flight engineer for not challenging the captain over his errors, while at the same time concluding that it was unable to determine the exact reasons why. The NTSB also noted that "problems associated with subordinate officers challenging a captain are well known."

That deference to authority was not unique to Korean Air, says Niall Downey.

"When I started flying, a lot of the very senior guys were ex–air force pilots—they were used to flying solo," he says. "They weren't used to taking input from junior people, or from anybody, really. In aviation, there were some captains who we just had to wait until they retired to breed them out of the system [so] it's basically people like me who don't know any better."

You can count Martin Bromiley as one of those pilots steeped in CRM because they "don't know any better."

As discussed in the introduction to this book, Bromiley's wife, Elaine, died of a preventable medical mishap. He's been an advocate for safer healthcare ever since. He comes to that advocacy from his perspective in aviation. Bromiley is a training captain (TC) on the Airbus A319, A320 and A321. That means he teaches and examines in the simulator and on real airplanes. His instruction covers both technical skills and non-technical skills, including CRM.

"For the geeks, I'm a Type Rating Instructor and Type Rating Examiner," he tells me with more than a hint of pride. "Although

I love every aspect of my job, probably my favourite part of being a TC is getting to train brand new captains. Or, as they're now called under European and UK legislation, 'Commanders.'"

Bromiley is also a qualified CRM trainer (CRMT), which means he teaches CRM in a classroom. It makes him uniquely qualified to know the ins and outs of CRM in the training of pilots.

Bromiley sees cockpit hierarchy as non-rigid and adaptable to the immediate circumstances. That includes flat-out emergencies, like a potential stall.

"One of the big things we teach is if you're flying the aircraft as the captain and something goes wrong, you hand it over to the more junior person because they can probably fly better than you anyway," says Bromiley. "It just gives you that massive capacity to sit there and watch and think about what is going on during the emergency."

I can't imagine a surgeon doing that in the OR.

The CRM principle of reducing, if not totally flattening, the slope of cockpit hierarchy makes it easier for pilots like Bromiley to hand over control of the aircraft. It also creates a safe space for someone who is not the pilot to make pertinent observations.

As we have seen, Visual Thinking Strategies encourages students (medical and otherwise) to say what they see and to use their critical thinking skills to explain why they see it. The idea is to make trainees feel comfortable volunteering observations.

CRM builds on that by making it the duty of the crew to speak up if something looks wrong. Years ago, Bromiley was in the co-pilot seat headed to Belfast. Hitching a ride in the cockpit jump seat was a pilot fresh out of school.

"We were descending towards Belfast and as we got lower, we had to change the pressure setting on the altimeters," he says. "The captain had said to me, 'Okay, set the pressure.' I set the pressure on my altimeter, and he set the pressure on his."

According to procedure, those settings are supposed to be identical.

"We cross-checked them and agreed they were correct," says Bromiley.

The grad in the jump seat disagreed.

"This young lad on the jump seat leaned forward and said, 'Can I ask a question?'" Bromiley recalls. "I said, 'Yeah.' He said, 'Why have you got different settings?'"

The two experienced aviators looked at the pressure gauges and realized that one of them had been set incorrectly.

"It was just that moment when this kid who didn't really know either of us did what to him was the normal thing to do," says Bromiley. "That is what CRM buys you."

See it. Say it.

CRM and other factors have improved aviation safety dramatically, despite a massive increase in the number of passengers.

"We've had about a 95 percent or more drop in the actual number of [passenger] deaths," says Downey. "What changed it was that people accepted that mistakes were going to happen, and that there was no shame in them. When we investigated accidents, we didn't really need to be looking for who went wrong, we went looking for what went wrong."

Neither CRM nor VTS turns groups of individuals into teams. But both pave the way for teams to emerge by freeing followers to say what they see and freeing leaders to listen without seeing that as a threat to their leadership.

"When I get on board, I'm the captain, but I actually see myself as the most senior member of the team," says Downey. "I'm still part of the team, and I don't know everything. I'm not expected to know everything. I can't see everything."

Downey sees himself as the team's coordinator. Team members bring him important information that he uses to help solve problems and make decisions.

"If I make a decision and other people aren't happy with it, it's going to be very hard to implement it and actually get it to the proper resolution. So you need to make sure that people buy in."

It works for aviation. It seems like a no-brainer for healthcare.

===

IN 2005, MARTIN Bromiley's wife, Elaine, went into hospital for a routine operation to fix a deviated septum. Her anesthesiologist and (eventually) several experienced colleagues were unable to insert an airway into her windpipe and unable to ventilate her with fresh oxygen. She suffered irreversible brain damage and died nearly two weeks later in the ICU.

As we learned earlier, what happened to Elaine is a well-recognized yet incredibly rare emergency in airway management called the "can't intubate, can't ventilate" scenario. The American Society of Anesthesiologists estimates the incidence at somewhere between two in 10,000 and one in a million scheduled surgeries.

In 2019, the rate of fatal accidents in commercial aviation was 0.11 per million flights. That's even rarer than "can't intubate, can't ventilate." In both nightmare events, the people on the front lines seldom have the benefit of experience.

Aviation adopted CRM as a way to prepare for rare disasters. Martin Bromiley thinks a CRM mindset might have prepared Elaine's doctors to anticipate an unlikely catastrophe.

"It would involve some form of briefing between the anesthesiologist and other operating room personnel," he says. "They could pick any scenario so that mentally they're thinking about what to do and who to call for help."

In a CRM mindset, operating room personnel would regularly do simulation training involving the "can't intubate, can't ventilate" scenario and make certain that a surgical airway tray is available should they need to perform an emergency tracheostomy.

Most important, Bromiley says the pre-operative briefing would get people in the OR thinking about the unthinkable. And talking about it.

"That pre-operative briefing not only sets what are you going to do but it also sets up a tone for the group working," he says. In that atmosphere, he says, OR personnel would feel comfortable speaking up if they notice a procedure going south.

You'd see the emergence of a team among OR personnel who observe the patient closely and—like the crew on board a passenger jet—stand ready to institute emergency measures.

"A team is needed because there are multiple tasks to be performed within minutes," says Dr. Johannes Huitink, the anesthesiologist and founder of Airway Management Academy. "The diversity of experience of the team members allows a team to see risks and opportunities from different angles so that it can come up with new solutions and adapt dynamically to changing situations."

In an emergency, a team helps dispel the panic that leads to tunnel vision. "These teams communicate clearly, prevent fixation error and never lose situational awareness," says Huitink.

That did not happen when Elaine Bromiley was under anesthesia.

"The argument in Elaine's case is that the anesthesiologist became fixated, which then drove the other anesthesiologist and the surgeon who joined them," he says. "That fixation with attempting to successfully place a breathing tube down Elaine's windpipe took away the anesthesiologist's situational awareness."

In the independent report into Elaine Bromiley's death, Professor Michael Harmer wrote that he suspected that the anesthesiologist was unaware of how much time he spent attempting to intubate her. The timeline suggests that he and colleagues spent twenty-five minutes on multiple attempts to secure the airway— an amount of time that all but guaranteed Elaine would have suffered serious brain damage had she survived.

"What we need is for somebody to recognize when that's happening," says Martin Bromiley. "And that's when the other members of the team, including the nurses and assistants, come in and say, 'Hang on, everybody. We need to stop and think about what's going on.'"

A related issue here has to do with leadership and (by corollary) followership. As Downey has said, even with CRM, aviation has an explicit hierarchical system in which the captain is in charge. Healthcare's hierarchy is more implicit. Doctors and nurses don't wear rank insignias on their lab coats. It takes an understanding of hospital culture to know who's who.

In healthcare, people are assumed to be leaders if they get accolades and honours, can quote facts quickly, are slick at doing procedures like intubation and have the most published research papers. Healthcare assumes leadership qualities in people who dominate discussion and dislike uncertainty.

By contrast, a team-based leader is not smart but wise. Instead of needing to show they have every answer, they know how to ask the team pertinent questions, empower their team to speak up and trust members when they act.

Martin Bromiley sees cockpit leadership in aviation. In healthcare, he's not so certain. At the inquest into Elaine's death, he asked his solicitor to quiz every health professional taking the witness stand who they thought was in charge.

"Sure enough, virtually every single person said, 'I don't know, actually,'" recalls Bromiley.

At a moment when Elaine's life depended on it, the people trying to oxygenate and ventilate her in a crisis didn't know who was in charge.

Had the anesthesiologist seen himself as part of a team, he might have stopped what he was doing and said to the others present in the OR, "I'm not sure what's happening. What can you see? What are you thinking?"

Those are precisely the kinds of questions Alexa Miller asks medical students in her VTS classes. Had those questions been asked, or had someone in the OR volunteered their observations, Bromiley says things might have been different.

"It would have taken a minute or thirty seconds, but it would have been the moment to have changed the complete course," he says. "We know that some of the other people in the OR could see what was happening. We know that two of them knew a surgical airway was exactly what was needed."

Would Elaine Bromiley be alive and well today?

"We can't say that for certain," says Bromiley. "Most importantly, I think for me, it's the leader, whoever the leader is, recognizing that there is a team of resources . . . a team of brains around you, and being able to access and use those. And that's what CRM would have brought, I believe."

CRM seems like the most obvious innovation for healthcare to embrace. But that is easier said than done.

= = =

EXPERTS IN AVIATION believe they have lessons to teach doctors about creating and maintaining a culture of safety. For years, Martin Bromiley and others have been teaching CRM to doctors. He says the response has been mixed.

"I choose my words carefully here because it's usually doctors we teach," says Bromiley. "I think when pilots go in and teach CRM to doctors, it's very popular. The feedback forms at the end of courses are fantastic. But it doesn't change the culture. That's the problem."

Bromiley says aviation had to go through the same kind of culture change, moving away from the "pilot as boss" model to a team-based approach.

"What we had in heaps was evidence," he says. "We could read the accident reports in great detail."

That sort of evidence may soon be forthcoming in health-care, thanks to a technological innovation borrowed straight from cockpit recorders. It's called the Operating Room Black Box, and I'll talk about it in detail in the next chapter. But its use is not yet widespread enough to know the extent to which it can change hospital culture.

Ten years ago, Captain Niall Downey returned to his medical roots. He started a company called Frameworkhealth Ltd. to bring aviation safety techniques like CRM to healthcare to reduce the number of patients being inadvertently harmed through human error. He developed training modules and recruited pilots to teach them.

Downey says he's had some success training individual surgeons, but it has not been an easy sell; nine years into it, the business had yet to break even.

"I had assumed that I would be welcomed with open arms," says Downey. He chalks up the lack of enthusiasm to differences in culture between aviation and healthcare.

"In aviation we are trained that we're going to make mistakes," says Downey. "In healthcare, the emphasis is that we don't make mistakes. And if you do make a mistake, that means you weren't working hard enough, so work harder next time."

Like Bromiley, he gets a polite response from healthcare insiders.

"People are prepared to listen, but it's trying to get them to take the next step then, to actually go, 'Yeah, we buy into that, and we would like to apply that,'" Downey says. "That's where I have the problem."

There is a fledgling movement to make simulation training a standard of continuing competence to practise medicine, in the same way it is to fly passenger jets. But medicine remains far behind aviation. Downey closed down Frameworkhealth Ltd. in the first half of 2021. He says he doesn't expect much funding for innovation as the healthcare system struggles to recover from COVID-19.

So far, I've shown mostly positive developments in the evolution of teamwork in healthcare. There are speed bumps, and CRM may be one of them. But healthcare is not the only domain that hasn't adopted CRM because the culture has a problem with flattening the hierarchy.

Downey has since moved off healthcare and turned his attention to the military, one of society's most hierarchical organizations. And this time, he has an ally.

=\=\=

GRAHAM HOUSE WAS once a military insider. He's been an officer, military commander and military pilot. Today, the Royal Air Force (RAF) wing commander (ret'd) is taking on the United Kingdom's military establishment culture as one of the founding co-directors of Justice4Troops (J4T). Launched in 2019, the not-for-profit registered community interest company is made up of former service personnel, all with brutal experiences of injustice within the UK's armed forces.

House's belief in CRM comes from having witnessed one horrific mishap and one instance of injustice that derailed his military career.

"I got involved in a dreadful accident in 2006, when we lost an aircraft over Afghanistan," House recalls. The incident occurred during the UK mission to Helmand province as part of the NATO-led International Security Assistance Force.

On September 2, 2006, a Nimrod aircraft operated by the RAF caught fire shortly after air-to-air refuelling (AAR). The fire caused the aircraft to lose control and crash. All fourteen on board were killed.

"It was our biggest loss of life in modern times on an operational sortie," says House. "It was also my fleet, so I knew those people. It had a big impact on the area, as well as that community."

A parliamentary inquiry led by Charles Haddon-Cave dealt mainly with technical issues related to AAR. The remainder of the inquiry's report focused on the people directly involved. It pulled no punches.

"Unfortunately, the Nimrod Safety Case was a lamentable job from start to finish," Haddon-Cave wrote. "It was riddled with errors. It missed the key dangers. Its production is a story of incompetence, complacency, and cynicism. The best opportunity to prevent the accident to XV230 was, tragically, lost."

As House describes it, Haddon-Cave "was focusing on the importance of the questioning culture that leads to a safety culture and a just culture."

By "questioning culture," House means the willingness to listen to underlings who raise issues of safety.

"A complaint in its purest terms is someone asking a question of the organization on the basis of something that you designed [that] hasn't worked," says House. Leaders, he continues, "need to be receptive in order to try and improve it."

He says soldiers typically do not feel safe enough in their jobs to "say what they see," in terms of CRM.

"You have half the audience in the armed forces who won't make a complaint because they're fearful that nothing will come of it," he says. "And the other half won't make a complaint because they're fearful of retribution if they do."

In the civilian aviation sector, CRM has succeeded by encouraging the crew to see the team's interests as their individual interests. It's a lot harder to do that in a more rigid hierarchy such as the military, where whistle-blowing, with all its attendant risks, may be the only way to speak up for what's right.

The Nimrod crash was the first experience that made House question the culture of the UK Ministry of Defence and the armed forces. But another episode led more directly to the creation of J4T and his call to bring CRM to the UK military.

It also cost House his job.

Following the mission in Helmand province, House returned to England, where in 2010 he became the base commander at RAF St. Mawgan, which at the time was used for defence training.

House says that one day, the mother of a thirteen-year-old female cadet on the base contacted him alleging that a female member of his staff had sexually assaulted her daughter.

"When she told me about this incident, my immediate thought was that it couldn't have happened," says House. "My second thought, in the same second, was, well, if it did happen, as the commanding officer, how's that going to impact on me?"

House says he took a deep breath while listening to the mother.

"And then the third thought was, well, exactly why I'm here as the commanding officer is to sort that out, learn from it, deal with it and move forward from it," he says. "It was the third thought that I would suggest as a moral component to my thinking."

House began a formal investigation, which was quickly quashed by higher-ups.

"They didn't want to touch it," says House. "They told me not to investigate it because [of] the reputational damage to the organization at that time."

As a pilot, House knew the dangers of not speaking up. He was aware of incidents in the past where co-pilots had been afraid to speak up in the face of a grave pilot error, with disastrous consequences. In this case, though, he could have let the matter go with no effect on his career or his life. Instead, he reported it to the local police. The staff member, a female RAF sergeant, was charged, found guilty and sent to prison.

For taking the matter outside the chain of command, House became the subject of a formal complaint and was effectively fired for refusing to cover up the assault. In 2015, he received a medical discharge from the RAF with what was characterized as an "adjustment disorder." One day later, House was committed to hospital under the terms of the British Mental Health Act out of concerns that he harboured thoughts of self-harm.

"It put a toll on me, I guess, emotionally, in thinking through that toxicity of the situation at the time," he recalls.

House complained to the Service Complaints Ombudsman (SCO), whose mandate is to provide independent and impartial scrutiny of the handling of service complaints made by members of the UK armed forces.

In January 2021, the SCO upheld House's complaint. The ombudsman found that House had been "unjustly removed from command" and "wronged."

"My complaint cost me my career, home and £80,000 in legal payments," House told the *Daily Mirror*. "If I found that brutal—definitely life-changing, and close to life-taking—with all my background, all my resilience and all my experience to draw on, God help the minority groups, women, BAME [a UK acronym that stands for Black, Asian and minority ethnic] and the junior ranks."

That crushing experience became his coming-out party as a political agitator. House told his story to a parliamentary select committee and provided testimony to a formal MP's inquiry into the treatment of women in the UK armed forces. He agreed to a request to publish his evidence.

"It was that publication that led to a lot of people coming to me with similar experiences," says House. "It became pretty quickly apparent that there are an awful lot of people out there whose cases have been deliberately silenced."

House collected stories and got the idea for J4T, guided by the principles of CRM. A former military pilot himself, House was quite familiar with its precepts.

"Effectively, you can equate a military commander as the heart surgeon or as the airline pilot," says House. "They're part of a team. I'm orchestrating an environment where people in that team need to feel safe to operate to the best of their ability. If they're not feeling that, then there's a risk to what we're doing, whether it's in the health world, in the aviation world or in the military."

House met Niall Downey, now one of J4T's independent advisors, through a mutual contact.

"He struck me as one of these inspirational characters who's trying hard to improve systems and is hitting resistance [from] people who would just deny it," says House.

It's obvious how CRM might prevent airline disasters. Grafting that mindset onto complaints of sexual assault in the military would require adopting that "see it, say it" mentality along the chain of command. It would also require those in authority to act based on what is reported.

House thinks Downey is the perfect advisor because the doctor has been frustrated trying to introduce CRM to healthcare. Success there would give House some hints on how to change attitudes in the military.

"As far as I know, every doctor has taken an oath that broadly says 'Do no harm,'" says House. "It is the same in the military, certainly for an officer, same for Canada. Sometimes that means telling people things they don't want to hear in a compassionate way. Effectively, Niall's going to tell me my heart isn't functioning and he's going to have to do an operation on me, and the risk of him getting it wrong means I don't make it."

That's how Graham House sees what Niall Downey has to offer. The challenge is to change minds on the inside of the UK armed forces.

"House seems to have hit as many barriers as I did in healthcare, if not more," says Downey. "He appears to be battling a senior leadership team, in both the government and the forces, who are totally divorced from the reality of the organization they are leading."

The statistics back Downey up. That MP's inquiry into the treatment of women in the UK armed forces found that up to

17,000 members (12 percent) have been physically, racially or sexually harassed by colleagues in the past year.

"The recent examples House has quoted on figures for sexual harassment and rape in the forces are very disturbing," says Downey. "I fear he is getting little support from senior leaders and politicians and is seen as an inconvenient whistle-blower sullying the reputation of the British Armed Forces. I think he is doing great work on an individual basis but is doomed to failure on the larger stage, as I ultimately was in healthcare."

Instead of asking why CRM hasn't succeeded in building teamwork in healthcare, law enforcement and the military, perhaps we need to find out why aviation finds CRM so appealing. The fact that crew and passengers share the same fate when the plane crashes may be the winning argument in the skies.

If a rigid hierarchy is the obstacle that prevents CRM from seeping in, perhaps the solution is to challenge the hierarchy through external (i.e., civilian) oversight. Perhaps CRM would stand a better chance if there were safer and more effective mechanisms to report abuses. And perhaps it's up to people like Graham House and Niall Downey to make the case that the reputational harm from failing to follow the logic of CRM is worth avoiding.

CHAPTER SEVEN

FLY ON THE WALL

Improving safety and teamwork in the OR
with black box technology

C REW RESOURCE MANAGEMENT has made aviation dramatically safer by improving teamwork cohesion and by flattening the hierarchy so that the most junior team members feel comfortable speaking truth to power.

Despite being a really good idea, CRM has not been a game changer within the walls of the hospital—or the local police precinct, for that matter. However, another innovation from the airline industry just might move the needle.

AN OPERATING ROOM thrums with activity. A scrub nurse and a surgical technician carefully lay out more than a hundred sterile instruments on two tables draped in blue. The anesthesiologist primes the anesthetic machine and checks the cardiac, blood pressure and respiratory monitors used to measure vital signs. A surgical assistant logs onto a computer and loads digital X-rays and a CT scan. There are overhead lights and monitors on handles with adjustable elbow joints, IV poles, carts with extra supplies and a solitary low, black swivel seat. All of it is crammed into a 650-square-metre space.

The centre of the room under the surgical lights sits empty and waiting for the patient to be wheeled in.

This is about as ordinary as any OR, but several things make it remarkable. The first is the existence of the footage I've used to describe this scene, captured unobtrusively by a camera with a fish-eye lens. Personnel move about their work, their faces pixelated and voices distorted so they can't be identified. Even so, it's striking that those in the room are aware of the camera but aren't paying attention to it.

Then there's the point of view itself. The camera is up high and tilted down. It sees everything. It's the perspective of the fly on the wall, or ceiling—one that stands a good chance of opening the hidden culture of the operating theatre, making things safer for patients and, yes, building teamwork.

The camera is part of a new piece of surgical equipment called the OR Black Box. It takes its name from the flight recorders used on passenger airplanes.

The forward-thinking surgeon in Toronto who grabbed the black box concept from aviation and brought it to the OR is Dr. Teodor Grantcharov, whom we met back in the introduction.

Grantcharov says the ORBB paints a picture of what really goes on in the OR, leaving less to the imagination and faulty human recall than ever before. He says the chair of surgery at North Carolina's Duke Health, one of the testing sites for the device, put it best.

"Before they launched [the ORBB] last year, he sent a video message to the entire staff," says Grantcharov. "He said, 'It's time for us to find out what we really are, not what we think we are.' Individual perceptions of what happened are often very different from reality. And once you see it, you understand the power of data and critical reflection."

More a platform than a device, the ORBB records the entire operating theatre from multiple wall-mounted cameras and ones installed on the laparoscopic instruments. Microphones pick up conversations between the surgeons, anesthesiologists, scrub and circulating nurses and anyone else who pops into the OR for even a moment. The system also captures the patient's vital signs, feedback from electronic surgical instruments and more.

A growing list of hospitals are installing the ORBB to analyze and improve efficiency and patient safety. Many, like Duke Health and Stanford, are among the best hospitals in America.

The term "black box" was first used by the British during the Second World War. Today, the devices are actually bright orange so they can be located quickly following a crash. The impetus for flight recorders came from a series of airline disasters in the 1950s. In 1957, a demonstration model of a flight recorder was developed by Dr. David Warren and his team of engineers in Australia. The device underwent further development in the United Kingdom, and in 1966, the British Ministry of Aviation ordered that the recorder should be carried on all planes. Two years later the devices became mandatory in the United States.

Since then, flight recorders have become mandatory in all major aircraft throughout the world. They have helped find the cause of many airline accidents and, like CRM, helped build a culture of safety in aviation.

There are two kinds of flight recorder devices. The cockpit voice recorder makes an audio recording of the conversation of the pilots and other members of the crew who visit the cockpit during the flight; it also records alarms and other sounds in the cockpit. The flight data recorder records time, altitude, airspeed, heading, aircraft attitude and much more.

Dr. Grantcharov's interest in developing the ORBB comes from his twin fascinations with mistakes made in the OR here on Earth and those made by flight crews at cruising altitude. He started thinking about a black box for surgery while doing a PhD alongside his surgical residency in Copenhagen beginning in 1997.

"The topic of my PhD was developing a system to measure the performance of the surgeon," he says. As part of his thesis, Grantcharov developed a virtual reality OR simulator to test surgical skills.

"I found that some surgeons were amazing, and some surgeons were terrible."

You may find that statement shocking, but Grantcharov doesn't. That's because surgery, like family medicine, cardiology and every other specialty, has long been taught by apprenticeship. Young surgeons learn good and bad habits from their mentors. It's hard to standardize training in that model.

That variability in quality also exists despite surgery's attempts to develop scores that evaluate technical skill. One such metric is called the Objective Structured Assessment of Technical Skill (OSATS), a comprehensive score comprising nine groups of tasks and four potential errors. It is to surgery what sabermetrics, or *Moneyball* baseball analytics, are to America's pastime.

The higher the OSATS score, the more proficient the resident.

Grantcharov took that scoring system and married it with video recording. He and colleagues did a preliminary study in which they analyzed the unedited videos of a common laparoscopic surgical procedure for weight loss. The videos were submitted by surgeons from around the world and analyzed separately by two observers who used OSATS to score the surgeons' technique.

An analysis of twenty-five videos entitled "Error Rating Tool to Identify and Analyse Technical Errors and Events in Laparoscopic Surgery," published in the *British Journal of Surgery* in 2013, was groundbreaking. In half of the videos analyzed, surgeons made thirty-five or more mistakes per operation.

To a patient and their family, that statistic no doubt seems frightening. Disturbingly, that paper was one of the first to publish any kind of surgical error rate.

A surgeon, critical care specialist or ER physician like me usually relies on recollection to piece together errors and bad outcomes. Memories are faulty, video cameras far less so.

"People believe that the variation in performance of a surgeon doing brain surgery in a modern hospital with modern equipment will be very narrow, but in fact it is not," says Grantcharov.

Better OSATS scores correlate with better surgical outcomes, but Grantcharov thinks the assessment is not robust enough to raise the bar on surgical skill. The black box just might be.

Grantcharov's journey from surgeon to inventor continued during a fellowship in minimally invasive surgery at Temple University's Western Pennsylvania Hospital in Pittsburgh. He had just completed his surgical residency at the University of Copenhagen, and a doctoral degree in medical sciences at Aarhus University in Denmark.

A newcomer to medical culture in the United States, Grantcharov assumed that most of his surgical colleagues played golf during their off days. He signed up for lessons from a golf pro. At the first lesson, the instructor surprised Grantcharov by setting up a video camera.

"The teacher said he wanted to record my golf swing so he could analyze and fix what I was doing wrong," he recalls.

It was a light-bulb moment for Grantcharov. Immediately, he began recording his operations, and has been doing so ever since.

"I've got terabytes of my own surgical technique," he says.

Videotaping his work made Grantcharov a more technically proficient surgeon, once he got past the discomfort of watching himself on a monitor at home.

"I found it embarrassing to watch," he says. "I couldn't watch till the end because I was very disappointed with myself. That for me personally demonstrated the power of video and the power of video analysis."

Grantcharov believes surgery can and must be made safer, but not at the expense of throwing colleagues under the bus. The only person he criticizes publicly is himself. And he's his own worst critic.

He joined the staff of St. Michael's Hospital in Toronto in 2006, where he began doing research on videotaping surgeons to standardize their training and evaluation. From the moment he started envisioning the OR Black Box, he wanted video recording to be part of it.

Flight recording is audio only. In 2000, the US National Transportation Safety Board proposed video recording to capture information such as the presence of smoke inside the cockpit and whether the pilot and co-pilot were incapacitated. To this day, however, video recorders are not mandatory in aviation. Cockpit crews have resisted it because they believe recordings lack context and are prone to misuse.

"If cameras were in the cockpit, it could change the way flying gets done," Doug Moss, a former test pilot and accident investigator, told *Wired* in 2014.

Grantcharov wanted the ORBB to include a video recorder because he wanted to marry surgical performance evaluation to the investigation of surgical mishaps.

Grantcharov has made himself a student of disasters in other domains.

"I was always fascinated by the process that the aviation industry uses to identify root causes and contributing factors" to help prevent future disasters, he says. Grantcharov founded Surgical Safety Technologies (SST), a start-up based in Toronto, and has obtained research grants from leading medical equipment manufacturers such as Medtronic, Ethicon Canada and Olympus Canada.

In hard dollars, it's a costly project. The 2014 prototype for the ORBB cost roughly CAD$20 million. Grantcharov estimates the total cost thus far at close to $40 million, with a monthly cash burn rate of half a million. He thinks the cost is small compared to what's at stake.

"How do you put a price on surgical complications?" he asks.

For other measurable outcomes, he says it's easier to show how the black box can save hospitals a lot of money.

"We can improve access by cutting waste," he says. "We can improve efficiency and we can improve education. We can do that not one surgeon at a time but many."

The ORBB is being tested at St. Michael's Hospital and four other hospitals in Canada. Since 2017, SST has partnered with leading hospitals in Amsterdam, Copenhagen and Ghent. In 2020, they were joined by the Long Island Jewish Medical Center and the William P. Clements Jr. University Hospital in Dallas.

Grantcharov and colleagues have begun to publish important research findings such as the sheer number of distractions that occur during everyday operations.

Dr. James Jung, a surgeon at St. Michael's Hospital, and colleagues studied ORBB data from 132 consecutive patients who had laparoscopic surgery for weight loss, gall bladder removal or cancer. Jung published the results in 2020 in the *Annals of Surgery*.

All told, the ORBB detected 3,435 errors and events, with a median of twenty errors per operation. These included applying too little force and misjudging distances. A total of 1,258 "events" (untoward outcomes) occurred during the operations. The most common was unexpected bleeding of any amount.

Surgery requires intense concentration and attention to detail. In 2016, the Committee on Perioperative Care of the American

College of Surgeons concluded there is a growing body of evidence that distractions in the OR harm patient safety.

The ORBB in Jung's study detected a median of 138 distractions per patient, or one distraction every forty seconds. For instance, the device detected an OR door opening forty-two times per patient—not just a distraction but a possible source of contamination and post-operative infections. Machine alarms rang a median of sixty-seven times, and loud noises sounded eighteen times per operation. In thirty-four operations, the surgical team was engaged in at least one irrelevant conversation. One out of every three operations studied had at least one distraction.

These are early studies, but already the ORBB is seen as a stupendous technological achievement. In 2019, *Time* magazine named it one of the best inventions of the year.

Other SST projects in development include Trauma Black Box, Sim Black Box and (since the pandemic) COVID Black Box. OR Black Box Explorer is a platform that enables surgeons to curate their own libraries of recorded operations to mark their progress and compare themselves to colleagues.

Some of the early wins from ORBB are remarkable. It's a serious and potentially lethal mistake to leave surgical instruments inside the abdomen. Nurses do a strict count so that the number of instruments taken from and returned to the instrument table match. Typically, a miscount is due to human error, often caused by distraction. At one hospital, the ORBB was able to narrow the moment when the miscount occurred to a five-minute window within an operation that lasted six hours.

Grantcharov and his team are also committed to standardizing the training of surgeons by using technology to discover the errors of today to help prevent those of tomorrow. All of this requires a level of teamwork involving different professionals that is seldom seen at hospitals.

Grantcharov and his many partners have much bigger plans too. They want the black box to detect errors during the operation before those errors cause harm. That is something even the engineers who design cutting-edge flight recorders have yet to implement.

To do all of that and more, he's assembled a team that is as eclectic as any I've seen in medicine.

===

AMONG GRANTCHAROV'S FIRST recruits were engineers at Air Canada. They're no longer involved in the project, but Grantcharov recalls vividly one piece of advice they offered.

"That the process has to be confidential and not punitive," he says. "The moment somebody gets punished because of black box data, that will be catastrophic. Imagine that we capture private data and we use it to fire a nurse because she didn't properly assemble a device. You've lost the entire profession right there. And then you'd go back to the dark ages of surgery where all the professions would be protecting themselves and no one would be comfortable sharing information."

Grantcharov took that advice to heart. That's why the faces and the voices of people in the OR aren't recognizable. In fact, every bit of data assembled by the black box is stripped of identifying information. This, he says, is one of the key features that makes it easier to sell the concept to hospitals and to the people who work there.

Pansy Schulthess, a former scrub nurse, is the manager of quality, patient safety and education for Perioperative Services at Unity Health Toronto, a hospital network that includes St. Michael's. Today, she describes herself as the device's number one fan. That was not her initial reaction, or that of her nursing colleagues, when Grantcharov proposed giving the ORBB a try at St. Michael's Hospital as part of a research project back in 2014.

"That meeting did not go over well," she recalls. "I think all anyone heard was that you're now going to be recorded on audio and video."

The nurses were concerned that the recordings might be used for disciplinary purposes in the event of an adverse patient outcome.

"Unfortunately, there's a culture within nursing that they always fear being blamed for things," she says. "No matter what happens, somehow it's always going to end up the nurse's fault."

She says Grantcharov listened to the nurses and allayed their concerns.

"We always felt that if it didn't feel safe or we had more questions we could come back and talk again," she says.

Shuja Khalid is a deep learning engineer and a key member of a team of more than thirty at SST. Deep learning (a function of artificial intelligence, or AI) imitates the way humans think. It does this by finding patterns in data that are then used to enable a computer to make decisions about, for example, what is or is not a surgical error. The ultimate aim is for machines to analyze the data without being closely watched by humans.

"The purpose of deep learning in this case is to use all of the sensory input data collected by the ORBB [such as the audio data and the video data] to directly extract information from these sources such that they can be used in downstream processes for things like quality improvement and safety procedures for surgical patients," he says.

Khalid is a PhD candidate at the University of Toronto, where his focus is machine learning. His interests include biomedical engineering, visual scene understanding, and explainable AI (XAI), which refers to methods and techniques in the application of artificial intelligence in which the solution can be understood by humans.

Khalid may or may not be able to tell the difference between Metzenbaum baby curved scissors and the consumer kind you use to cut toenails. And his first deep learning project in university sounds more germane to the general manager of a National Hockey League team.

The project involved the NHL's Trade Deadline Day. That's the last day in the NHL seasonal calendar in which teams can trade players. Good teams stock up on players in anticipation of a deep playoff run. Bad teams dump players on expiring contracts in return for draft picks and prospects.

Khalid's objective was to use deep learning algorithms based on recent performance metrics to help general managers decide whether to trade or retain players.

"What I developed could potentially predict how likely it was that a player would get traded at the trade deadline," he says. "The idea was to be like an assistant general manager that could determine who would most likely be available from other teams at the deadline."

Grantcharov heard about Khalid's project and wondered if he could do the same with surgeons and nurses, but with one huge difference: instead of looking at past surgical performance, Khalid was asked to evaluate OR personnel in near-real time.

"That's when I got really excited about this project, and that's how this marriage sort of came to be, where I started looking at deep learning solutions," Khalid says.

Khalid and his colleagues at SST are attempting to use deep learning to extract meaningful information from videos of surgeons doing operations. That might mean estimating how much bleeding has occurred or quantifying the skill of an individual surgeon.

That's not as easy as it sounds. While there are numerical measures of surgical skill, the number assigned to a particular surgeon based on video evidence depends on the human who is looking at it.

"If you give that same video to multiple surgeons, chances are that they might give it different scores," says Khalid. "That's something that is deeply troubling to us. We want to be able to quantify surgical skill based on objective measurements."

However, that doesn't mean Khalid and his fellow data engineers ignore the opinions of surgeons. Far from it.

= = =

IN A DARKENED room at SST, Dr. Sherman Wong and ten colleagues peer at a large computer monitor. Like Wong, most are young general surgeons from some of the finest residency programs around the world. Throw in a gynecologist and a plastic surgeon and you've got a fairly broad range of opinions. Which is exactly what Shuja Khalid and his fellow data engineers want.

They're looking at a video from a critical moment in a nephrectomy, the surgical procedure to remove a cancerous kidney or one damaged by trauma. The procedure often causes bleeding, and the estimated blood loss from a partial or complete nephrectomy ranges between 200 and 555 ml.

"There's bleeding here," says one of the general surgeons.

"There's definitely bleeding here," another agrees.

"That's a lot of blood," says a plastic surgeon.

A straggler gives the images a careful second look. As a trauma surgeon, he's used to seeing a lot of blood.

"That's not a lot of bleeding," he says.

Though contrary to the team's early assessment, that outside perspective demonstrates how Dr. Wong and colleagues play a critical role. If the deep learning algorithms of Shuja Khalid pick up possible indicators of trouble like bleeding, then these young surgeons add a human perspective.

"It's kind of a recursive process," says Wong. "The AI will give us what it thinks is happening, and human interpretation will improve that. That in turn helps improve the AI, and there's kind of a continuous process for the AI to continue to learn from the cases that we see and that it sees."

Most often, this group determines whether the bleeding is expected or unusual. The group dynamic reminds me of the Visual Thinking Strategies approach used by Alexa Miller to teach budding doctors at Harvard Medical School.

Khalid sees his job as augmenting Dr. Wong and his fellow analysts. Maybe more.

"Clinical analysts look at videos [of surgeons] and rate them," says Khalid. "What I'm trying to do is create an agent that can do this in their place."

Khalid and his colleagues at SST are clearly getting somewhere. Grantcharov says there are early indications that deep learning algorithms may be better than flesh-and-blood surgeons at picking out things worth noting on the video footage of an operation.

There are good reasons why deep learning may sometimes be better than humans at poring over hours of surgery on video. The task can be tedious. A human analyst might be too fatigued or even too bored to pay constant close attention.

The next logical step for the ORBB is to help uncover the reasons why errors such as instrument miscounts occur. Once again, surgeons like Sherman Wong aren't there just to look at clinical things like bleeding during surgery. They also examine the stretch of video during which a miscount occurs and look for factors that might have distracted the people in the OR.

"There might be a lot of conversation going on," says Wong, hypothetically. "The person doing the count might have their attention diverted away."

Information like that can be fed back to the OR team so that they can reflect upon and streamline practices that might contribute to distraction.

Using deep learning to make things safer and more efficient in the OR is one goal. Khalid says another is to turn deep learning and the OR Black Box into something a surgeon can use to improve individual performance.

Until Grantcharov came along, there was little if any video recording of surgeons whatsoever—and no deep learning algorithms for evaluating performance. Surgical residents kept copies of the recorded camera feed from the laparoscope camera to review. Grantcharov says they would store them in a box or drawer on anything from VHS cassettes to USB keys. And quite possibly never look at them again.

OR Black Box Explorer enables surgeons, inexperienced and otherwise, to store all of their procedures in the cloud, where deep learning algorithms can point out their training needs and can pit them against thousands of other surgeons.

≡ ≡ ≡

So FAR, I'VE said that teamwork between surgeons and deep learning engineers has been fundamental to the development of the ORBB. But there's another kind of teamwork that's just as essential.

Spend any time in an OR and you see not one but several interconnected things going on.

There's the surgical procedure itself. That may be what patients and families think of as an operation. It's also the focal point of TV shows like *Grey's Anatomy*.

Then there's the anesthesia. An anesthesiologist orchestrates a complex set of procedures that begin before the patient is put under anesthesia, intubated and placed on a ventilator, and end after the patient is extubated and awakens in the recovery room.

And there's one or more scrub nurses. In addition to assisting the surgeons, they set up the operating room for the patient.

They open the surgical trays and set up the instrument table so that all of the sterile instruments are ready to go. They hand tools to the surgeon and accept them back when the surgeon no longer needs them.

As noted earlier, one of the most essential duties of scrub nurses is to keep a strict count of instruments, sponges and other items to make certain nothing is left inside the body when the incisions are closed.

All three domains—surgery, anesthesia and nursing—carry on during the operation. They are coordinated and largely contingent on one another. But knowing a lot about one of them doesn't tell you about the other two.

The ORBB is uniquely situated to keep track of all three. But to do that, the people behind the black box must create a much more inclusive team than what many of us in healthcare are used to.

Pansy Schulthess knows all about that. Before she became a manager, she spent much of a twenty-year career as a scrub nurse in the OR in British Columbia and later at St. Michael's. "We kind of joke that OR nurses have OCD [obsessive-compulsive disorder] when it comes to a lot of things," she says, "but I want to say patient safety in particular."

That makes a lot of sense. Scrub nurses are the keepers of surgical instruments. But as Schulthess explains, they do so much more. When they arrive at work, they look at the OR list of the day. They check the history of the patient. They make sure the OR is stocked with equipment and supplies. They check in with the anesthesiologist to see if the patient needs special medications and IVs. Then they take part in the preoperative safety check and give patients emotional support while bringing them to the OR to meet the staff. They position the patient on the OR table and get them ready for the anesthesiologist and the surgeon.

"If I was that patient, I would want my nurse and my team to have OCD with the care that I'm being provided," she says.

Initially, Schulthess says, she and her nursing colleagues watched what they said when they worked in an OR with the black box equipment. Soon, they forgot it was there.

A few years later, Schulthess became the team leader for general surgery, and asked Grantcharov how the recordings and the data were being used.

"He was explaining to me about some of the feedback they'd given to the surgical residents and some of the staff surgeons," she recalls. She asked why they hadn't given any feedback to the nurses.

So Grantcharov and Schulthess curated ORBB video snippets of interest to the nurses. They showed recurring issues like distractions caused by technology and personnel, as well as challenges with communication, effectively bridging the three silos by showing those in each how surgeons, anesthesiologists and nurses distracted one another at critical times during the operation. The breakthrough was demonstrating that the critical times for each silo did not coincide.

Take abdominal surgery. For the surgeons, the critical part of the operation is stitching two loops of bowel together and making sure there are no leaks. For the anesthesiologist, it's inducing anesthesia and putting the patient on a ventilator, and then doing the reverse at the end of the operation. For the scrub nurse, it's counting surgical instruments near the end of the procedure to make sure none have been left inside the abdomen.

"A critical phase for the surgeon may not be [a critical phase] for me as the nurse," Schulthess says.

What the ORBB demonstrated is that many of the distractions were experienced by one of the three groups performing a critical function while the other two groups did the distracting—for example, by playing music loudly and filling the room with unnecessary talk about, say, the hockey games they planned on watching on the weekend.

Grantcharov clearly remembers the day a nurse told him he was seeing the critical aspects of the operation only from the point of view of the surgeons and not the nurses.

"'When we enter the nurses' critical phase, you don't care,'" Grantcharov recalls the nurse telling him pointedly.

Schulthess says the ORBB also showed when conversations between the nurses were bothering the surgeons.

"Sometimes two nurses in the room would start talking to each other about the next case or the next steps or something related to the case," says Schulthess. "In one of the videos, Teodor actually stops [during the operation] and says, 'This is really distracting.'"

Grantcharov was determined to address distraction from all sides. He brought in human factors engineers to zero in on critical moments and how to prevent distractions during those times.

"We brought engineers and we brought AI and data people," Grantcharov says. "We started really understanding not only how complex it is but also how exciting it is and how many amazing opportunities we have to understand and mitigate risk, understand and improve performance and [ultimately] improve safety."

"Just hearing each other's perspectives opened people's eyes," Schulthess says.

But what is it about the ORBB that makes it possible for surgeons, anesthesiologists and nurses to find that common ground in ways seldom seen before?

Before the ORBB, they documented mistakes. What the black box does is show the environment surrounding the mistake and provide the essential context that explains how it happened.

As we've discovered, the game Friday Night at the ER encourages team behaviour by making each player aware that actions in one hospital department have consequences in other departments. Likewise, the ORBB boosts teamwork in the OR by demonstrating that actions by the surgeons have impacts on the anesthesiologists and nurses, and so on.

Before the black box, people relied on faulty and biased recollections. The black box tells them what actually happened. Without cameras and deep learning, none of that would be possible.

===

SHUJA KHALID FIGURES he's approaching the halfway mark towards his goal of creating actionable data for surgeons. Like Grantcharov and Pansy Schulthess, Khalid believes the key to success so far has been teamwork. At SST, he says, there are deliberate efforts to break down silos.

"The biggest thing about this teamwork is to ensure that we have multiple people with multiple backgrounds working on a specific project," he says. "It's to ensure that we can bounce ideas off of each other."

That teamwork is reflected in the entire organizational culture at SST. There are four main groups. They include administration; clinical analysts like Dr. Sherman Wong who evaluate surgical procedures on video; a front-end engineering team that creates apps for the clinical analysts; and an AI engineering team that works on deep learning. All of them work in one large, open-concept room.

"There's constant collaboration with the different groups that exist within SST," says Khalid.

Khalid doesn't do surgery, just as the surgeons aren't experts in AI. But by working closely with one another, they are able to gain a greater understanding of each other's strengths and limitations.

"The more we collaborate, the less annoyed we get with one another," he says.

A second factor that encourages teamwork at SST is a flat hierarchical structure. Khalid has worked at siloed companies where the CEO was almost always too busy to interact with employees. At SST, he says, Grantcharov sets the tone.

"Dr. Grantcharov does not sit in his office," says Khalid. "He sits outside so that he's more accessible to people . . . Whether it's personal stuff or project-related, he's happy to make the time. There are times when I'm working late, and he has come by and talked to me about how my day is going."

===

THE GROWING PAINS at St. Michael's Hospital have taught Grantcharov and his team valuable lessons on how to improve and develop the ORBB, how to scale it up and how to increase buy-in by colleagues and hospitals.

The key to gaining acceptance is for each hospital to develop its own implementation plan, with wide input. It means ensuring that nurses and other staff aren't forced to work in an OR with the black box. It also means informing patients of the black box's existence and giving them the option to have the device switched off.

At a virtual conference held in February 2021, the Surgical Safety Network (SSN) Roundtable Sessions brought together ORBB early adopters and researchers from Canada, the United States and the European Union. Patterned after informal meetings held by airlines in which errors and near misses are discussed, SSN is designed to highlight early wins and challenges in implementing the black box.

Delegates learned that in August 2020, UT Southwestern Medical Center in Dallas installed the ORBB in five of its operating rooms. In November 2020, Duke University Medical Center had the black box up and running in two of its ORs.

To me, one of the most impressive things about the SSN Roundtable Sessions is that they have healthy representation from surgery, anesthesia, nursing, human factors engineering and computer science, all together.

Introducing guest speakers and commenting on the proceedings, Teodor Grantcharov beamed as he watched his dream of an OR Black Box in every operating room of every hospital take flight.

"It's turning into a movement," he says. "We've got some of the best hospitals in the world who have adopted it, and it's growing. It's nice to see the changing culture of the operating room."

= = =

BLACK BOXES AND crew resource management are two long-standing features of aviation that are essential to passenger safety. But while teachers of CRM have encountered turbulence as they share its precepts with people in healthcare, the ORBB seems to have reached cruising altitude with far less chop.

There are several reasons why, and most of them have a bearing on teamwork.

CRM is delivered to healthcare mainly by aviation experts who are outsiders to medical culture. The ORBB was developed by Dr. Teodor Grantcharov, a surgical insider who understands that medical culture demands scientific proof of innovations.

Another reason has to do with objectives. The main goal of CRM is better patient safety. Few in surgery would argue with that, but patient safety is not the imperative that airplane safety is in aviation, where everyone on the plane shares the same fate should a crash occur.

In developing the ORBB, Grantcharov learned a lot from aviation. I would argue that his black box and its various iterations have gone much further than the ones on airplanes. That makes me wonder what aviation can learn from him.

"They can learn a lot," he says. "The way we process data, the way we study teamwork and the way we proactively develop strategies to mitigate risk—we're doing it in a much more systematic way now than they do in aviation."

At the end of the day, it takes a well-informed and lively guest speaker to teach CRM to doctors. It takes a team to bring the black box to the OR. I'm betting on the team.

CHAPTER EIGHT

SWISSAIR

Building a team in trying circumstances

W E'VE SEEN PARAMEDICS join forces with family doctors and nurse practitioners to provide more comprehensive primary care in Ontario's Renfrew County. And we've seen ex–Navy SEAL Brian Ferguson and colleagues at Arena Labs moulding groups of immensely skilled individuals at places like Cleveland Clinic into high-performance teams. Those efforts come from the predictable needs of patients who require everything from primary care to open heart surgery. But sometimes, a crisis takes a special kind of leader to build a team on the fly and create order out of chaos.

===

WEARY FROM AN evening cracking the textbooks, Trevor Jain went to bed early. A phone call from the operations officer at 36 Canadian Brigade headquarters in Halifax woke him from a deep sleep. The bedside clock said 3:15 a.m. It was September 3, 1998.

"Trev, it's Rick." Jain willed the cobwebs from his mind as Captain Rick Dykens tried to rouse him. "There has been a plane crash and I need you at Shearwater."

"Rick was known to be a bit of a prankster," Jain recalls. "You have to realize back then there was no internet. I couldn't just hop on a computer and see CNN or CBC News."

Jain hung up and went back to sleep.

Dykens called a second time, at 3:30 a.m.

"Rick, I got class tomorrow early," Jain told Dykens.

"Trevor, it's not a joke," Jain recalls Captain Dykens telling him. There had been a plane crash, and Jain was to report to the military base at Shearwater, Nova Scotia.

Jain had barely enough time to change into his military uniform before an RCMP officer knocked on the door.

= = =

SWISSAIR FLIGHT 111 departed from John F. Kennedy International Airport in Jamaica, New York, at 8:18 p.m. eastern daylight time on September 2, 1998.

It was a misty and mild evening, with light rain recorded on the ground, scattered clouds above and thunderstorms to the west and northwest, moving eastward. Two minutes in, the flight crew requested a heading diversion to stay clear of stormy weather, then ascended to cruising altitude.

The wide-body airliner carried 229 people—215 passengers along with 14 flight crew en route to Geneva, Switzerland. United Nations officials frequently used this flight to travel between New York and Geneva, the UN's two largest sites. Also on this flight were business executives and scientists with the World Health Organization.

The aircraft, a McDonnell Douglas MD-11, had more than 36,000 hours of recorded flight time, and up-to-date maintenance reports. The pilot-in-command (captain) and first officer had thousands of hours of total flying time. Words like "quiet," "friendly," "calm" and "professional" were used to describe them.

Around fifty-three minutes after departure, the first officer noted an unusual smell—a final observation preserved by one of two flight recorders that Canadian navy divers pulled from the seabed. Seconds later, the captain said, "Look," noting what aviation experts charged with reconstructing the crash would report was likely a wisp of smoke.

The "most likely" cause? An arc of electricity linked to power cables for the in-flight entertainment system had ignited highly flammable insulation. Invisible to the cockpit crew, the resulting fire in the ceiling, or "attic," was spreading above and behind them.

Minutes later, smoke became "discernable" in the cockpit and the crew asked to land in Boston, then agreed on Halifax. At 9:24 p.m. EDT, the in-flight recorders began logging ninety-two seconds of continuous systems failures, cutting power to parts of the plane, including the lights in the passenger cabin, where the flight crew used flashlights to prepare for landing.

With control panels shutting down and fire burning overhead, the captain and co-pilot declared an emergency and alerted air traffic control in Moncton, New Brunswick. They were starting to dump fuel and needed to land immediately.

Then communication ceased.

Roughly five minutes later, at 9:31 p.m. EDT (10:31 p.m. local time), the plane hit the ocean off Peggy's Cove, Nova Scotia. All 229 passengers and crew on board died, making it one of the worst aviation disasters in Canadian history.

===

ROYAL CANADIAN AIR Force Base Shearwater is located 8.3 kilometres southeast of Shearwater on the eastern shore of

Halifax Harbour. At the time, it was called Canadian Forces Base (CFB) Shearwater. The RCMP driver, lights flashing, drove Jain onto the base at about 4 a.m.

"The whole base was chaotic," Jain recalls. "Everybody was running around."

A medical officer approached Jain.

"Are you the guy with pathology experience?" a military doctor asked Jain. A member of the staff put a medical brassard, with its distinctive red cross, on Jain's arm.

At the time, CFB Shearwater was a military base buttressed by a sea jetty to the southwest, fenced on all sides and guarded. Past the main gate, office buildings, crew quarters, messes, gym and chapel was the operational side, where a grid of runways mainly served as a rest stop for Sea Kings, the "workhorse" of military helicopters.

Close to the runway were two giant aircraft hangars.

Jain was taken to Hangar B.

When Swissair 111 crashed into the waters off Peggy's Cove, doctors and other first responders were mobilized to rescue passengers from the chilly waters.

Jain spotted a flight surgeon he knew—a doctor from CFB Greenwood, located in the Annapolis Valley.

"He was just sitting on his rucksack," says Jain. "They had been flown in. I asked what was going on, and he said they were flying home because there were no survivors."

By 4:30 in the morning, a rescue operation had turned into a recovery operation.

"Picture walking into a large, empty warehouse with 110 people running around," Jain recalls. "Picture the chaotic noise of heavy metal music playing, even though it wasn't, but that's what it felt like. Multiple organizations running around. And no purpose."

Just then, a truck driver entered the hangar and asked if anyone knew how to get a portable X-ray machine off the back of the truck he had just driven to the base. In hospitals, radiology technicians drive these self-powered X-ray machines on wheels to the patient's bedside in the ER, the wards and the ICU. To get the machine off the truck, any X-ray technician would have known to power it up and drive it down a ramp.

"I actually knew how to do it," says Jain. "It's all about helping where you can."

That was one problem solved. The next would be a lot trickier.

When Jain parked the X-ray machine in a corner of the hangar, he noticed a tarp with long black hair trailing out from under it. That was when he first realized he'd be identifying bodies from the crash.

Jain took a sketch pad out of his pocket—the kind soldiers carry to write down orders, plans, dates and locations of meetings, contact information and other things. Jain sketched out the basic requirements of an autopsy room: plumbing for water and drainage, a source of electricity and a long table.

Swissair 111 had crashed into the ocean off the coast of Nova Scotia. Under Canadian federal law, it fell to the chief medical examiner of the closest jurisdiction to recover and identify the victims. At the time of the crash, Nova Scotia's chief medical examiner was Dr. John Butt.

When Butt first heard about the Swissair disaster, he'd just come home from a trial in New Glasgow.

"I just so hoped that it wasn't true," he recalls. "I was hoping that even as I drove into Halifax at about 11:30 p.m. It was horrible in terms of the dismemberment. It's just crazy how terrible it was."

Butt had to quickly assemble a 150-member team to identify the remains, most often by matching recovered body parts with DNA samples taken from family members.

It was Butt who decided on CFB Shearwater as the place to conduct autopsies, take X-rays and gather tissue samples from the victims.

"I remember that John Butt had surveyed the scene from one of the ships," Jain recalls. "He got word back that he needed a morgue."

Dr. Butt called upon Nova Scotia's Emergency Management Office (EMO), which is responsible for emergency planning and coordinating emergency responses in the province. At Hangar B, EMO contractors gathered to build the morgue. But they didn't know how to begin.

"A carpenter walked up to me and asked if I was the guy with pathology experience," says Jain. "I took them to the hood of a truck that was near the hangar. I held out my field message pad and I said, 'Here's what we need to do. We need twelve-by-twelve suites with hot water and drainage. If you can start there, we'll be miles ahead.'"

For the second time, Jain was the man with the plan. The contractors started cutting wood, laying electrical cables and laying PVC piping for water.

"When they saw me do that, people started asking me more questions," Jain says. "It kind of snowballed. And what we say in the military, that's a leadership void that was being filled."

The next day, Dr. Butt arrived with his assistant to inspect the mortuary, and Jain was asked to show him around.

"Oh, Trevor, you can be my assistant," said Dr. Butt, taking in Jain's youthful appearance.

"No, you don't understand, John," said the assistant. "Trevor has set up your mortuary for you."

"He did what?" Dr. Butt looked incredulously at Jain for what felt like an eternity. "Well then, you're my pathology operations officer."

And that's how Jain was put in charge of building and operating the temporary mortuary for one of the worst aviation disasters in Canadian history.

The "guy with pathology experience" was twenty-eight years old. And he wasn't even a doctor. At the time, Jain had just three years of medical school under his belt.

===

THE STORY OF how Trevor Jain ended up overseeing the largest makeshift morgue in recent history is equal parts medicine and military. He's been doing both since he was a teenager.

Jain, born in Ontario in 1970, comes from a blended family. He has a stepsister who is ten years older. The family moved to Wolfville, a town in Nova Scotia's Annapolis Valley, when his father became a professor at Acadia University.

"My father was Hindu," says Jain. "You can imagine growing up in rural Nova Scotia as one of the only two brown kids with mixed parents."

Jain remembers being bullied by other kids.

"I was called 'Hindu,' 'Paki' and 'Gandhi,'" he recalls. "I had school projects destroyed by classmates. I don't know how I survived junior high [middle school]."

Those experiences gave him empathy for teammates with disadvantages or who lack privilege.

Leaders sometimes rely exclusively on the best and the brightest in the group. But the most effective team leaders get help from everyone, including those who are the least advantaged. Due to his own experiences as a middle-school student, Jain sees this ability as his secret power.

"Everyone needs to feel valued and able to see themselves as contributors," says Jain. "This brings more firepower to any problem. A leader knows how to do this."

Jain joined the Canadian Armed Forces' Reserves as a seventeen-year-old in secondary school. The infantry was a respite from the intolerance he experienced growing up.

"I was with a diverse group of people," he says. "It didn't matter provided you could shoot, communicate and move. And I had a brand-new family of brothers and sisters."

Jain was with the West Nova Scotia Regiment, an old and storied unit of the Canadian Militia. Tracing its history as far back as 1717, it was part of the Canadian Expeditionary Force during the First World War; the unit was also among the first Allied soldiers to invade the European continent during the Second World War.

In 1990, Jain completed an eight-week officer training program at Camp Aldershot, an army training facility north of the Cornwallis River. There, he had his first test of leadership as a platoon commander with the rank of second lieutenant and thirty-seven soldiers under his command. The training was gruelling, an experience Jain wrote about in the book *Everyday Heroes*: "We had started with thirty candidates and were down to fifteen and I was exhausted, going on sheer willpower," he wrote. "But since I was a West Novie, there was no way I was going to be RTU [returned to unit] without a passing grade."

Jain's culminating assignment was to conduct a deliberate attack on a fortified position. He used a standard approach to planning the attack, from initial reconnaissance to deploying soldiers and wielding support weapons.

He was just twenty-one years of age, but he passed.

"It was the best day ever in my life," he recalls. "The day that I'm most proud of is when I got the rank of lieutenant in a Canadian infantry regiment."

Jain says lessons learned back then were critical to building and running the temporary morgue at Hangar B.

"The number one lesson I learned is that a platoon commander is responsible for the welfare of your troops," he says. "If you don't look after your people, they are ineffective. If they're ineffective, it affects the firepower of the platoon, the company and the battalion."

That meant making sure they had adequate provisions, rest, sleep and even proper footwear. It meant that they got appropriate leave when they needed it. It also meant that they got emotional support.

Around the same time, Jain got his pilot's licence, and got a degree in biology at Acadia University.

"The first couple years I wasn't a good student, but always knew I wanted to end up in medicine," says Jain. "So I pulled up my socks the third and fourth year."

Jain developed an insatiable curiosity about the human body. He wanted to be able to correlate the clinical signs and symptoms of a heart attack to the death of heart muscle cells as seen on a microscope slide.

He began volunteering at the Valley Regional Hospital, a small facility in Kentville, Nova Scotia. There, Jain spent time with patients with life-threatening illnesses. His interest in how the body works in health and fails in disease steered him towards pathology.

"I was attracted to pathology because of the experiences that I had as a volunteer," Jain recalls. "Why does somebody die? What's the disease process?"

Jain began volunteering in the hospital's pathology lab. He asked the hospital's chief pathologist, Dr. Roland Jung, if he might be permitted to watch an autopsy.

The pathologist—who received his medical degree from the University of the West Indies in Mona, about eight kilometres from Kingston, Jamaica—took a shine to Jain and invited him to learn how to do a post-mortem. Jain says Dr. Jung painstakingly explained the purpose of autopsies and the inner workings of a morgue. Jain's apprehension at the thought of seeing a dead body was eased by his mentor's calm demeanour.

"With utmost professionalism and care, he began the autopsy and was quickly able to delineate and confirm why the patient had died just a few hours before," wrote Jain in *Everyday Heroes.*

Jain says Dr. Jung showed him how to close up the body in preparation for transfer to the funeral home. Jain thought that part of the process was quite like plastic surgery, which, at the time, he was considering as a career choice. Jain saw both fields as creating order out of chaos.

"During the first part of a surgical operation, you have a chaotic surgical field in front of you," he says. "Then you have reconstruction. After that, things are back to where they were. Same with pathology, where we make the body look presentable. That's how I was attracted to both."

Eventually, Jain got a paying job as an assistant in the pathology department so he could support himself while attending Dalhousie Medical School.

Dr. Jung became Jain's mentor in both pathology and team building.

"Roland Jung was just an amazing individual," says Jain. "One thing that I learned from him is that he talked to everybody. He talked to the custodial staff, the nutrition folks, the cashier and the women who ran the gift shop at the Valley Regional Hospital Auxiliary. He talked to everybody regardless of their position in the social hierarchy of the hospital. It was legitimate, it was warm, and it was kind."

Jain says this kindness was pervasive.

"He showed kindness during autopsies," says Jain. "People think it's very robotic. I have never seen anybody handle somebody who's passed away with such respect. And it really hit home with me how much I wanted to be [like] him."

As we've seen, crew resource management helps prevent accidents in aviation and in medicine by flattening the hierarchy so that everyone feels comfortable pointing out errors and other potential problems.

Jain says the hospital cafeteria was the place where Jung would take the opportunity to chat.

"He didn't sit at the doctors' table, the nurses' table or the administrative table," says Jain. "He could sit anywhere, and anybody could sit with him. You were part of the team bubble. In the world of pathology, he was the top dog. But socially, as human beings, we were all the same."

Jain saw in Dr. Jung an example of leadership that he could use as a reserve officer with the Canadian Forces.

"It really stuck with me because it was similar to what it means to be a lieutenant," he says. "You need to know the folks under your command."

Dr. Jung died in 2006 at the age of fifty-six, his life cut short by bowel cancer. But he lived long enough to see Trevor Jain become the kind of leader who made him proud.

That outsized impact and other influences are what permitted Trevor Jain to rise to the challenge of building the temporary morgue at Hangar B in the aftermath of Swissair 111 crash. And those influences became even more essential when it came to the near-impossible task of identifying the victims.

= = =

Today, retired brigadier-general Rick Parsons is a part-time military historian who lives in Nova Scotia. In 1998, he was a colonel in the reserve.

Following the Swissair crash, Parsons was asked to provide soldiers to help set up the temporary morgue at CFB Shearwater.

"Trevor was dispatched to determine what assistance we could provide," says Parsons. "He had the medical experience and some medical school, so he was the obvious choice."

By then, Jain had worked as a paid pathology assistant with Dr. Roland Jung on close to one hundred autopsies, handling human remains, autopsy procedures and other logistics.

Jain was tasked with setting up the temporary mortuary at CFB Shearwater on September 4, 1998, just as he started his senior year at Dalhousie Medical School. His clinical rotations would have to wait.

Amidst the chaos in Hangar B, Jain was able to fill a leadership vacuum. But that in itself didn't compel the soldiers and contractors in the hangar to follow him. Jain thinks that began as soon as he was able to drive the X-ray machine off the truck.

"It sounds like a small thing, but in the military, we always say the most powerful soldier in a platoon is the one that knows how to work the radio," says Jain. "You can be a general, but if you don't know how to use the radio, the private who does is the most powerful in that whole unit at that moment."

Jain's medical and pathology expertise made him the soldier with the most valuable expertise in the entire hangar. And he wasn't even the ranking officer.

"Not by a long shot," he says. "But I had knowledge and I had the demeanour. When they saw me organize with the contractors, and it was a team effort, I helped them see that the job was doable."

Jain's training prepared him to visualize the autopsy suite where he worked with Dr. Jung. With that expertise, he was able to figure out how to build one temporary autopsy suite, and then twelve.

Dr. Butt says he believed in Trevor Jain from the moment he met him a day later in Hangar B.

I asked Butt if he had any reservations about giving Jain so much authority, given his age.

"I didn't realize he was twenty-eight at the time," says Butt.

What the chief medical examiner saw was a young man apparently in charge.

"What I noticed about Trevor is that he didn't demur from anything," Dr. Butt recalls. "I think that his behaviour was officer-like. He was certainly capable of handling anything in that hangar that came his way in the mortuary, as we called it. And that goes back to the confidence that you can, just to make a metaphor, smell in people like this. He was good at it."

For Jain, the next step was assembling the personnel necessary to do autopsies on the remains of 229 passengers and crew.

As chief medical examiner, Dr. John Butt was in charge. In the organizational structure, there were four divisions that reported to Butt. Jain was put in charge of pathology operations. His job was to coordinate medical and dental examinations, mortuary operations and X-rays.

Jain began to assemble pathology teams, each one staffed by a pathologist, a nurse with expertise as a medical examiner, and an RCMP scribe. Jain also had to recruit technicians with expertise in gathering tissue samples for DNA analysis.

And how did Jain know who to recruit? Instead of telling them what to do, he asked those around him lots of questions.

"A good leader knows their weaknesses and blind spots and asks for top cover from other people that have that knowledge," he says.

By leaning on people with greater expertise than his own, Jain says he got things organized quickly.

"We had a fully functioning autopsy suite in the middle of a hangar and the first autopsy was done twelve hours after the plane went down," says Jain. "That's incredible if you think about it."

Not everything went so smoothly. The human remains gathered by divers at the crash site were far from intact. Mere hours after the crash, they were already badly degraded by salt water, jet fuel and other chemicals from the plane; almost all were unidentifiable. What was recovered was placed into large body bags.

It was up to Jain and his teams to open the bags, do the autopsies, and identify and tag the jewellery and other personal items that came with the remains.

And this wasn't the straightforward kind of autopsy he'd assisted in a hundred times. It was a forensic autopsy.

"The first body bag took sixteen hours to complete," says Jain. "So that night we modified our protocol because it was going to be a mission fail. That's not a failure. That's a success, that you recognize that it doesn't work and you're going to pivot."

Ultimately, they used DNA analysis to confirm the identity of almost every passenger and crew member.

By gathering ante-mortem data on the passengers, they were able to identify some by certain distinguishing characteristics. For example, Jain says he was able to identify a former member of the Swiss Armed Forces by a distinctive tattoo.

"Everything blanked out for about five seconds when I saw the tattoo," Jain recalls. "It was like having a five- or ten-second time that stood still. That could have been me, or that could have been one of my twenty-seven-year-old buddies that has a similar tattoo."

They were able to identify people on the flight in other ways too.

"We identified one person based on the serial number on an artificial hip," Jain recalls. "We called the biomedical company and gave them the number. They told us which hospital that particular device was sold to. Our liaison people in medical records called that hospital. They looked up their records and told us which patient received that implant, which they confirmed with the passenger manifest."

Identification by artificial joint was a rare win. More commonly, they matched passengers and crew with dental records.

"This is a story that hasn't really been told," says Dr. Butt. "There was a significant need for dental identification, and we just didn't have it until the military stepped in with their whole unit. It was like night and day."

Trevor Jain was instrumental in recruiting dentists.

"I'm sure Trevor got along very well with these people," says Butt. "The military people just brought everything with them, not only their equipment but their discipline, their comradery. There were about six or eight of them, and they did a class job."

Jain says there was one dentist he had to fire. He explains that he had permitted health professionals to take photos of their forensic work for teaching purposes, provided they would be careful about where they had the films processed. The dentist he fired got careless.

"He took pictures of all these remains and took them to the drugstore, where a seventeen-year-old girl processed them," Jain recalls. "The RCMP were called because they thought they had a serial killer. They didn't link it to Swissair. I took the dentist into the office and fired him."

Jain says he also fired a master corporal whose attitude Jain believed was detrimental to the team's morale.

Besides staffing the post-mortem teams, Jain arranged for food rations and quarters. As a leader, he provided emotional support. Given the difficulty of a recovery effort like this, Jain says he used several techniques to keep his teams focused on the grim task. One of the most effective was humour.

"You had to use dark humour to cope with a horrific situation," says Jain. "To get somebody to laugh or to smile creates that momentary endorphin release in your brain and it makes you human."

Like the time they prepared samples they thought came from one of the victims only to find out the tissue came from a dolphin. The next day, Jain found his autopsy room festooned with photos of animals carefully labelled so he wouldn't mistake them for humans.

"There was a lot of dark humour in there that was not being disrespectful of the victims," he says. "It was being respectful of the situation and the horrible task that we're asked to do."

"Trevor's got a good sense of humour," says Butt. "And you needed to have a bit of gallows humour. He'd express it quietly, but it was a survival tool. It is recognized as a survival tool amongst cops, for example. You have to be careful about it, but it's good to have it. Yeah, that's Trevor."

As Jain's commanding officer, Colonel Rick Parsons paid a visit to Hangar B.

"I had contacted Trevor to let him know I was coming," Parsons recalls. He says he wanted to get a sense of what the post-mortem teams were facing and what resources were needed. Parsons says Jain stood out among those who were older and much more experienced.

"When I arrived on the scene, it became clear to me that there was a lot of gravitation towards Trevor in terms of his expertise," says Parsons. "It seemed to me that he had a presence of mind and clearness of his thinking processes, where he could harness his knowledge from the medical side, but also his military skills, and begin to put order into chaos."

I keep trying to picture Jain as a twenty-eight-year-old man who was not even a fully qualified physician.

"Well, I think it's very unusual," says Parsons. "I think we were well on the way through this experience before we realized the overall responsibility that he had assumed there as well as what was placed on his shoulders. Some people can operate in terrible situations, others can't. He just seemed to flourish. Indecision is often the harbinger of disaster. And he could make decisions."

Parsons chalks up Jain's success to "clearness of thinking, analytical capability and decisiveness," plus an extraordinary ability to manage teams.

"I'd say teamwork was of paramount importance," Parsons says. "You can tell that someone is thinking in that vein, and I left there reassured that whether we can provide trucks, stretcher bearers, security staff, whatever, that they were getting the best they could out of the military because Trevor was deploying them that way."

The results of the work done by Trevor Jain and the seventy or so people under his command speak for themselves. By

December 11, 1998, just fourteen weeks and a few days after the disaster, all 229 passengers and crew had been identified.

Dr. John Butt chalks up much of that astonishing success to Trevor Jain's leadership and his grasp of teamwork.

"I think it was the lubricant in the machinery," he says. "There were no solo operatives there."

For Jain, it began by taking an X-ray machine off the back of a truck and filling a leadership void.

"We knew that a thousand people were directly affected by these 229 individuals," he says. "They needed to know. I was given a mission to keep my team focused and to get everybody invested so that we could walk out of there and say that we did it."

Jain did it by leveraging skills gleaned from medicine and the military. By knowing what it's like to grow up being excluded because of the colour of your skin. And by learning from his mentor in the pathology lab to listen to everyone on the team. Especially those least advantaged.

Jain recalls the lone custodial worker in Hangar B.

"He was an older gentleman with a full moustache and brown eyes," says Jain. "He wore a dark-blue shirt and pants and always seemed to have a mop in his hands. His face had a thousand-yard stare. He would scrub and wash the floors while being exposed to sights that I would imagine were quite foreign to him."

Jain says that nobody talked to him. Then he recalled the way Dr. Roland Jung would sit and talk with anyone who worked at the hospital regardless of title or profession. He asked the custodial worker how he was feeling and asked him for suggestions.

"I said that he was the most important part of the team," Jain recalls. "Without him, we could not do quality-grade autopsies on the victims and give them the respect they deserved."

Jain says the man's face lit up.

"He started to smile," Jain recalls. "Better yet, other members in the mortuary noticed us talking. They asked me his name. The next day, other team members started speaking to him. He was brought into the fold."

Six months after he finished his assignment in Hangar B, Trevor Jain graduated as a physician. His family, along with Dr. Roland Jung and his wife, attended. That night Jain was awarded the Meritorious Service Medal (military division) from the governor general for his work following the Swissair crash. At that time, just ninety-three Canadians had ever been awarded that medal.

He and Dr. Jung shared a celebratory drink.

"Trevor-man, you done good. I am very proud of you," Jain recalls his mentor telling him.

"The weight of the words behind his beautiful smile and huge soul meant the world to me. I miss him greatly."

But the mission came at a huge emotional cost for the young doctor and for many of those involved—a cost that required a different sort of team leader to address.

===

WHILE JAIN COORDINATED efforts inside Hangar B, the RCMP marshalled the force's interfaith chaplains, many just a few months into the volunteer position.

When Rev. Bill Newell got the call in Yarmouth, he and twenty newly appointed chaplains were taken by bus to Peggy's Cove. Their mission was to provide emotional support to whoever needed it. Families and individuals looking for loved ones. Military and civilian workers searching for remains and families.

Rev. Newell remembers that the stench of jet fuel hung heavy in the air. Media were staked out and the site was a tangle of equipment and packed with service personnel. Behind barricades at the water's edge the search and rescue teams worked, tethered to the rocks as protection against rogue waves.

Hundreds of relatives began to arrive, bringing with them "enough grief to fill an ocean bay," as Newell recalls a fellow chaplain saying at the time. One person collapsed on the rocks and was taken to hospital. Another threw flowers into the sea, and then tried to cast themselves into the water and had to be restrained. "That was the type of thing you had to be on guard for."

Canada's East Coasters have earned their hardy reputation while still managing to make each visitor, in grief or good times, feel like they've come home. "We are seafaring people," Newell says. "You may have trouble today, [and] it could be my family in the same mess tomorrow."

Newell says he and his colleagues always felt part of the larger team of professionals at Peggy's Cove. Those collective efforts were noticed by the loved ones of those who perished and became something of a curiosity to American personnel.

"They couldn't get over the interconnectedness between the coast guard and the army and the navy and the RCMP and fisheries," says Newell. "They said in their country that wouldn't happen. Everyone is so territorial [and] trying to build their own empire. They forget that they're part of a bigger team. Pulling and working together."

Going in, the chaplains had worked out a plan. "We were told to stay out of the way, be available, and don't look unless you had to. Save yourself a lot of nightmares."

Inside Hangar B, Trevor Jain had no choice but to look.

"We had twins on board," says Jain. "We had children on board. One of the things that bothered me was each of the autopsies I had to do on a baby."

At the time, Jain was young and single. He says anytime his teams were asked to identify the remains of infants and children, he made certain that parents of young kids were excused. Sometimes, Jain did all the tissue gathering by himself.

"I'd always check in with my team," he says. "It was just some-thing in me to do that."

Still, team members who were parents were traumatized by the work.

"I had a nursing officer who couldn't hold his own child," Jain recalls.

Jain says a lot of the people he worked with in Hangar B would later be diagnosed with post-traumatic stress disorder (PTSD).

"I had twenty-seven medics; two of them have committed suicide since Swissair," he says. "I know some of my dental col-leagues are still struggling."

Rick Parsons says Jain took good care of the emotional needs of those under his command.

"I had no reservations in my mind that the soldiers under the command there were being well taken care of," he says. "Trevor brought to my attention the degree of pressure and stress that was on these soldiers."

Jain says he also had PTSD. For years, the experience in Hangar B triggered feelings of rage.

"If anybody talked about Swissair on TV, I just got angry, because they weren't there in the morgue."

Rev. Newell acknowledges that the people who worked in Hangar B were at greater risk.

"I can only speak for our group as chaplains," he says. "I was only there for one or two shifts, so it was not a major issue on that end for me."

Dr. John Butt, who stayed in contact with Jain for many years following the disaster, knows about the emotional fallout of work-ing inside Hangar B.

"There were lots of people that had that. Some people were terribly encumbered by it," he says.

That includes the divers who collected human remains.

"Some of the Canadian divers were sicked out of the service of the navy," he says. "An air force psychologist who came down to work with us from Greenwood, Nova Scotia, lost his whole career in the military."

Rev. Newell says many local people who participated in the recovery operations are still affected by it.

Today, dealing with the emotional aftermath of traumas like the Swissair disaster is a high priority. Stress counsellors now have a better handle on how to alleviate suffering among first responders than they did back in 1998.

"We did not do critical incident stress properly back then," says Jain. "They had eighteen critical stress counsellors. They were so aggressive at the time. Their heart was in the right place, but I kicked them out of the mortuary because nobody wanted to talk to them. They wanted to talk to each other."

Rev. Newell says back then it was rare for people to disclose traumatic memories even when provided with counsellors.

"I think a lot of the older veterans dealt with it with a forty-ouncer," he says. "Supervisors need to be aware of some of the signs that people have when they are going through it and be able to provide some intervention."

He knows that's easier said than done, even now.

"Mental health services in Nova Scotia are atrocious. And the waiting lists are months long. If someone is in crisis, I'm sorry. That's not good enough."

Trevor Jain says he still bears the emotional scars of that experience to this day.

"For anybody to walk away from that experience and say that they weren't [affected] is lying. I haven't had a reasonable night's sleep since that experience."

= = =

MORE THAN TWO decades after running the temporary mortuary in Hangar B, a fifty-one-year-old Trevor Jain is a star in medicine. An ER physician at the Queen Elizabeth Hospital in Charlottetown, Prince Edward Island, he also teaches paramedics. He continues to serve in Canada's military as the 36 Canadian Brigade Group surgeon and the deputy commanding officer of the Prince Edward Island Regiment.

He has completed five deployments overseas, including stints in Bosnia and Herzegovina as well as the 2001 G8 Summit in Genoa, Italy. The most recent deployment, in 2018, was in northern Iraq as the senior medical authority at the special forces' Role 2 hospital. Its mission was to do damage control resuscitation and surgery to special forces, and to evacuate the wounded to a trauma centre for further treatment and rehabilitation. The temporary hospital was built from a converted airport terminal. It had four trauma resuscitation spaces, a blood bank, a small laboratory, one operating room and a small ICU beside it.

Jain says he was tasked with directing twenty-five Canadians, including nurses, medical technicians, a pharmacist, a dentist and a command team. Also deployed there was a team of surgeons from Germany.

"My mission orders were to be the trauma team leader for this facility and the senior medical authority," Jain recalls. "There were periods where you're busy and there were periods where you weren't doing anything, which really could be hard on the team. If your team is not doing anything and they're not feeling like they're contributing to a mission or the bigger picture, morale is degraded."

Jain's boss at the Role 2 hospital was Lieutenant-Colonel Cher Goulet. An ICU nurse by training, Goulet showed aptitude early on as an administrator and quickly stepped into a leadership role. She was a critical care nursing officer deployed to Afghanistan in 2003; she returned in 2008 as a senior nurse before moving into leadership positions at a large military clinic in Ottawa as well as military headquarters.

"We were in northern Iraq relatively close to the Iranian border," Goulet recalls of the 2018 deployment. "We had the capability to get patients out and medical evacuation capability that's close by so we could get folks out really swiftly."

Goulet first met Jain during their pre-deployment training in Canada.

"Before we go on a mission, we always have individual training to do, but probably the most important part is having those team trainings," she says. "Folks start working together and develop a camaraderie for how each other is going to work in bad situations where there's expectations that need quick interventions."

She says she liked Jain from the start.

"He was really animated and easygoing," she says.

Jain arrived at the hospital in Iraq on a sweltering summer day and got to work building the same foundation of good teamwork he'd fostered in Hangar B.

Lesson number one could have come from the improv training exercises explored in chapter three: make your partner look good onstage.

"Lieutenant-Colonel Goulet set me up for success by giving me the resources, the personnel, the structure and all that," says Jain, who in turn reciprocated.

"I wanted to set my boss up for success," he says. "When the rest of the facility sees the senior medical authority and the commanding officer gelling and working hard together, it filters down."

Goulet says she and Jain clicked immediately.

"He and I established our own rapport as the senior medical authority [Jain] and the actual authority over the hospital [Goulet]," she says. "That was the synergy that was created between Trevor and I right away."

Jain decided that his main objective was to boost the capacity of the hospital and the medical team to respond to mass casualty incidents. He took stock of the capabilities of each medical unit attached to the mission. When he visited those units, he took Goulet with him.

She says Jain accomplished all of that in just one week. She says laying down a logistical foundation like that is important because of the emotional burden of being close with the wounded soldiers.

"This is like our family coming through the door," she says. "We see these people where we eat, we see these people where we live, and we see these folks in the gym. And all of a sudden they become our patients."

She says other things also marked Jain as a leader.

"Keeping that team at a good level of intensity I think is part of that physician leadership role," she says.

Intense yet calm.

"You just knew that everything was calm. It was something to see."

As he did in Nova Scotia. Jain used humour to diffuse both the tension and the occasional boredom while deployed in northern Iraq. And he taught the medical team how to do ultrasounds of wounded soldiers at the bedside and ran tabletop mock disasters and simulated mass casualty incidents—all of it designed to boost the team's readiness to handle the real thing.

As it turned out, Jain wasn't there to see the fruits of his labour. A mass casualty incident involving three soldiers who were shot took place less than a day after his deployment ended. Cher Goulet sent him a text that he received as he landed in Canada.

"Thanks to your leadership during the last two months, the team performed extraordinarily," read part of the text.

All three soldiers were successfully resuscitated and survived.

"When it came to providing the care to the casualties as they came in the door, the team knew exactly what they needed to do," Goulet says.

In November 2018, Major Jain received the Order of Military Merit (officer level). At the time, Jain was the only Islander to receive the award, one of just five people out of 26,000 soldiers in the Canadian army to receive it. The soldiers in his brigade nominated him for outstanding military service.

"To be nominated by your fellow soldiers and supported by senior leadership in Ottawa is an incredible honour," Jain told the SaltWire news network in 2018.

From Hangar B to northern Iraq, Trevor Jain is an exceptional team leader.

"The military gave me the discipline, organization skills and leadership to manage chaos," he says. "Medicine gave me the clinical acumen, the credibility, empathy and insightfulness into the human condition. My upbringing gave me the importance of feeling valued and feeling part of a group."

Combined, these attributes are a potent combination that allows a team to excel under the most trying of circumstances.

CHAPTER NINE

THE CAR MECHANIC AND THE JOURNALIST

Making the end user part of the team

I N THE WORLD outside of healthcare, astute managers and leaders build better teams by envisioning the customer not just as a consumer of products and services but as a member of the team. Treating patients like a member of the team is, however, a relatively new development—even if Dr. Carl Allamby learned the lesson a long time ago. Allamby is a budding ER physician who thinks like a car mechanic. And unlike other ER physicians, he gets the analogy right away.

In an automobile repair shop, the first person you meet is a customer service agent or a service manager.

"A service manager is like a triage nurse who works in the hospital to get information on the patient when they first walk in the door," says Allamby. "They pass that information on to the technician and the technician is tasked with addressing the customer's needs so that we're fixing the right thing effectively."

Allamby also thinks there are very strong parallels between ER patients and car owners in need of emergency repairs. The tow truck brings the car just as the ambulance brings the patient. In both cases, it's a customer or a patient who needs help fast.

"People come in and they're flustered," he says. "They don't know what's wrong with their car, they don't know how much it's going to cost, and they don't know how long it's going to be down. They have a bunch of stuff going on in their lives that they have to contend with. They're stressed."

Allamby envisions the ER physician speaking to a patient or family member in the same way as a service manager would speak to a car owner.

"The first part is calming them down," he says. "Get the story, find out what's going on and what the symptoms are, how often they occur and what makes them better. It's exactly the same thing I deal with every day."

All of this makes a lot of sense, but the thing is, until Allamby said it, the analogy was one I didn't want to make. That's because my mentors harped constantly on the exceptionalism of physicians. In that way, comparing patients to car owners trivializes what healthcare professionals do. It never occurred to me to just accept the analogy and gain wisdom from it.

Dr. Carl Allamby knows all about teamwork in healthcare. While he exploits that wisdom as a physician, he learned it in a completely different line of work. By the time he earned his medical degree in his late forties, Allamby had spent most of his life working as a car mechanic and as the owner of a successful car repair business.

"I can't tell you how many people would show up to my counter crying, distraught and in despair," he says. "Like they just had no idea what life was going to be like [since] their car had failed them."

Dr. Allamby just might be the only doctor on the planet who did his pre-med in carburetors and shocks.

===

CARL ALLAMBY GREW up in the city of East Cleveland. It's the first suburb of Cleveland, Ohio, and is located in Cuyahoga County. Partly founded by Scottish immigrants, it became a city in 1911. It's home to Nela Park, the world's first industrial park, which in 1975 was declared a historic site. The suburb was once the seat of "Millionaires' Row," a tranche of estates along Euclid Avenue that included the 248-acre home of Standard Oil founder John D. Rockefeller.

The 1960s saw a surge of African Americans fleeing rural southern states and seeking a better life and employment opportunities in cities such as Cleveland. By 1984, it was one of the largest predominantly Black communities in the state. Rust-belt factory shutdowns, targeted segregation and a failure to invest in housing after white people moved out made it one of the poorest cities in the nation.

"The high school that I went to is now ranked dead last in Ohio," says Allamby.

By the time Allamby graduated from high school in 1989, the city was ravaged by an epidemic of crack use and the impact of a zero-tolerance approach to drug use.

"I can still remember walking around the neighbourhood, and you'd see people strung out on drugs and walking in the streets like zombies," he recalls. "There was a huge police presence, and a lot of my friends sold drugs, did drugs and died from being in the drug game."

As Allamby remembers it, East Cleveland was a very challenging place to grow up, and without too many opportunities to make a living. Working on cars was a notable exception.

"I was pretty much self-taught," he says. "My dad says that even at age four or five years old, I used to stand under the hoods of cars and point out different [parts]. I was just mesmerized by everything that was under the hood."

By the age of twelve, Allamby was working on his dad's and his sister's cars. He got his first job thanks to a man who owned a car parts store who knew Allamby's dad.

"He hired me on and I worked at the parts store making minimum wage," says Allamby. "I was probably about . . . seventeen years old, and in high school, and I was lucky to find a job in my neighbourhood."

After Allamby started working at the parts shop, he supplemented his hands-on experience by attending what was then called the Ohio Auto/Diesel Technical Institute, but ended up leaving for family reasons. The school, which opened in 1969 as the Ohio Diesel Mechanics School, offered a six-week course in Cummins four-stroke engine, Detroit two-stroke engine and basic diesel fundamentals. The school went through various name changes in the 1970s and '80s as new courses were added to the curriculum. In 1984, the school added automotive diesel, an automotive technology program and a motorcycle and small engine training program, and took on the name that Allamby remembers it by. After about a year, he shifted to night courses in automotive training at Cuyahoga Community College, making it easier to juggle school and work.

"I started getting customers who would come into the car parts store, and they would buy a starter and alternator and ask, 'Hey, do you know somebody who puts these parts on?'" Allamby recalls.

The owner of the store let the teenage Allamby repair cars on his own time and in the store parking lot. Soon, the repair bit was taking up more and more of his time. By the age of nineteen, he'd saved up enough money to start a business. That, plus a Sears credit card with just a $500 limit, enabled him to buy more tools.

The only thing he still needed was a location. Allamby remembers a cold winter day in the parking lot when he was fixing a Chrysler.

"This guy walked by and he saw me out there and he's like, 'Hey, Carl, I got a few extra spots in my garage if you want to pay me some rent,'" Allamby recalls. "It was like three hundred a month."

The garage space had once been one of the largest General Motors dealerships in the United States. That first year in business, Allamby made $8,000 while paying $3,600 in rent. At the time, he had little interest in higher education. He enjoyed fixing cars. Besides, he saw his sister going to college out of town and having a hard time making ends meet.

"College was a gateway to struggling and barely surviving," he says. "For me, it was either trade school or go work in a factory or join the military."

The car repair business grew so quickly that Allamby asked his landlord if he could rent additional space. He ended up opening a used car business at the same location and eventually took over the entire building. He was all of twenty-one.

During that time, Allamby learned lessons about teamwork that he would eventually apply to the ER. Some of those lessons came by making mistakes. One lesson was what to call the business. The name of his first shop was Allamby's Auto Service. But when he opened a second shop in a more affluent city nearby, he named it Advanced Auto Care.

"If you want to be successful and grow a business, the last thing you want to do is name it after yourself," says Allamby. "Every customer wants to see the guy whose name is on [the sign] and not the technicians who work there."

The second lesson? There's a world of difference between fixing cars and running a successful car repair business. The former he could do solo; the latter required a team.

"It's like the conductor of the orchestra [who] makes sure everyone is in the right harmony and at the right time," he says. "Just because you're good at doing something doesn't mean that you're good at running a business. You can be a great cook, auto technician or even doctor, but it doesn't mean that your business is going to be successful."

Allamby started with four employees—his brother was his first hire—and grew to thirteen. But instead of working less, he was working more.

"At one point, I was thinking of walking away from the business, because I was just working all the time," he says.

The key to working smarter and not harder was more teamwork. Allamby sought advice from a company based in California called Management Success. A big revelation was that he wasn't charging customers high enough rates for the work performed by his service technicians.

Allamby thinks some teamwork lessons are taught and others come by intuition.

"There are some foundational things you have to learn, like how to make people work together," he says. "I can be good at fixing cars up to a certain point, and [then] I need training to become more efficient. I think it's that same way with being a doctor and almost anything in life. It takes constant training and a constant commitment, along with a little bit of intuition."

Over the next few years, Allamby's business grew nicely. In 2006, he started taking management courses part time at Ursuline College, a Catholic liberal arts college based in Cleveland that was founded in 1871. His career plans included growing his business and possibly joining corporate America by working his way up the ranks of a major corporation.

But Allamby was about to change his career plans entirely. Ever since childhood, he'd been quite curious about the inner workings of the human body.

"I remembered as a kid sitting in class in ninth grade that I used to write 'Dr. Allamby' on the top of my page of whatever work I had done," he recalls. "My teacher was so upset at me writing my name on there. I had dreams of becoming a doctor at one point but lost it just coming up through such a rough educational system. There was no training that would put you on that path to become a doctor."

Of all places for Allamby to rekindle his interest in medicine, Ursuline College was probably one of the best, because it has very strong programs in basic sciences and nursing. As part of his management degree, Allamby had to take a basic biology course, which was taught by Dr. Micah Watts, at that time a senior resident in interventional radiology at Cleveland Clinic—the very same place where ex-Navy SEAL Brian Ferguson taught high-performance teamwork to heart surgeons.

"When he came to teach us he just lit up, and you could tell how excited he was about medicine," Allamby recalls. "Within the first hour in his class, I knew what the rest of my life was going to be like. I came home and told my wife."

He graduated from Ursuline College in January 2010. Two weeks later, he signed up at the Cuyahoga Community College, where he had taken those automotive night courses. But this time, he was a science major who graduated with a GPA of 3.98.

Allamby started looking for college programs that would help him become a nurse or a physician assistant. Pushing forty, he thought he might be too old to become a doctor. But one of his science teachers suggested he go for it.

"I was shocked that he even said that," says Allamby.

At the time, Cleveland State University had set up a new program in conjunction with the medical school at Northeast Ohio Medical University (NEOMED). What made the school attractive to Allamby was its Post-Baccalaureate Early Assurance Pathway. This two-step process to admission to NEOMED College of Medicine is offered to students who hold a bachelor's degree and have an interest in community-based medicine and ties to northeast Ohio. Students take all the prerequisites to the medical school at NEOMED, and accepted applicants are promised a place provided they maintain a minimum GPA and Medical College Admission Test (MCAT) score.

"It took the risk out of applying to medical schools in a traditional way," Allamby says. "That takes a huge stressor out of the equation."

Allamby bet on himself as a physician. But he needed a team of sorts to finish. At the time, he had to support two teenage sons from his first marriage and two much younger daughters from his second marriage.

"I was doing pre-med, and the Post-Baccalaureate program," he says. "I was still running the auto business and working every day and then being a dad and a husband, so definitely a lot to juggle."

When he graduated from medical school and began his residency at Cleveland Clinic, he knew what he wanted to do.

"I wanted to go into emergency medicine because it resembled my automotive shop," he says. "When I'm at work at the hospital, I get flashbacks to my automotive shop."

Allamby has brought several things from the car service bay to the trauma bay in the ER. One is a knack for calming patients, many of whom share a sense of utter discombobulation with car customers, albeit for very different reasons. Another is his uncanny ability to connect with people at their worst. The third thing he brought from the automotive industry is an exceptional ability to lead a team.

"They kind of look to me for leadership already," he says. "They know that I was a business owner and that I had employees. They also know I have children and a life outside of medicine. So, in a lot of ways, I'm able to give good advice to people and be somebody they can emulate."

From the car business to the ER, the proof of Allamby's leadership qualities is an ability to inspire trust.

"You need to build rapport and to offer sound advice," he says. "That doesn't just come naturally. Say I'm talking to a family about a very sick patient, and they're on the fence as to whether or not they want to sign a do-not-resuscitate (DNR). You have to tell them the reasons why it benefits that person to relieve suffering or they're not going to do it. In so many ways, you have to sell yourself, and my business has really taught me a lot of those things."

Unlike many seasoned health professionals steeped in the hierarchical culture in hospitals, Allamby was sold on the value of teamwork long before he got his MD. In the shop, he wanted his technicians to tell him when they felt he was giving bad advice. He also empowered them to do more.

"I always encouraged my employees who came to me with a problem to also come with a solution," he says. "If you have ideas of what's wrong, you should also have ideas of how to make it right. I wanted their input."

He sees the culture that resisted teamwork in healthcare changing.

"The Cleveland Clinic seems like it's been making a very nice transition," says Allamby. "I see people actually working together. I see nurses giving pushback if they think that [a treatment] is not the most optimal care for the patient. I see physiotherapists and occupational therapists taking leadership responsibilities when it comes to patient care. And I see doctors backing down from their positions based upon what a nurse or somebody else in the department may think."

Dr. Allamby's journey into medicine isn't unique solely because of his prior business. As an African American, he has joined a culture in which he is in the minority.

"Medicine is suffering for a lack of African Americans, for people of different minorities," he told National Public Radio (NPR) recently. "I'm trying to play a part in reversing that . . . I want them to look at me as an example of what they can do if they really want to. With the proper support and love from your family, you can achieve so much more than what you could ever believe."

Allamby arrived in medical school as an outsider from a business whose success depended on fashioning a team that both includes and serves the customer. That he has been able to become a physician in midlife despite many challenges probably says much more than mere words about the shift towards teamwork in healthcare.

On the journey from fixing cars to fixing patients, Dr. Carl Allamby brought with him the habit of including customers as part of the team. Medicine has slowly recognized the importance of doing the same with patients. Journalism has likewise moved slowly, but it's getting ready for a revolution.

===

It's OCTOBER 2019, and close to 250 journalists and other interested parties have come to a conference at 501 Union. It's a chic meeting place for weddings and corporate events on Union Street near Third Avenue in Brooklyn. They're here to take the first steps in learning how to think differently about delivering the news. And they're here to get past a common rut in journalism that begins with hearing about a story, collecting data that confirms it and then rushing like heck to be the first to get it in the paper, on TV or on the website.

Hearken's Engagement Innovation Summit is a call by journalists for wisdom from what organizers referred to as "adjacent" industries. Hearken is an innovative company that helps media, colleges and universities, and community organizations accomplish more by learning how to listen to and get feedback from their end users and anyone else with a point of view worth considering. They have cleverly invited experts from outside the media to drive the message home.

Caitlin Moyer, the director of new media for the Milwaukee Brewers baseball club, talks about building a fan base through tailgate parties and shareable social media content.

Jennifer Godzeno, director of engagement at the National Association of City Transportation Officials (NACTO), walks the audience through something called "participatory budgeting," which is a process that gives members of the community real power to make suggestions on how to influence the spending of public money by politicians. Godzeno describes how the process works in the Connecticut city where she resides.

Hearken has also invited someone we've already met: Alexa Miller, the artist who has used Visual Thinking Strategies to open the minds of countless medical students and health professionals. She's here to deliver the same message. Only this time, it's for journalists.

"They had me come and do a workshop for journalists in the basics of diagnosis and how good diagnosticians do things like frame a problem appropriately, check their thinking, or even approach a diagnosis not as an answer but as a process of information gathering and information synthesis that integrates a lot of perspectives," says Miller.

She took journalists through the same VTS process we did at dotMD 2019 in Galway, Ireland, and got them to see beyond their cognitive biases. By looking at and commenting on art, she got them to examine critically how they frame stories. She got them to put aside the habit of identifying the nut of a story immediately and to think first about developing a hypothesis. She also got them to recognize the unconscious biases from which hypotheses are generated and to ask themselves what other hypotheses might be more accurate. Most important, she got them to pause before jumping to journalistic conclusions.

Election news is a telling example of the kinds of habits and biases this conference is trying to address. It's common for news organizations to frame coverage in terms of which candidate is leading or trailing. Lurking under that common trope may be a more nuanced story—provided the journalist is willing to take a closer look.

Miller's approach with these journalists sounds exactly like what she's trying to do with doctors and diagnosis. In medicine, we call the result a misdiagnosis; among journalists, it's getting the story wrong.

"It's definitely something I want to do with this research," says Miller. "To not just make it available to medicine and people within medicine who need to learn about diagnosis. The number one cause of suffering in our world is inaccurate representation. Great diagnosticians are just aware there's two ways of thinking and two ways of seeing, and they're both good, but you have to have checks and balances around it to be masterful. If you don't, people get hurt. And either it's a bad diagnosis or it's a news story that's perpetuating the wrong thing."

It was Jennifer Brandel who invited Miller to the conference. She's the co-founder and CEO of Hearken and a leading thinker in getting journalists to engage in a two-way dialogue with their audience.

"When I started learning about Alexa's work of teaching doctors to pause and think differently and to question some of their pattern recognition, I thought immediately that this applies to journalism," she says.

Brandel says they got a lot out of Miller's session.

"I think she probably got through half of what she wanted to say because people just kept wanting to talk about journalism," she says. "You know, diagnosing a patient and diagnosing what the story or what the problem is are so similar and have very similar pitfalls."

For Brandel, hearing Alexa Miller speak was like meeting a kindred spirit. For close to a decade, Brandel has been on her own personal and professional quest to make journalism more open-minded.

The award-winning scribe took the conventional route to journalistic success, reporting for NPR, CBC, the *New York Times* and *Vice*. In 2012, however, she did something rather unconventional. Brandel founded *Curious City*, a groundbreaking series on Chicago's National Public Radio station WBEZ 91.5. The series is an ongoing news experiment with a mission to include the public in deciding what stories to cover, while simultaneously making the show's journalism more transparent.

She describes how it all began.

A funding initiative was the launching point for "a year to experiment and do a public-powered approach," says Brandel.

A decade later, that "experiment" is still on the air.

"This works, and in fact, the stories that result are more original, more nuanced, more complex, and people like them a lot more," she says.

Brandel wanted to see if she could take the idea behind *Curious City* far beyond one show on WBEZ 91.5 to news organizations themselves.

"I was actually interested in holding news organizations, which are very powerful, to account," she says. "To help them see the ways in which the *culture* of journalism is complicit in perpetuating processes and narratives that consolidate power, uphold white supremacy and limit the democratic imagination."

The key to accomplishing that goal was to increase the depth and the relevance of audience engagement. In 2015, she started Hearken. Its mission is to advise news and other organizations how to listen more fully to the communities they serve.

Journalists in newsrooms tend to work in isolation. Brandel says the way Hearken operates is the very embodiment of teamwork.

"The process that we have with Hearken and public-powered journalism is that there are feedback loops at every major moment of decision making," she says. "At the pitch phase, a lot of people are putting in their ideas, [and] not just the folks in the room at the assignment phase. A lot of people are weighing in. . . . You are constantly checking yourself against other people and making sure you're bringing in diverse perspectives. In the actual reporting process, you are checking back with the person whose question you're answering to make sure you got it right and that you interpreted their question correctly. You have these checks and balances so that you're not running solo down a road and then later finding out that you weren't targeting the right thing someone needed."

Hearken helps organizations build two-way relationships with their audiences and clients, in effect by teaming up with them.

The Hearken Engagement Management System (EMS) is a software platform that helps companies figure out the kinds of stories that readers, listeners and viewers want to consume. It does so by gathering, analyzing and organizing audience data and by showing journalists how to use that data to produce coverage in efficient ways.

The platform turns the usual way most news organizations have of pitching and executing stories inside out. Instead of generating story ideas from the editorial room and delivering them to an audience, EMS enables news organizations to use audience feedback to generate story ideas.

A second Hearken platform is called the Switchboard Community Management System (CMS), which was developed by the company Switchboard. Hearken and Switchboard merged in 2020. CMS is aimed at colleges as well as member-based and grass-roots community organizations. It uses a software platform known as "asks and offers" that enables community members to ask for what they need and for people to offer to help.

Among the 250 news organizations around the world that have used Hearken's tools are the *Seattle Times*, WBEZ 91.5, the *Philadelphia Inquirer*, Gannett and the British Broadcasting Corporation. Clients from academia include Oregon State University, William & Mary and Santa Clara University.

Hearken has success stories. In 2017, New York City began two months of track repairs at Pennsylvania Station, causing disruptions on New Jersey Transit, Long Island Rail Road and Amtrak. WNYC and *Gothamist* joined forces (WNYC acquired *Gothamist* a year later) and hired Hearken to help them on a project called We the Commuters.

They used the Hearken platform to create a survey that identified accessibility in the transit system, biking and homelessness as the three topics people wanted covered. A weekly *We the Commuters* newsletter got 95,000 subscribers after one year, and a series on homelessness doubled page views for *Gothamist*.

Audience engagement fuelled by the Hearken platforms is good for the bottom line. North Carolina's public radio station WFDD saw member donations go up substantially. Listeners follow an increasingly predictable path from consumers to subscribers to donors. The key seems to be direct audience feedback that leads to stories that more closely serve the needs of the listener community.

These are powerful examples of change in journalism and elsewhere. But they're in the minority.

"At the end of the day it's a cultural thing that is around change management in newsrooms, where the technology becomes useful after you start thinking of the public as a partner and not a consumer," says Brandel. "And that takes a long time."

As I've said elsewhere in the book, the culture of medicine has been slow to adopt things like crew resource management, patient engagement and teamwork. Brandel says she sees the same slowness to adopt audience engagement and more open-mindedness in journalism. She thinks there are some striking similarities between journalism and medicine. For example, both face the same kinds of pressures and challenges. Doctors care for patients with increasingly complex diseases and treatments, just as journalists tell increasingly complex stories. Both fields operate under time pressure, which can force people to reach conclusions that might be too simplistic.

"As a journalist [and] as a doctor, you're already in a system that's rigged against you trying to find complexity, nuance and truth," she says. "You have deadlines, quotas [and] numbers you need to meet. That's a reality."

Brandel questions the need for speed in journalism, just as some are questioning the same in medicine.

"If we were able to change the operating system of the news from being optimized for efficiency, speed and distribution to being optimized for relevance, truth and trust, then you would approach your reporting very differently," she says.

Privilege is yet another link between medicine and journalism. It explains who gets to be doctors and journalists.

"Well, it's like journalists and doctors both are taught [to be] and get so much power out of being authorities and being certain," she says. "At times, both of those things are really dangerous."

That power emanates from the fact that most newsrooms don't reflect demographically the communities they serve, just as most doctors don't reflect demographically the patients and the communities they serve.

The implications of changing that fundamental power dynamic would be huge.

"I don't know the lived experience of the people I'm trying to serve, so I need them to lead," Brandel says. "I need them to be part of this to be accurate and not assume that just because I have a bunch of training and I've done something for a long time that I'm going to be the only person that can help them. In fact, doing that approach is a paternalistic system that then perpetuates people feeling disempowered."

Brandel sees changing the culture of journalism to more openness, more inclusivity and more teamwork as a long-term project.

"I think this is generational work," she says. "The good news is [that] there's a lot of dissatisfaction with the status quo. There's no way of going back, because we know what doesn't work. We don't know what works yet, but I have faith that there's a shitload of people out there who have been doing experiments that hold promise that just aren't known yet or haven't gotten the funding or the spotlight."

Brandel believes the Hearken approach increases the odds that those promising experiments can find their way into the light. But just as in medicine, getting the people who hold journalism's levers of power to want and accept that feedback and adapt to it requires change agents like her and like Alexa Miller to team up and help change the world.

As an ER physician, I've learned to stop and listen to my patients. At the end of most encounters, I strive to summarize what I think I've heard the patient and family tell me, and I ask if there's anything I've missed. As the host of *White Coat, Black Art*, a show about the patient experience within the culture of modern medicine, I know our best show ideas come from recent and former patients and their loved ones.

For me, experiences in one domain inform the other. In both, I've learned to make sure the end user knows they're an integral part of the team.

CHAPTER TEN

ENTERTAINERS

*Using teamwork to cross boundaries
and expand horizons*

THERE ARE HEALTH professionals whose passion is building teamwork within the medical field. That's what drives Dr. Teodor Grantcharov to perfect the OR Black Box. It's also what excites Chief Mike Nolan as he sets out to make community paramedics the eyes and ears of family doctors in rural and remote parts of Renfrew County. Then again, there are health professionals who take hard-learned lessons from inside the hospital walls and use them to build better teams in entirely different domains.

You may be surprised to learn just how many doctors think their brand of teamwork works well in the world of mass entertainment, and vice versa. I certainly was. Their stories and backgrounds are eclectic. Their mission is teamwork.

===

A WOMAN WALKS through the front door of a nondescript office building off a nondescript street. The only distinguishing feature is a Bed Bath & Beyond nearby. This is Hollywood, but there's no big "Hollywood" sign anywhere near this place. The TV networks rent lots of spaces like this.

The woman is in her late thirties, carries a youthful energy and glow, and takes the stairs two at a time to the second floor and a large office space. Some people have office doors and some work in cubicles. Beyond is a large room dominated by a big whiteboard with lots of cards featuring code words. It looks like an idea farm.

Dilapidated couches look like they belong in a college dorm. An open kitchen is piled high with snacks from Trader Joe's.

Two people recline on the couches, while others work in their offices. All of them are dressed in hoodies, overpriced T-shirts, jeans and fancy sneakers. The woman thinks she overdressed. A close friend has already said as much.

"You can't wear any of this," her friend told her earlier that day. "You can't look this professional. You've got to look cool. You don't have anything cooler?"

She ended up choosing smart pants and flats, not heels. She didn't want to look too tall. She just wants to look like a regular person on an interview. She's there to pitch stories to one of Hollywood's top-rated medical series, *The Resident*.

The woman may or may not be cool by some Hollywood standards. But she *is* a doctor.

= = =

THE DOCTOR IS Daniela Lamas, the ICU specialist we met in the introduction. Lamas is a respirologist and critical care physician at the Brigham and Women's Hospital in Boston and a clinical researcher. She's also a medical journalist who writes for the *New York Times* and the *Atlantic*. Her first non-fiction book, *You Can Stop Humming Now: A Doctor's Stories of Life, Death, and In Between*, was published in 2018.

Her description of the writers' room at *The Resident* was quite vivid. "I paid my way to go to LA to pitch stories to them," she recalls. Lamas has long nurtured a love of scripted medical dramas, from *ER* to *Grey's Anatomy*.

"Over the years, in moments of frustration, I've reached out to doctors in Hollywood who have been involved in medical TV shows and been like, 'Help. How can I be you?'"

Most of the time, they didn't respond. But the head writer for *The Resident* gave her a shot, hiring her as a consultant who checked scripts for accuracy.

"That's how I got involved," says Lamas. "It was essentially just hounding a lot of people for a lot of years."

Having read her non-fiction, I'd figured Hollywood had sought her out.

"I've just given myself away," she confesses. "I'm not that cool at all."

Lamas has been a staff writer on *The Resident* for two seasons. In the 2019–20 season, she was a staff writer for all twenty-six episodes. Between 2019 and 2021, she had five "written by" credits. So far in 2021, she's been story editor for five episodes, one of which she also got credit for writing.

"It's really fun," she says. "It's a different type of team, and my role on the team is totally different, given I had specific knowledge, but in terms of writing TV I was the lowest person on the team."

When she's writing non-fiction pieces, Lamas is alone in her thoughts, at a computer. TV scribes don't work that way.

"It's a totally different way of thinking. You don't have that same degree of autonomy at all," she says.

It's often said that writing for television is not brain surgery. I was surprised to learn just how well Lamas thinks the ICU prepared her for TV.

"I think there are ways that it is much more similar to the way that we come up with a treatment plan for a patient," she says.

When it comes to critical care, Lamas knows what she's talking about.

"The ICU is an extraordinarily team-based specialty, which is probably one of the reasons that it appealed to me initially, and perhaps one of the reasons that being a solo doctor in an outpatient practice is so much less appealing to me," she says.

Lamas says the ICU where she works has a medical hierarchy yet is highly collaborative. She thinks both are critical to the smooth operation of the team. When she's working in the ICU, Lamas leads a team that includes a fellow training to be like Lamas, followed by residents and medical students. The rest of the team is made up of nurses, respiratory therapists, pharmacists and social workers, plus physiotherapists and occupational therapists.

"You need everyone to be there," she says. "You need somebody at the bedside, you need somebody to be able to respond quickly to events, and then you need a family who's aware of what's going on so that they can know these realities, so that you can help them make the right decision for people who can't speak for themselves."

She says teamwork in the ICU is founded on several principles.

"I think that shared purpose is really important," she says. "I think leadership is also important."

As she began working in the writers' room at *The Resident*, Lamas saw the same kind of dynamic when she pitched ideas based loosely on real patients.

"I'll have this notion to tell the story about this [particular] patient in my head," she says. She calls that the nugget of an idea. It could be about a disease or a moment in the life of a patient. She pitches it to the team. One writer talks about a show she's been scripting. Another remembers a major character in the show who is going through what's known in the writing business as a dramatic arc—a dramatic journey spanning several episodes that transforms the life of the character. On a medical show, it could be an accusation of malpractice, an opioid use disorder or a divorce. Someone suggests a major character that interacts with the patient whose story is being told. If the nugget is a disease, sometimes the disease is given to one of the major characters.

"You begin with this nugget, and then a lot changes around it," says Lamas. "But it's neat. I like that."

As with critical care teams, that collaboration doesn't happen without a skilled leader in the room.

"The good upper-level writers are really good at hearing something somebody says, taking some aspect of it and building on it," she says. "Then somebody else takes that [idea] and builds on it. It's that sort of iterative process that creates these stories that really are an amalgam of a lot of different people's ideas."

In the ICU, Lamas is an attending. In the writers' room, she's the intern. But the team dynamic is very much the same.

"There's a clear hierarchy," she says. "I was initially worried about speaking up, but a good leader empowers everyone to feel like they have something to add."

Lamas may be the intern among experienced writers, but she has plenty to teach TV writers about teamwork. Starting with her passion for finding original medical stories that Hollywood writers may not be aware of.

Take vent farms, for example. The phrase is slang for a ward or an entire hospital for patients who are on a ventilator long-term. Some of these patients have irreversible brain damage or diseases like amyotrophic lateral sclerosis (ALS) and can't breathe on their own.

As an ICU doctor, Lamas cares for these patients and their loved ones. Lamas was passionate enough about the story to pitch it to *The Resident*.

"We created a fictional long-term vent facility in this show," says Lamas. That's the ending of the story. How the writers' room got there is the stuff of teamwork. It turned out that a different writer had already written an episode in which she depicted a mother with advanced cancer undergoing a massive operation.

The patient survived, though viewers didn't actually get to see where she ended up.

The vent farm gave the patient a second act that would pack a punch while also enabling Lamas to get her nugget of an idea into a show.

"A different writer was like, 'What if we see that patient from [the earlier] episode, and we realize she was there at the vent farm the whole time?'" says Lamas.

That dramatic element was thanks to Lamas's nugget, the work of a fellow writer and a team willing to pivot.

"I remember thinking how cool it was that we tied together this storyline about the woman that we had started without even knowing where it was going," she says. "It was a neat use of an idea that I brought to them based on the fact that I'm a doctor and I've worked in places like that."

Lamas brings an insider's ICU perspective to the writers' room at *The Resident* in much the same way I bring my experience as an ER doctor to my CBC Radio show *White Coat, Black Art*. Lamas's work in the ICU has real-life consequences. She brings that level of intensity to her writing colleagues on *The Resident*.

There is something about trying to make a difference in the outcome of a patient hovering between life and death that (under the right leadership) facilitates teamwork. What Lamas brings to her fellow writers makes them aim higher, work harder to help one another more and accept fewer compromises. And it brings teamwork to another level.

===

OVER A TWENTY-YEAR period that ended in 2016, the Tragically Hip was the bestselling band in Canada—a powerhouse rock band right up until the day lead vocalist Gord Downie died of a form of brain cancer known as glioblastoma multiforme.

Surviving band members guitarist Paul Langlois, guitarist Rob Baker, bassist Gord Sinclair and drummer Johnny Fay aren't recording new material, though in May 2021, the band released *Saskadelphia*, a collection of six songs originally recorded for 1991's *Road Apples*. In June 2021, they gathered at the Juno Awards, in Calgary, to receive a Humanitarian Award for their philanthropy, and reunited onstage with Canadian pop star Feist.

As a lover of Canadian pop music, I was heartbroken when Downie's diagnosis was announced at an emotional news conference in 2015.

Dr. Max Montalvo felt that way too. Montalvo and I are both ER physicians. I work at Sinai Health System in Toronto, and Montalvo practises in the ER at Kingston Health Sciences Centre (KHSC).

He is also a filmmaker. Montalvo directed the music video for "In a World Possessed by the Human Mind," the first single from the Tragically Hip's 2016 album *Man Machine Poem*. In 2017, Montalvo's video took home the Best Rock/Alternative Video Award at the iHeartRadio Much Music Video Awards, in Toronto.

Montalvo's concept was a "lyric video," in that the lyrics of the song appear on everything from handwriting on a page to text on a microscope slide.

But Montalvo realized he could make the words part of a story. Previously, he had done a nostalgic film about using a microscope in a high school biology class.

"I just took one of my hairs out and I looked at [it] under the microscope," he recalls. "I was blown away by just the way it looked."

He asked colleagues to provide clinical bits, some of which might be viewed under a microscope. Montalvo recorded the video on his iPhone, along with photographs. He blended all of these images and some added colour. The finished product was accompanied by classical plus some atonal music.

"It was just for fun, nothing that I put out," he says. Montalvo used a serious version of that "fun" in the concept for "In a World Possessed by the Human Mind."

By the time the video was shot, Downie was too ill to appear in it. His brother Patrick took his place.

"You see somebody who I thought would be Gord looking through a microscope, and you only see that it's him at the very end of the video," says Montalvo. "When he kind of looks up, it's sort of like [he's] discovering things and making notes of what he's saying."

As Montalvo tells it, the late singer and songwriter liked the idea of the main character being himself at that precise moment in his life.

"I didn't have a very long friendship in terms of a relationship with Gord," says Montalvo. "But the time that we had was really special in terms of [having] great respect for what he did and the way that he approaches art. He was always very complimentary and very engaging when talking together about ideas, which I loved, loved doing."

Montalvo has the same love for emergency medicine that he does for directing films. That he excels at both says a lot about his facility with teamwork.

===

MONTALVO WAS BORN and raised in Mexico City. In 1982, the family settled in Oakville, Ontario, an affluent town on the shore of Lake Ontario. He was fifteen.

"I don't think there were any other Mexicans living there," Montalvo recalls. "It's not a diverse community."

Montalvo says he was already used to being an outsider. As a Jew growing up in Mexico City, he was "certainly experiencing lots of anti-Semitism."

Montalvo remembers rocks being thrown at the school bus he took to Hebrew school. One rock broke through a window and injured a child. Experiences like that strengthened his Jewish identity. Another formative lesson? "There's strength in numbers."

In Canada, Montalvo cultivated a love of soccer, which he had learned to play in Mexico.

"It was well beyond just how to learn to work in groups," he says. "There was a real comfort and forming friendships with the common feeling of loving [a] game. It was the process of collaborating, practising, and getting together to do that. It was just really a healthy way to channel all those emotions"

Montalvo was named to Maccabi Canada's soccer teams that participated at the thirteenth and fourteenth Maccabiah Games. Held every four years in Israel, it's been called the third-largest multi-sport event in the world.

In 1993, Montalvo nearly tried out for a professional team in Israel, but the political turmoil in the Middle East made him think twice. Instead, he went to medical school at Queen's University and became a physician in 1997.

The lessons in teamwork from soccer carried over into medicine. After his MD, Montalvo did a residency in emergency medicine at Queen's, then went on to work at various hospitals near Kingston. Eventually, he joined the ER staff at KHSC and became an assistant professor in the Department of Emergency at Queen's School of Medicine.

Like me, Montalvo has combined careers in medicine and the arts. I'm a self-taught writer, and Montalvo has been a self-taught filmmaker since childhood.

"I loved grabbing my dad's Super 8 camera and just playing without any film," he recalls. "I loved that sound the camera made and just looking through the glass."

When his dad shot footage on family trips, Montalvo says he enjoyed viewing, labelling and assembling the footage.

"I loved the whole aesthetic of that," he says.

His first grown-up videos were satirical takes of medical students and residents making fun of their attending physicians. He says he takes after his mother, who was a visual artist.

"A lot of my video or filmography actually comes from art as influenced by my mom," he says. "At night I paint. I take drawing classes too."

For his first serious effort in filmmaking, Montalvo directed *El Payo*, a feature-length documentary on the life of Toronto flamenco guitarist David Phillips, a Northern Ontario–born virtuoso who arranged two of Liona Boyd's most well-known flamenco pieces, "Malagueña" and "Granada." Phillips died in 2002 at the age of sixty-seven.

As Montalvo tells it, he had just completed his residency in emergency medicine and was looking for a creative film project. He was also taking flamenco guitar lessons from Phillips's best friend, Martin Sprissler. The more Sprissler talked about Phillips, the more Montalvo was determined to tell his story.

Montalvo directed, wrote and shot much of the 2011 film on a used Beaulieu Super 8 camera he brought via the internet.

Rob Baker of the Tragically Hip was the executive producer of *El Payo*. Montalvo and Baker have known one another for years. Baker also wrote original music for the film and narration. Montalvo's connection to the Tragically Hip followed naturally from his friendship with Rob Baker.

===

UNLIKE MANY PHYSICIANS I've known over the years, Montalvo gets the teamwork model in the ER, just as he gets it when he's shooting a documentary or a music video. The teams he leads in either domain function in remarkably similar ways and with similar objectives.

He approaches the patient as if they are the protagonist in a film. Take the patient who comes to the ER with the sharp end of a fishhook stuck in her hand. Montalvo sees that common clinical scenario as something like a story in a film, except that the patient's story is real. Painstakingly, he constructs the patient's narrative, right down to what kind of fishing tackle was used and exactly how the hook got embedded.

"The concept for a video is a story that has a beginning and an end, and this is exactly what happens with patients," he says.

Both of us think that, far too often, patients are seen as collections of symptoms and signs. Looking for the patient's story means understanding more holistically the person and the impact of their medical situation on them and their loved ones.

As we've seen, there is a technique that greatly increases the odds that healthcare professionals figure out that story—Visual Thinking Strategies.

Like the first-year medical students Alexa Miller taught at Harvard, Montalvo encourages his teams to "say what they see" about the patient and the patient's story to enrich their understanding of the individual and, through that, provide a higher quality of care.

Like practitioners of VTS, Montalvo is a big believer in getting students and residents to look at works of art. He points to a 2017 study by Dr. Jaclyn Gurwin, published in the journal *Ophthalmology*, in which students who received art training from professional art educators were better at making specific observations about art, and deeper observations about patients.

Montalvo thinks that the study shows the power of observation in medicine, with the very same implications for teamwork that I've written about in this book.

But even he needs an occasional kick in the pants to re-engage in expanding his own powers of observation. Montalvo tells the story of visiting a free exhibit in Kingston, Ontario, celebrating the early works of Rembrandt—produced after the master artist returned to his native city of Leiden in the Dutch province of South Holland at the age of nineteen.

"I must have gone through it fifteen or twenty times and looked at it at different times," Montalvo recalls.

But then Montalvo and his partner signed up for a session on the exhibit led by a guide who is blind. The guide made him appreciate elements he hadn't really noticed before.

"I realized that is exactly what we do in medicine all the time," says Montalvo. "We're framing a picture of what happened based on someone else's words."

Montalvo thinks thorough physicians try to capture the story of the patient at the bedside just as the artist tries to capture the essence of a dynamic pose from a model in the studio.

Montalvo's ability to reconstruct the stories of patients goes hand in hand with his ability to tell stories in his documentaries and his music videos. He challenges viewers, on the one hand, and doctors, on the other, to look deeper by getting them to question the certainty of what they observe.

That was the main point of "Land of Greed," a music video directed by Montalvo for a song by soul and blues artist Miss Emily from *In Between*, her fifth studio album.

The video features Miss Emily singing for patrons at a venue named Artaud's Café. Montalvo says the video was inspired by Vincent van Gogh's *Le Café de nuit* (*The Night Café*) and René Magritte's *La Trahison des images* (*The Treachery of Images*), a painting that shows a pipe in full frame with a caption below it that translates to "This Is Not a Pipe."

The resulting video is a mashup of both images. It begins with a sequence of close-edited handheld shots showing patrons in period costumes at a French café. We hear fragments of conversations in French. A quick close-up of the words *Café Artaud*, written in chalk on a chalkboard, tells us where we are. These sequences are shot in black and white.

Abruptly, we see a woman shot in colour and wearing a modern dress; she looks directly into the camera and says, "Ce n'est pas le Café d'Artaud" ("This is not Artaud's Café").

It's a bit on the nose, but the message is clear: look beyond what you think you see.

Montalvo showed the video and the painting by van Gogh to young doctors during a teaching session. He says he was trying to encourage his charges to overcome a type of cognitive error known as "confirmation bias."

"You're looking at something, and the moment that you analyze it with a particular perspective, you ignore clues that don't fit that perspective and just support the ones that do," he says.

The young doctors told Montalvo it was his best session of the year.

Montalvo took that valuable lesson from the blind guide who showed him what to look for in a Rembrandt exhibit, and he started teaching the technique to medical students and residents. That same approach then went into his "Land of Greed" video, a project he would later use as a training tool when teaching young doctors about confirmation bias and how to look past that first impression. Call it a case of medicine imitating art imitating life. And the glue that held it all together was teamwork.

= = =

THE 2020 CANADIAN film *Beans* tells the story of the Oka Crisis—also known as the Kanesatake Resistance or the Mohawk Resistance—through the eyes of Tekehentahkhwa, a twelve-year-old Mohawk girl nicknamed "Beans" who comes of age during the standoff. The film is directed by Mohawk filmmaker Tracey

Deer, who lived through the crisis; it was second runner-up for the People's Choice Award at the 2020 Toronto International Film Festival.

The Oka Crisis of 1990 was a seventy-eight-day standoff between Mohawk protesters and the Sûreté du Québec (the provincial police force), the RCMP and the Canadian Armed Forces. It took place in Kanesatake, on the north shore of Montreal near the town of Oka. In 1989, the Club de Golf Oka announced plans to expand their course by nine holes. The proposed expansion would have occupied disputed land in Kanesatake that included a traditional burial ground.

A sometimes violent standoff between Mohawk protesters and authorities began on July 11, 1990, and ended on September 26, when the golf course expansion was cancelled and the federal government agreed to purchase the disputed land.

When writer and director Tracey Deer wanted to film scenes that depicted the violence that left two people dead, she hired a stunt coordinator. The job entails designing and choreographing stunt sequences, casting stunt performers and ensuring they are properly trained and equipped to perform.

"If there's a risk of being hurt physically, we are obliged to have a stunt coordinator present to choreograph everything so that it is absolutely safe," says Deer. "It's going to look fabulous and brutal onscreen, but nobody's actually gotten hurt in the making of it. This is a standard that we all believe in."

But when Deer wanted to film a scene in which the titular character, played by young Indigenous actor Kiawenti:io Tarbell, fends off a sexual assault, she hired an intimacy coordinator.

"Because we were shooting multiple very violent and traumatic scenes, I did not want to re-traumatize anyone or cause trauma in the making of a story about trauma," she says.

Stunt coordinators manage the risk of physical harm. Intimacy coordinators navigate the risk of emotional harm.

The first and quite possibly only person in Canada qualified to do the job is Lindsay Somers—Canada's first intimacy coordinator, and one of the first in North America.

"We're giving a name to this very important role to help create boundaries for all the actors in the future," she says.

An intimacy coordinator oversees scenes of intimacy, nudity and simulated sex. From casting to shooting of intimate sequences, they facilitate communication between the producers, writers and performers while respecting the performers' personal boundaries.

Deer was surprised to learn that intimacy coordinators are relatively new.

"I'm shocked that we have not required that same amount of safety for the emotional and psychological well-being of our actors when we ask them to do very difficult things," she says. "I think their emotional safety is just as important as their physical safety."

As someone who has worked on film sets for fifteen years, Lindsay Somers thinks intimacy coordinators are overdue additions to the set.

"I've witnessed many situations where performers are left to their own devices to choreograph and break down the scene on the spot in front of people who probably didn't need to watch," says Somers. "I have felt uncomfortable watching the performers at that moment."

Somers believes it was a blind spot in the film industry, where incidents of sexual harassment and assault have long taken place but were rarely addressed, and were even accepted. While the #MeToo movement created an opening, the direct catalyst for intimacy coordinators was a series of round table discussions and a town hall called #AfterMeToo, held in December 2017. Its purpose was to discuss sexual misconduct in the film industry.

"It was glaringly obvious to me that there needed to be someone like a third-party advocate present [during film shoots]," Somers says.

Under a pilot program at HBO in 2018, Somers in Canada and Alicia Rodis in the United States were hired as the inaugural intimacy coordinators in North America.

"HBO made a media splash announcing intimacy coordinators would be a standard on all of their shows moving forward," says Somers. "And that's how it was launched."

By 2019, Somers was consulting on thirty productions. The ages of the actors involved made *Beans* one her greatest challenges.

The first thing Deer did was to consult extensively with the parents of Kiawenti:io Tarbell and D'Pharaoh Woon-A-Tai, who plays Hank, the older teen who has a sexual encounter with Beans.

"I was very nervous about that scene, as were the parents," Deer recalls. "I wanted everyone to know what they were getting into . . . what would be required in regard to the entire film."

Deer hired body doubles for the most intimate moments. She and her director of photography, Marie Davignon, figured out how to film the scene so viewers couldn't tell when they were used.

"I was able to go back to the actors and their parents with the plan," Deer says. "And they were all on board with it."

This is when Lindsay Somers joined the team to choreograph the intimate scene and prepare the performers.

"It's very similar to a dance with multiple rehearsals," says Somers.

As the intimacy coordinator on season three of *Designated Survivor*, Somers choreographed a sequence between two male performers. She met with the performers, the director, the assistant director and the director of photography to work out the choreography in precise detail. "[Even] before rehearsals, I've talked with each performer about their personal boundaries, and we work that into the rehearsal."

Somers did the same thing on the set of *Beans*.

"It was very important to work with those minors and their parents and to ensure proper communication the whole way through," she says. "Making sure every player in this sequence understood what we were doing and why we were doing it was really important."

Tracey Deer says the filming went smoothly.

"The kids were super professional," she says. "There were the normal nerves that I can sense but nothing out of the ordinary. Once we were rolling, their performances were extraordinary. I credit them because they're awesome. And I credit the work Lindsay did with them in order to get us to that level of performance."

Somers's job continues long after the director yells "Cut." If anything, that's when she becomes even more important to the actors.

"Performers might still be in a moment of vulnerability," she says. "They might be in an awkward position or be semi- or fully nude. We're trying to give them that extra time to have wardrobe come in and clothe them."

That means closing the set to all but essential crew to give the actors privacy until they are clothed. Even then, some actors may not be ready emotionally to move on to the next scene. Somers's job is to help give them the time they need.

Sex scenes aren't the only ones that call for an intimacy coordinator. Any scene that involves nudity may require one, such as birthing scenes or sequences involving patients in hospital on a gurney.

Frequently, the job requires someone with advanced medical knowledge.

"Everything I've learned from the medical community has been helpful in intimacy coordination," says Somers. "Everything I've learned has created the foundation of my being able to do this job."

To say that Lindsay Somers was made for the job of intimacy coordinator may not seem obvious. It gets easier to appreciate when you find out she once trained as a paramedic.

SOMERS RECEIVED HER Advanced Emergency Medical Care Assistant certification in Ontario. But a funny thing happened on her way to becoming a paramedic; she discovered she was better suited for film work.

That insight came from Bob Lewis, a fellow paramedic who supervised her as a student and who has a side gig as a set medic.

"I got her hooked up," he says. "I basically brought her into what I do and got her doing movies."

Lewis thought Somers was perfectly suited to the job.

"She's very energetic and very personable," says Lewis. "She likes to talk to people. Those are good things that work well on a movie set."

Lewis also saw that Somers was good at working in teams.

"The ability to communicate well with people and basically have an energetic feel about you," he says.

Somers followed Lewis's career advice.

"The first day on set as a medic, I absolutely knew this was the route I was going to take," Somers recalls. "I was very happy."

Somers took her natural team-building ability plus knowledge of paramedicine and became a set medic. In many jurisdictions, a certified paramedic or nurse is required on set to provide medical assistance for everything from injuries to heat stroke.

Somers got good reviews in the role and started her own medical consulting company, Ready Set Medic Inc. She provides medical advice and double-checks the accuracy of film scripts. When she can't answer questions herself, she recruits physicians to the team.

She began choreographing medical procedures on the Canadian TV series *Remedy* in 2014, followed by *Designated Survivor* in 2017. Somers got to arrange the medical scenes after the president, played by Canada's Kiefer Sutherland, was shot in the chest during a failed assassination attempt. It was originally meant to be a single episode, but Somers got the producers to expand the story into a two-episode arc.

"Suddenly we had a very much more realistic approach of what would happen if the president was shot, which was really fantastic," she says. "They took that feedback very well."

Adding a second episode meant writing more of the trauma resuscitation into the script. There were scenes in the ER, the OR and the ICU. It meant a lot more choreography from Somers. It also meant incorporating the teamwork part of trauma resuscitation, with an understanding of how to position the film crew to shoot the scene accurately.

"It's all part of this big dance that we choreographed," she says. "On *Designated Survivor*, we had multiple rehearsal days to make sure that the director was getting what he needed for his shots and that the realism stayed in place. When we brought the shooting team in with the cameras on, it was flawless."

Without time learning her craft as a set medic and medical consultant, Somers would not have become Canada's first intimacy coordinator. Both came from team-building skills she learned as a paramedic.

But what specific lessons from healthcare has Somers brought to films?

"A director asks for something," she says. "The idea is always to say, 'Yes, let's figure this out.' And if they must be presented with a no, then it should be, 'No, but how about this?'"

That sounds a lot like the "Yes, and" technique medical students learn in improv classes. It also sounds like the way cockpit crews and high-performance surgical teams are trained to communicate with one another in extreme pressure situations.

"I think that is my journey of how medicine got me to where I am," says Somers. "And I think that my days as a medical consultant really showcase why I was chosen to be Canada's first intimacy coordinator."

When Dr. Niall Downey trained to be an airline pilot, he brought his perspective as a cardiothoracic surgeon along to remind himself and fellow trainees that their decisions in the cockpit have real consequences on passengers.

Lindsay Somers saw first-hand the consequences for patients of the accidents and traumas she witnessed as a paramedic. That gave her an appreciation for the emotional impact playing intimate scenes can have on actors.

Dr. Daniela Lamas brings the teamwork skills she learned in the ICU to the writers' room in Hollywood, along with knowledge of the real-life situations that patients face.

Dr. Max Montalvo reconstructs the patient's story in the ER and in the films and music videos he directs.

Having empathy for clients, patients and fellow team members is an essential skill in teamwork. It takes a great deal of team-building skill to do that in two extremely different fields of endeavour, as all three of them have.

CHAPTER ELEVEN

THE UNTANGLER

The glory and ecstasy of teamwork—and showbiz

I T'S A CLEAR late-summer evening in 2019, and the Philadelphia Episcopal Cathedral is pulsing with activity. The City of Brotherly Love may have been founded by Quakers, but this house of worship was run by Anglicans until 1992, when it became part of the Episcopal Diocese of Pennsylvania. The church, which was previously called the Protestant Episcopal Church of the Saviour, is an iconic house of worship for the African American community in West Philadelphia.

The exterior is Romanesque, but the interior is wide open thanks to a 2002 renovation that makes it all the better for a highly memorable live theatre performance. Three hundred patrons are seated on chairs facing a stage that spans the longer left side of the trapezoidal room—an arrangement that gives the cast of twelve performers and two musicians ample room to perform while allowing for a large backdrop to project films. The clever design also creates a warm and intimate feeling in the room.

"I was the first person in my whole family to be born outside of China." Salena Cui stands and speaks with confidence to the audience. The third-year medical student, who was born in Canada, wears a simple yet elegant white blouse and navy-blue skirt.

"I had two loving parents, but when I was young, they couldn't afford to raise me. They asked my grandparents to bring me back to the Chinese province of Xinjiang, 9,000 miles away. I can't imagine what it was like for them to say goodbye to me as a baby."

Cui tells the audience that Mandarin was her first language. She was separated from her parents until a year and a half later, when they brought her to live with them in Canada. She tells the audience how she experienced the double loss of the memory of her grandparents and her fluency in Mandarin.

"I wonder now," Cui asks the audience, "how do we lose a language and a culture so quickly?"

The question holds a deeper meaning as Cui begins to tell the story of how she met Diane and Paul. Diane is an older woman she came to know during her medical studies. Paul, the woman's husband, had late-stage dementia.

"I have found great similarities between myself, a woman two generations older than me, and a man living with Alzheimer's," says Cui. "We were all suffering from a loss of languages, and we were all blessed with people we loved enough to make our hearts ache. I know now it is possible to fall in love with anyone."

The audience cheers loudly. Some are crying. Many are family and friends of the cast. A good number have a stake in the tragedy of dementia, as do the people onstage.

Just offstage, Jay Fluellen, a pianist who wrote the score for the show, lifts his fingers off the keyboard.

"I think that's the beauty of using real people telling their stories," Fluellen tells me. "The audience can really connect with the cast on so many different levels and different ways. Every person's story has those moments."

The show is called *Tangles in Time*. It's a multimedia collection of stories and reflections enhanced by music, dance and video. The stories are all about the experience of dementia from three related points of view—the person, their partner and their care provider—and are arranged in a way that mirrors how the disease is experienced. It's a bit like working on a jigsaw puzzle, with its brief moments of satisfaction in the assembly and great understanding and pleasure only when the puzzle is complete.

As with any great team, the *Tangles in Time* production is much greater than the sum of its parts, for it joins cast members, stage crew, the production team and the audience in a shared feeling of ecstasy.

The title is a nod to the neurofibrillary tangles found inside the brains of people with Alzheimer's disease. The tangles are caused by threads of a protein called tau that collects inside brain cells. Researchers believe these tangles impair memory and cognition.

Tangles in Time is the culmination of a two-year collaboration between the arts community, academia and philanthropy to build empathy through the arts. But at its core is a living example of multidisciplinary team building at its best.

"You're seeing everything untangle," says Fluellen. "Everyone is able to experience the final production without knowing all of the different components, the process that we went through to put it together."

We've just caught a glimpse of a giant jigsaw puzzle fully assembled. Now it's time to meet the genius who put it together: a writer, theatre director, team builder and untangler named Teya Sepinuck.

= = =

"It is my baby," says Sepinuck, a dynamo of seventy years with short brown hair and dark eyes. "It's what keeps me up at night and what wakes me up in the morning."

Sepinuck came to the theatre by accident. She trained as a dancer in the late 1960s at a liberal arts college in Bennington,

Vermont. After college, she taught improvisational dance at Swarthmore College in Pennsylvania. She stopped dancing after she had her children, then took her career in a different direction.

"I felt like I didn't know how to say what I wanted to say about humanity and love through dance, but I found this other form," she says. "Or it found me."

What found her was an original form of live drama in which she used audiotapes as inspiration for improvisational dance.

"That audio and the connection it created felt like it was way more successful than the dance on its own," she says.

It was when she was honing this technique that Sepinuck first became interested in doing a show about older people. She assembled a group of lay people to talk about aging. She got a grant, and the work took shape over the course of a year.

"It was so joyous all working together, and the ideas just kept copping from each other, and the stories started to intersect," she says. "I realized I want to be in a room with people where I am going to learn a lot. That's what this work has done over the years: I get to be in the room with people that have become my teachers."

Tangles in Time is just the latest of more than thirty-five original multimedia plays Sepinuck has written, co-produced and directed as a Theater of Witness production. Since 1986, Theater of Witness has been a vehicle for performances created and performed by real people whose stories invite audiences to bear witness to suffering, transformation and peace.

The mandate is to empower people who may be otherwise invisible or at the margins of society. Like *Tangles in Time*, these productions blend spoken word with music, movement and video. Most follow a pattern of telling stories of people on opposite sides of a conflict, or, in the case of *Tangles in Time*, people with dementia and budding health professionals.

For the 2009 production *We Carried Your Secrets*, Sepinuck was asked to go to Derry (known to some as Londonderry) to write and direct a play about the conflict in Northern Ireland known as the "Troubles." The bloody dispute between nationalists and unionists, divided along religious lines, cost the lives of more than 3,000 people over roughly thirty years. It ended in 1998 with the Good Friday Agreement.

Sepinuck conducted in-depth interviews with roughly forty people who'd been directly involved before settling on seven whose stories formed the backbone of the show.

In "The Role of Art in Processes of Reconciliation," Paul De Bruyne and Yves De Maeseneer wrote of Sepinuck's method: "This is a precarious process, because the participants choose to share their most hidden experiences with their 'enemies,' while not even having shared these traumas with friends, family, or sometimes even themselves."

What's interesting to me is that Sepinuck is not a health professional, yet she sees the work she does as "deeply healing for the people that are in it." Not infrequently, they're witnessing their own story for the first time.

"They're getting somebody to deeply listen, because it starts one-on-one with me, and then the group, and they build this community," she says.

Back in Philadelphia, Theater of Witness caught the eye of Megan Voeller, director of humanities at Thomas Jefferson University. Voeller sat in the audience for one show and immediately reached out to Sepinuck.

It's a leap from theatre that provides a form of therapy for people impacted by war and sectarian violence to theatre that serves the same role for people with dementia and their healers. Turns out the forerunner to *Tangles in Time* was something called HeART Stories: Building Empathy through the Arts. It's an optional course offered by Jefferson Humanities & Health that connects medical students with members of the Philadelphia community living with dementia and their care partners.

Teya Sepinuck became one of the course instructors. One of the most intriguing aspects of the program is that community members with dementia and their family caregivers mentor students on what it's like to live with or care for a partner with dementia.

This is how Salena Cui joined the cast of *Tangles in Time*.

"I signed up for the class because I was interested in dementia," Cui recalls. "I just loved the idea of being paired with a community mentor who could teach me something about what it means to be a caregiver and how the patient experiences disease."

Cui's performance was inspired by her relationship with Diane and her husband, Paul.

"I would meet up with Diane, and we got really close," says Cui. "When the class ended, she invited me to go visit Paul with her. He was living in an assisted living facility at that time. I ended up going back with her a couple of times. I really felt like I was getting to know him through her, and I also got to meet him in person."

Sepinuck told Cui about *Tangles in Time*.

"I was already familiar with her work by that time, and it sounded like the perfect opportunity," recalls Cui.

Nora and Bill Dougherty were HeART Stories regulars who also joined the cast. At the time, both were seventy-six years old.

"We were married for fifty-six years, but we knew each other for sixty," says Nora. "That's a lifetime."

A pharmacist by training, Bill worked for thirty years as manager of outpatient pharmacies at Jefferson Health. Nora also worked at Jefferson Health as a hematology medical technologist and a phlebotomist.

"I think he was one of the last good guys," she recalls. "He was everything, so I was very fortunate to have him and have us together that long."

When Bill was in his early seventies, he began showing signs of dementia.

"He would tell stories and they were so opposite of what really happened," she says. "We would bicker when we had company." It was a shift in behaviour also noticed by their children.

Nora suspected hearing loss, and Bill went to the doctor twice, but nothing came of it.

It was only when Nora went with Bill to the doctor that they started getting some answers. Eventually, Bill had an MRI of his brain. Nora remembers hearing from the doctor.

"He said there were vacuums where brain cells should have been." She shudders as she says it. "He said it was Alzheimer's."

From that moment, Nora saw herself as Bill's caregiver.

After Nora saw a pamphlet for HeART Stories at a geriatrician's office, both she and Bill became mentors to student doctors, occupational therapists and (not surprisingly) pharmacists.

"He was well enough that he could talk about pharmacy," she says. "He could talk about having dementia for a time. He liked to be the centre of attention. He liked to be the ham. He was humorous."

By this time, Sepinuck was looking for stories for *Tangles in Time*. Salena Cui provided the voice of a medical student, but something was missing.

"I realized that I needed to get to know these mentors," Sepinuck recalls.

She recruited Nora and Bill to a recurring group for people with dementia and their partners.

"Teya would always open her sessions by ringing a little bell to calm us down and do a little meditative moment," Nora Dougherty recalls. "Bill took over that bell."

Sepinuck noticed Bill's face light up at the sight of it. She asked if he'd like to be the bell ringer.

"He would ring it whenever he felt like," she says. "We would just let him ring it."

Through a painstaking process lasting a year or more, Sepinuck began to assemble a cast of non-actors for *Tangles in Time*.

"What I'm not interested in is when somebody wants to be in a theatre piece," she says. "They have to want to tell their story as a way of service and hope it will help someone else. They have to want it enough to go through the suffering of telling that story, maybe crying onstage, and getting really vulnerable."

Sepinuck says she's looking for people who want to tell their story because they wish someone had been there to provide that perspective in their hour of need.

"I can tell you what happens in the audience afterwards," she says. "They come up to the performers. The real people. They're just sobbing, and they're saying thank you."

===

DIFFERENT WORLDS WERE starting to come together to make for a memorable show and a therapeutic experience. Having come up with the raison d'être for *Tangles in Time*, the next step was assembling the team. Megan Voeller had already brought Teya Sepinuck into the humanities program at Jefferson. It made sense that Voeller co-produce the play with Sepinuck.

Before *Tangles in Time*, Voeller had no experience in theatre production.

Much of the work she does with Jefferson Humanities, she says, involves meeting local arts organizations and getting them to partner with Jefferson on special projects. "I know that's maybe a little bit bananas in its organicity, and it's not scientific," she says. "Still, we tend to meet people, realize that they are amazing, and decide that we're going to do something together."

That is exactly how Sepinuck likes to operate, and what made Voeller the perfect person to co-produce the show.

"Megan knew everything about Jefferson and the medical students," says Sepinuck. "I couldn't have gotten into that system and gotten the incredible people that I got. None of that would have happened. She was an excellent producer. She's an artistic curator and she gets it. She's a humanitarian with a deep heart. She would come up with ideas that I wouldn't think of. It was a real joy to work with her."

= = =

WITH VOELLER'S HELP, Sepinuck cobbled together a cast of student doctors and nurses, residents, people with dementia and their caregivers. Chief among her requirements was that each participant have a unique and resonant story to tell—something that would help unpack what it's like to have dementia or to care for someone with dementia.

Sepinuck spent hours getting to know each cast member.

For Salena Cui, finding her performance meant delving into her own extraordinary life.

Salena was born in 1993. Her parents are first-generation immigrants from China. They had a tough time getting established in Canada. So, when Salena was eighteen months old, her grandparents took her back to the city of Ürümqi in the Chinese province of Xinjiang.

"The first language I learned to speak was Mandarin from my grandparents," she says. "And that's a part of my life I no longer have. I don't really remember it."

In 1996, her parents brought her back home to Canada.

"I started going to daycare, started learning English, and very quickly lost my Mandarin," she says. "It's kind of weird to think now about Mandarin being my first language, because I feel like I can barely speak it."

It's that sense of having a lost identity, culture and language that, years later in medical school, compelled Cui to connect with people who have dementia, and made her a natural fit with Teya Sepinuck's vision for *Tangles in Time*.

"In dementia, you have loss of memory and language," says Cui. "I had that as well, but it was never really something that I had thought about so much before I had that conversation with Teya."

The connection the med student made between losing her ability to speak Mandarin and the loss of language that occurs in people with dementia was deepened when she met Diane and Paul through the HeART Stories course.

Diane told Cui that the couple had loved listening to "Chances Are," a pop ballad written in 1957 by Robert Allen and Al Stillman, and made famous by singer Johnny Mathis.

One day, Cui visited Paul at the nursing home. At the time, Paul could not speak. Cui spoke to him but got no reaction. Then, she took out her smartphone and played "Chances Are."

The reaction was immediate.

"We listened as the music filled the room, and from my perch on the side of his bed, I noticed his peaceful smile," she says.

Cui and Paul had discovered a common language and a bond. It was music.

She and Sepinuck crafted a story about that bond and called it "Loss of Language."

For her performance onstage, Cui recited the words while her fingers played on an imaginary piano keyboard. Turns out the medical student had also been a talented pianist but had abandoned the instrument as her medical studies took up more and more of her time.

On performance day, Jay Fluellen, who wrote the score for the show, accompanied Cui onstage.

"I actually wrote Salena a piano piece," Fluellen recalls. "She's not only a great pianist, but she's also a really beautiful dancer. She just has this natural presence. In her scene, there's this moment where she actually is playing the piano. We had music that was inspired by her movements in the air."

Fluellen, a full-time music teacher, first met Sepinuck when he composed the score for a 2017 Theater of Witness production called *Walk in My Shoes*. It explored the relationship between the police and the public, and the fear, mistrust and anger that can exist between them.

"She and I just had a really deep connection," says Fluellen, who joined *Tangles in Time* as soon as Sepinuck finalized the script.

"Everyone rehearses their text, and then I create the music that's going to go along with it," says Fluellen, who composed a score called *Tangles in Time* for the production. "For me, it was so powerful that I was able to be a part of the process as they were developing their stories, and then I was able to really connect with it musically."

The 2019 show had a wide range of performance pieces. John Best, a neurology resident at the University of Pennsylvania, performed an illustrated essay of the human brain. John's partner, Sunny Lai, a family physician at Thomas Jefferson University, performed a piece about the regret she felt at not being on the wards when a terminally ill patient of hers died. Sunny also played a violin piece composed by Fluellen.

For Sepinuck, it was straightforward to write a script from interviews with young medical students. Crafting a role for Bill Dougherty, whose dementia had by then progressed to the point where he needed long-term care, was a far more challenging task.

But Sepinuck remembered the look of pleasure on Bill's face when he rang the bell at the weekly group meetings. That inspired her to pair Bill with a percussionist. And not just any percussionist, but Josh Robinson, whom we met in chapter three and who teaches the Language of Music: Improvisation in Sound to medical students at Jefferson.

Robinson served as director of percussion for the show. He remembers bringing one of his handpans, and how Bill picked it up immediately.

"We soon realized Bill had this natural rhythm pattern that he could play very steadily and very well," Robinson recalls. "I started to create music with him around that and also would sometimes try to bring him into new rhythms and spaces."

Robinson created a percussion piece that gave Bill a space in which his improvisational rhythms sounded perfect. He even created a space for Nora to improvise in counterpoint to Bill's work on the pans.

"Nora was lacking a little confidence at first," says Josh. "So I set up gongs and chimes and things that were not dependent on rhythm and told her to play whenever and wherever she wanted. It was amazing to watch her listen to find the right spot, and it was like she was sending Bill these sonic hugs. They always felt like they were in the right place, and together, we created some really heartfelt and natural music."

As opening night approached, Bill's condition had deteriorated to the point that Sepinuck wasn't sure he'd be able to perform. She brought Bill, Nora, Robinson and a film crew to the Philadelphia Episcopal Cathedral to record their collaborations.

"I wanted to just try to film them and see what would happen," she recalls.

The film crew caught Bill on a good day.

"That was a time of such joy for him," says Sepinuck. "He would have stayed there all day."

Afterwards, the film crew went back to the Dougherty home, where Sepinuck got the couple to reminisce and to talk about how dementia affected them. The result was a short film called

"Music is the last thing to go," which became a standout moment in *Tangles in Time*.

It was only when Nora saw the completed film that she recognized what Sepinuck was trying to accomplish.

"I did not have a clue," she says. "Bill was just having fun. I could see it on his face when he would finish a piece. He would just glow. He was happy and that's all I cared about. If he had ten minutes of happiness in a day, I was thrilled. That's how good she is."

Sepinuck gives much of the credit to Josh Robinsion.

"Josh is so sensitive," she says. "He is always listening and connecting to people and loving people. He is one of the most extraordinary human beings."

Bill's participation in the project left a lasting memory for his family.

"Bill and Nora's son came to a video recording session once," says Robinson. "He came up to me to thank me for letting him know his dad is still in there, because there is a moment at the end of our video where we are talking, and Bill was clearly present. The family thinks it was the last sighting of the real Bill. It was quite an emotional moment for us all, and such an honour to be a part of facilitating a glimpse into that window, even if only for a brief moment."

Bill Dougherty could not attend the premier of *Tangles in Time*. By then, he had been living in long-term care for more than ten months. He died in 2020 during the COVID-19 pandemic.

But he's up there onscreen, thanks to his wife, Nora, Josh Robinson and Teya Sepinuck.

===

TANGLES IN TIME made its debut with two performances at the Philadelphia Episcopal Cathedral on September 13 and 14, 2019.

In addition to her appearance on video with her husband, Bill, Nora Dougherty was also a cast member during the live performance. She got to do a bit of business onstage with Salena Cui; in effect, she subbed in for Cui's mentor Diane, whose husband, Paul, had dementia.

Nora was nervous. But she says she was surrounded by a team of stagehands, many of them budding health professionals like Cui.

"There were babysitters with me that made sure I would get up onstage at the proper time," says Nora. "I think I had one line at the end. Thank God, I could remember it."

Diane was in the audience on the second night. "She was sitting on the side in the front row," says Cui. "I could see her face when I was on stage doing my part, and I didn't expect that to feel so hard, but it really was. That was the performance that I cried onstage, and it felt good, but it also felt really hard."

Diane was crying too.

"She was really moved," says Cui. "There were definitely tears in her eyes when I went to go see her afterwards."

Teya Sepinuck says there was a lot of laughter during rehearsals. But she says she knew the cast was starting to come together as tears began to flow.

"I'm sure everybody cried in *Tangles in Time* at different times," she says. "Some cried all the way through the performance. Until somebody cries in the group, I don't think we really are a group. I think of it as building a family and a community."

It's a community Sepinuck hopes will live on long after the live performances. A website holds biographies of the cast plus the filmed pieces from the show itself and additional pieces about the cast members.

Tangles in Time is too modest a production to change medicine itself. But the people who worked on it hope it helps leave a legacy in healthcare.

For Salena Cui, the budding neurologist who wants to help find a cure for dementia, it's an invitation to team up with patients and the people who love them.

"We need to look to patients and caregivers to be our teachers," she says. "I think a lot of the time, we're so wrapped up in our own scientific world of treating this disease. We can run the risk of having our expert hats on and forgetting that each patient, and caregiver, and family is unique. And that they will have something to teach us as well."

Nora Dougherty says it's a wake-up call for kindness.

"I hope that educators, healthcare workers, lawyers, power people, little people get to see it, learn from it and live it," says Dougherty. "It can change who we are."

As an exercise in team building, Sepinuck says *Tangles in Time* was among the most complex productions she has ever attempted. For one thing, the show had twelve cast members, far more than the six or seven she'd cast in prior productions. She also had to work with performers who had diminished cognitive abilities.

And that's just the cast. There were many others involved in the production too.

"I would have the performers in one circle and then I would have the composer and the ethnographer who we were working with and the assistants in a concentric circle around [them]," says Sepinuck. "Everybody watched each other do their part many times."

There is an alchemy about team building. You assemble the pieces and hope that they gel. That doesn't always happen. With *Tangles in Time*, it did. Sepinuck isn't exactly sure why this team was so sublime, though she has a theory.

"There was something about working with the medical students and the healthcare students," she says. "I've done intergenerational work before, so it's not just that. But it was their caring. It was their thinking at the beginning of their studies and of their careers. They had the patience to do this, and they were so excited for themselves and for each other. All of it just made me very, very satisfied. We created love here."

Teya Sepinuck created love by making connections. Between student health professionals and patients with dementia and their caregiver-partners. Between amateur performers and theatre professionals. Between words and musical notes and dance moves.

Neurofibrillary tangles disconnect brain cells and rob people with dementia of memories and cognition. Through *Tangles in Time*, Sepinuck built a team that re-established those connections. And in so doing, she created moments and performances that, for the cast, crew and audience, will not soon be forgotten.

CHAPTER TWELVE

MEDICAL ASSISTANCE IN DYING (MAID)

The team that helped a near stranger defy the odds and have a medically assisted death

THE OVERHEAD SUN casts a warm glow on the snowy landscape. It's a mild winter day on the outskirts of Peace River, a small town in northwestern Alberta where close to 7,000 people live. The snow makes a crunching sound on the walk to a two-storey house sitting on some acreage. Wood chippings cover the pathway to a walk-out basement flat—the detritus of furniture, lamps, carvings and knick-knacks. Every one of them has been cut, carved, assembled, sanded, stained and shellacked by a man I'll call John. (I'm not giving John's real name because he has a criminal record that he can't defend for himself.)

This is John's place. A recent arrival from out of province, he's been living here for six months. This is a special day for John. And for the health professionals who are gathering.

Through the basement doors and up three steps there's a long rectangular room with a dark ceramic-tile floor. A kitchen and a laundry room are beyond a closed door. To the left is a black leather sofa; to the immediate right, a leather loveseat pushed into the middle of the room. The room is warm and glowing and smells of woodsmoke and cigarettes.

John sits on his walker facing the centre of the room, parked as close as he can possibly be to the fire without being consumed by it. He grips his flannel button-up and T-shirt and jeans tight to his weakened body. His pale-grey skin hangs loosely about him. John's glasses are on, though his eyes are mostly closed. He winces occasionally in pain.

Two of John's brothers and his best friend are here. John moves gingerly to a grey recliner in a corner of the room. Each of the brothers sits on the floor close to John and takes one of his hands.

Kneeling in front and slightly to the right is a young family doctor barely out of medical school named Adam Mildenberger. He examines the IVs in John's right hand and right forearm to make sure they're running. Dr. Kylan McAskile, another GP, stands beside him. A pharmacist holds several syringes in hand while seated by John's feet.

Several off-duty health professionals—a second pharmacist and a student from the local hospital—make the room feel crowded.

An off-duty paramedic named Tyne Lunn takes all of this in as she sits close to one of the brothers.

Now, all eyes are on Dr. Mildenberger and John.

"All right, enough of this shit," says John. "It's time."

Dr. Mildenberger injects the drugs that end John's life and his suffering.

The brothers begin to cry softly. Tyne comforts one of them. She's here at John's request, as is another paramedic named Amber Bagan.

It's Tyne's first medically assisted death. She expected to be upset, but what she feels instead is a sense of peace, relief and exhilaration for a task she's helped along to a satisfying conclusion.

This is the story of a remarkable team of health professionals who banded together to help a near stranger arrive at this moment, despite some very daunting odds.

= = =

TYNE LUNN AND Amber Bagan are the two community paramedics who work in Peace River. In Alberta, community paramedics operate under a mission similar to what I observed in Ontario's Renfrew County. They provide and coordinate urgent medical treatments, referrals and supportive care to people at risk of needing emergency services and admission to hospital.

Tyne has been a paramedic here since 2004. A youthful thirty-six, she is full of energy. She's also quite used to not following a straight and narrow career path. At one point, she was planning on becoming a physiotherapist.

"When I started with my schooling, I was going to be an advanced care paramedic," Lunn recalls. "If that's the top here in Alberta, that's what I'm going to try and do."

Lunn graduated as a primary care paramedic—the kind that transports patients to the ER or between hospitals. She planned on taking additional training so she could qualify as an advanced care paramedic (ACP), but a job as a flight paramedic came with a chance to do medical evacuations from rural and remote parts of Alberta's far north to the city.

"That was completely by accident," she says. "It was just the northern rural area that I moved to at the time. The only place that had a full-time job available was the air."

When she handed in her resumé, they pointed out that she had no experience.

"Well, I need a paycheque and you need a paramedic," she recalls telling them. "Let's see how this goes."

For six years, it went rather well. During that time, Lunn completed her schooling to become an ACP. Having a baby and (eventually) becoming a single mother made the twenty-four-hour flight shifts impossible to do. So she started looking for her next career move. She spent some time filling in as a paramedic assigned to a fire brigade, where she found herself calling on patients with underlying chronic conditions and looking for ways to avoid having to transport them to the ER.

"That's what turned me on to looking into community paramedicine," she says.

Lunn was born in Edmonton but grew up in Spirit River, a small farming community in northwest Alberta. She went to college in Grande Prairie and moved to Peace River in 2004 to be with the man she was dating, the father of her daughter. They got married but divorced when Lunn's daughter, Ava, was two.

"The sole reason I remain in Peace River is to co-parent with my ex for the benefit of my daughter," she says. "However, serving my career rurally between air, ground and community clinical practice settings has afforded me unique experiences and allowed me to cultivate multidisciplinary relationships that I might not otherwise have."

Lunn says being in Peace River has shown her the "immense value of rural and remote teams." Especially working with fellow community paramedic Amber Bagan.

Bagan is in her late thirties and has been a paramedic for twenty years. Like Lunn, she's spent most of that time working in small rural communities in Alberta.

"I got paid next to nothing to do something that we enjoyed," says Bagan. "Over the years, it's kind of nice that this profession has developed into more of a career."

Unlike Lunn, Bagan has worked as a supervisor of paramedics. In that role, she was instrumental in getting community paramedicine up and running in the Grande Prairie and Peace River area. Lunn was the first community paramedic assigned to the region. For round-the-clock coverage, the town needed a second paramedic.

The second position went unfilled until Bagan decided to fill it herself.

"I regretted not applying for the position the first go-around," she says. "So, when it came up again the second time, it was like coming home."

Because Bagan and Lunn are the only two community paramedics in Peace River, it means they're never on duty in the same place at the same time.

"We try to keep a team dynamic by doing an email hand-off at the end of every shift," says Bagan. "We share what we experienced to maintain that continuity."

They make a tight little team, but like Matt Cruchet and Matt Rousselle in Ontario's Renfrew County, community paramedics in Alberta partner with a much bigger ensemble.

Lunn reckons that she's the eyes and ears of twenty or more family doctors, plus specialists. As the community paramedic in the client's home, she works with a large team that includes a family doctor or nurse practitioner, one or more specialists, a home care coordinator, personal support worker, pharmacist, registered dietitian and often many others.

Like family doctors and ER physicians, Bagan loves the variety in her work.

"You're not trapped in a box," she says. "You can actually do what the patient needs, whereas the [first responder] paramedic has these rigid protocols, and if you deviate a little bit, now you've got to justify it and write all this paperwork."

Local family doctors, nursing assistants and home care nurses refer patients to them. Sometimes, a paramedic flags the client during a first responder call. Many of them have poorly managed chronic conditions. Often, an acute problem like an infection reveals a medical problem Bagan and Lunn can deal with.

Sometimes, the two get confused with home care nurses. In fact, they get referrals from home care because they have a greater scope of practice than home care personnel. They also garner a lot of respect.

"When we call [on a client], home care nurses tell me that doctors pay more attention to us than the nurses," says Lunn.

Bagan and Lunn have earned their title as the "eyes and ears" of family doctors.

"If we want to spend two hours with this patient, we have that luxury and we can get that better, bigger picture," says Bagan. "We can draw the blood and look at the values and play that into part of our assessment when we call the docs. The time that we can spend is a luxury that I appreciate."

That time has also enabled them to be difference makers for some very complex patients. Recently, the duo cared for a woman in her early thirties who had had intermittent fevers and unexplained abdominal pain for close to two years. The symptoms persisted even through a pregnancy and vaginal birth.

Lunn and Bagan got involved in the woman's care after her doctor diagnosed an abdominal infection and ordered a long course of powerful antibiotics to be given by the paramedics at the woman's home. Another crew might have just administered the antibiotics and "stayed in their lane."

Not Lunn. She decided to retake the woman's history.

"This is so above my pay grade, but I'm thinking she needs to see an infectious diseases doctor and an ob-gyn," Lunn recalls telling Bagan.

They told the patient to go to the local ER, and gave a heads-up to the ER physician on duty.

"That emergency physician had her headed down to Edmonton to see the specialist within the hour," says Lunn.

It turned out the patient had an abscess on her ovary that required emergency surgery. The doctor who sent Lunn and Bagan to the woman's home to give IV antibiotics was grateful that two very attentive paramedics were his eyes and ears.

That same attentiveness was awfully handy when it came time to care for John.

===

IT'S HARD TO write about a man you've never met.

John was born in a province east of Alberta.

He was closest to a brother nearly fifteen years his junior, a man I'll call Doug.

"Most of the family is fairly tight," says Doug. "I'm tighter with the rest of the family than he was, but they got tighter over the years and he was pretty close with my brother-in-law."

What the two brothers had in common was carpentry.

John's oldest friend is a middle-aged man I'll call Sam. They met through a martial arts instructor.

"John was definitely always trying to be good at carpentry," says Sam. "He was fairly good at it but he had his limits."

Sam knew all about John's past.

"I could tell you he was around motorcycle guys back then when he was younger," says Sam. "But when I was around him, he was always about work. And for some reason I used to be able to keep him working. When I got someone good to work with him, he enjoyed working."

According to Statistics Canada, the oil and gas boom meant that more jobs migrated to Alberta through the 2000s than to any other province or territory. Some workers moved there permanently, but many keep their primary residence elsewhere.

Sam moved to Peace River and established himself as a project manager for a company building residential homes. He invited John to join him.

"From the first time he came out I knew there was something wrong with him," Sam recalls. "He started losing his body weight. I was just thinking it was too much weight."

In November 2019, John was admitted to the hospital, where doctors diagnosed him with metastatic prostate cancer.

"He was admitted to the hospital in crisis," recalls Dr. Adam Mildenberger. "I think they flagged him as someone who was in high need of a family doctor."

Mildenberger and his wife, Dr. Kathryn Wood, arrived in Peace River in July 2019 as new GPs and set up shop at the Peace River Medical Clinic. Mildenberger became John's family doctor during that hospital stay in November 2019. He recalls vividly the first time he met John.

"He had that grey, snow-peppered short hair with a beard," Mildenberger recalls. "And he had little reading glasses that he would give you small smiles behind. I think he was more interested in chatting about life than trying to solve his problems."

As Mildenberg quickly realized, John's medical problems were considerable. His body was severely weakened by the cancer that had metastasized to bones, causing severe pain.

"He had an allergy to anti-inflammatory drugs, so pain control was always a very challenging goal," he says. The fact that he couldn't prescribe anti-inflammatories meant that opioid pain relievers were John's best shot at relief.

"I think we ended up rotating three or four different opioids just to try to get him comfortable," Mildenberger recalls. "A couple of times I think he ended up getting delirious."

Sam says John realized he was dying.

"I tried to keep things stoic because that's just how he wanted it," says Sam. "He would only get overcome by emotion, probably I'm going to say three times. But other than that, he faced it quite well."

Sam says they talked about carpentry. John became too sick to work but could still putter around.

"I was out splitting wood so he could have the fire burning," he says. "The fire seemed to keep his mind a little bit occupied."

Sam says John used pieces of wood to build lamps and an armoire. The thing he was most reluctant to do was to seek medical care.

"He wanted to do it on his terms," says Sam. "I tried to encourage him to go to the hospital as much as I could. He was the type where you've got to help him make his decision on his own, if you know what I mean. [John] was his own person for sure."

John was about to come to the most important medical decision of his life. To do that, he needed help from a team led by someone special, someone with whom he could forge a unique connection.

= = =

To PROVIDE CARE for John at home, Mildenberger referred him to Home Care services at the Peace River Community Health Centre. The Home Care coordinator took one look at John and figured Amber Bagan and Tyne Lunn should see him.

"Home Care gave us a phone call," says Bagan. "They gave us the heads-up that he's cranky and that he might swear at us."

Lunn paid her first of many visits to John in his basement apartment. She remembers that one vividly. It was early winter, and there was snow on the ground.

"The first time I came in to see him, he just looked hardened," Lunn recalls. "You could tell he was cold down in that basement suite. He had on multiple layers of clothing and had been trying to keep a fire going in the fireplace. He had moved his chair and everything as close to the fireplace as he could."

An older fellow with tattoos all over is what she recalls. Forewarned, she expected him to be cantankerous.

"I remember he swore a lot the first day," says Lunn. "I sometimes cuss back in conversation. I remember hours, and hours, and hours of conversation with him. I'm certain he shared stories with me that he's never told another soul in his life. And that was so necessary for him to get some of that out before he was going to die."

Bagan says she met the real person behind John's crusty demeanour.

"He was a real gentleman," she recalls. "I just remember he always sat in his little recliner and had the wood fire going. He was fairly pleasant for the most part, but you could tell he was still uncomfortable."

Lunn thinks one reason why John was respectful of her was because of her blue paramedic uniform. She remembers something else.

"He was at a point where he was having healthcare providers tell him his decisions were wrong and that his approach was wrong," she says. "He had been told he's doing things wrong his whole bloody life. And this was the last thing he needed to hear."

Lunn sat on the sofa beside him instead of standing over him. She says it was a gesture intended to dismantle the power dynamic between them.

Bagan quickly figured out that John wasn't taking his pain relievers as prescribed because the combination of long- and short-acting opioids was too complicated to follow. Helping John manage his pain was the main priority.

"We wanted to keep him comfortable," she says.

The Canadian Cancer Society's five-year survival rate for patients with stage IV prostate cancer is 28 percent. But that didn't matter to John. One thing Bagan and Lunn discovered early on was that he was not interested in advanced treatment of his prostate cancer.

"He absolutely refused to go to the ER," says Bagan. "That was him standing his ground. Whatever happened, he was staying home. He never wanted to go to a hospital again."

John didn't want to go back to the hospital, and he didn't want chemo, radiation or any other active treatment of his cancer. That made it much harder for Dr. Mildenberger to control his bone pain.

Since John wasn't coming to Mildenberger's office, Lunn suggested that they do a house call. On a snowy day, Mildenberger hopped a ride with Lunn in the truck ambulance she took on her community paramedic appointments.

"I got to see how he was doing at home and functioning," he recalls. "From there we got to spend a lot of time discussing his goals."

Lunn and Bagan spent more and more time trying to help John deal with unbearable pain and nausea. They couldn't get him to follow their carefully laid-out care plan.

"So my next questions to him were, what mattered to him? What did he want?" Lunn recalls.

"'This cancer is going to kill me,'" Lunn remembers John telling her. "'I don't want to spend the rest of my days following a little sheet of all the different medications I need to take.'"

"Okay, well, how do you want to spend the remaining days?" Lunn asked.

Slowly, in the face of probing questions like that, John began to open up to her.

"I spent a lot of time listening to this man," she says. "That was the most apparent therapy that I think he needed. He had lived such a lonely, hard life. He was physically unwell, suffering and in pain . . . It was more a recognition that he needed a friend. He needed some human connection in those final days."

Then John said he wanted an assisted death. Lunn was there.

"He knew he was going to die," she says. "He wanted to die by MAID. He had a very clear idea of the date he wanted, and why he wanted it. And he just wanted to not be suffering up until then."

Bagan says she'd had a feeling John wanted MAID from the first time she met him.

"He was pretty isolated," Lunn says. "It was an odd situation. Most of your palliative patients have six or eight family members that you're trying to coach through the process as well. He had one really good friend that had taken him in to get him through this."

Mildenberger had been trained as a MAID provider but had little experience.

"He was one of my first ones," says the family doctor, who also was not surprised by the request.

"To be honest, it seemed reasonable for this gentleman, who really prioritized his independence and did not want to ever end up in a hospital. I could see his logical reasoning."

Helping John die at home would require Mildenberger's expertise. Helping him survive to that day in relative comfort and with a mind still lucid enough to give consent required a team.

===

IN 2016, LEGISLATION made medical assistance in dying—or MAID—legal in Canada. Those eligible had to be at least eighteen years of age, with a "grievous and irremediable medical condition" that causes "enduring physical or psychological suffering that is intolerable" to them. They also had to be in an "advanced state of irreversible decline" in which their "natural death has become reasonably foreseeable."

According to Health Canada's "First Annual Report on Medical Assistance in Dying in Canada (2019)," in 2019 alone, 5,631 Canadians had an assisted death. That's two out of every one hundred people who died that year. The provinces have reported that more and more Canadians are choosing it, with a nearly even split between men and women. The average age of those who opt for a medically assisted death is just over seventy-five years. Like John, two-thirds have cancer. Their first choice is to die in hospital, with MAID at home a close second.

At the time John requested MAID, he was eligible, according to federal legislation, because he was over the age of eighteen and capable of making healthcare decisions. His cancer met the test of a "grievous and irremediable medical condition." He was in an "advanced state of irreversible decline," he was suffering from intolerable physical or psychological harm, and his death had become "reasonably foreseeable."

Patients requesting MAID must be able to give informed consent after having been informed of the means that are available to relieve their suffering, including palliative care.

Dr. Mildenberger is one of just under 1,300 providers of MAID. Most are family doctors, followed by palliative care specialists and anesthesiologists.

Paramedics are not permitted to perform MAID itself; only doctors and nurse practitioners may do so. Thus, their role in the process is quite limited.

"The only place within our policy where paramedics are allowed and approved is to convey patients from point A to point B to receive it," says Lunn. "That's it."

As is the case for other health professionals, there is also a protocol for conscientious objectors. Should a paramedic not wish to take part in transporting a patient to receive MAID, they are permitted to refuse, provided another paramedic can be found to transport the patient.

Since John wanted to receive MAID at his home, transfer by paramedics was not an issue. But it would not have been an issue even had Lunn been asked to get involved within her scope of practice.

"I'm fully supportive of MAID as an option," says Lunn.

In Renfrew County in northeastern Ontario, community paramedics like Matt Rousselle are part of the team that provides palliative care to patients near or at the end of life. Rousselle's boss, Chief Mike Nolan, says paramedics in Renfrew are already playing a bigger, albeit quiet, role in helping MAID providers.

"We are playing an informal role in that process today," says Nolan. "It's not uncommon for us to get a call from a medical aid in dying team to come and assist with an IV start. If paramedics can start an IV upside down in the ditch, we can start an IV on somebody who has end-of-life wishes. It's part of the strength of the partnership amongst all the healthcare providers that we get those calls."

Like Matt Rousselle, Lunn has a major interest in palliative care.

"I'm very passionate about palliative end-of-life care," she says. "We do some of the most palliative care in our whole province in our area. I make sure that we show up for those referrals instead of handing them off to another one."

Her interest in end-of-life care and her uncanny ability to foster teamwork would be put to the test helping John achieve his goal of having a medically assisted death.

His challenges were daunting. John's body was being eaten alive by a prostate cancer that was metastasizing rapidly. He had severe pain that was getting harder to control by the day. He had other symptoms caused by the cancer and his palliative treatments. Nausea became a problem. The cancer invading his spine and his hips released calcium into his bloodstream, causing abdominal pain, kidney stones, constipation and agitation. The more opioid medications he needed to stay comfortable, the higher the risk that John would become so confused and delirious that he would be unable to consent to an assisted death.

Meanwhile, John's body was weakening. He lived alone in a basement flat with only his best friend, Sam, for support. He had just arrived in Alberta, and most of his extended family was living in another province.

To all of that, add John's determination never to set foot in a hospital again.

"It was difficult to manage him," Lunn recalls. "With all my previous palliative patients at home up to the end of life, we were only able to sustain them at home if we had caregivers, family members or children to help deliver round-the-clock care. Our team had to make decisions about what capacity we had, because we couldn't be here eight hours at a time."

But a group of committed individuals can replace a family when they work as a team. And if Lunn wasn't the team leader, she was certainly the team catalyst. After consulting with Home Care, a plan emerged.

"Home Care would visit him Monday, Wednesday and Friday," says Lunn. "If he was having urgent symptoms or needs anytime in between, they would call for us to go get things under control."

Most of the time, that meant little tweaks to medications to keep sudden jumps in acute pain and nausea under control. It also meant sanctioning John's use of cannabis to control his nausea.

"I found out that he was supplementing with medicinal marijuana, which was totally good," says Lunn. "But too much of a good thing can sometimes not be good, and that was contributing to his nausea."

Amber Bagan recalls that his bone pain was so severe it threatened to derail John's plan to stay at home.

"With the bone metastases getting into his hip and his pelvis, his mobility was declining a lot," says Bagan.

Because they visited him frequently at home, Bagan and Lunn could see he was having trouble moving. They told Dr. Mildenberger, and he prescribed a medication called pamidronate. It is used to treat bone metastases that occur with prostate and other types of cancer. Pamidronate has to be given by IV drip. The Home Care nurses couldn't do IV infusions, but Lunn and Bagan could.

"That made a big difference," says Bagan. "Without that, I don't think he would have been able to tolerate being at home. I was really impressed with how well that carried him through the last two months."

Medications, no matter how powerful, were not enough to keep John comfortable at home in Peace River, where the average daily temperature in January is minus nine degrees Celsius. At first, John could fell a tree and chop it into firewood.

"He just couldn't do that anymore," says Lunn. "So I just figured out who could actually deliver a cord of wood, so that this guy could keep having his fires."

When John's health deteriorated further, Lunn redrafted the plan.

"I had a spare space heater in my basement," she says. "I brought that and other small comfort things to him."

The team played a major role at that point.

"We had lots of ongoing conversations with Home Care in which they would be in and out of his house helping him more with his activities of daily living . . . showering and things like that," says Lunn.

As the days inched closer to John's preferred date for MAID, he got weaker. He needed more medication to keep his pain under control.

"My biggest concern was to get him to the [preferred] date," says Dr. Mildenberger. "At any moment I felt like I was going to change his meds and he would get too confused and [be] unable to give consent."

He had another worry for John.

"I felt like he was going to have a fall and end up in the hospital," Dr. Mildenberger recalls. "I think that was the most anxiety that I had with it."

It's only now, in retrospect, that the young physician can appreciate how all-consuming a task it was to keep John going.

"It was a while there that I think every week we were touching base with Tyne," he says. "I made the joke that he was taking up 20 percent of my workload for one patient, just to get him to his preferred date."

Lunn and Bagan say they spent a lot of time with John, who talked about his early life.

"He shared his childhood and his family story," Lunn says. "He shared [that] with me because I kept asking about [his] family. He ended up revealing that [by intention] he was not keeping his family informed back home. He didn't want them to worry about him. He didn't want them to see him suffering."

Lunn encouraged John to reconnect with his family.

"I worked on him a little bit, and just let him share about it," she says. "He started figuring out some things [for] himself."

John reached out to his family. Just days before he died, John's brother Doug came to visit him.

"I had seen pictures over Facebook and stuff," says Doug. "He looked like the spitting image of my father before my father passed away from lung cancer. It was heart-softening, that's for sure."

Doug says John feared he would try to talk him out of MAID, but Doug put John's mind at ease.

"I thought the poor man feared he was going to die alone," Doug recalls. "That turned out not to be a fact. Nobody deserves to die alone."

As soon as Doug met Tyne Lunn, he realized his brother wasn't alone in the least. He says he saw a lot of the team as they spent increasing amounts of time caring for John in the days before he died. Especially Lunn.

"It was almost shocking how caring [she was] and [how] she just kind of relaxed him, if you know what I mean," says Doug. "She spent lots of time with John and looked after him very well, mentally and physically. I can't really say enough about her. She, the nurses and pretty much everybody I met that had anything to do with John's care were fantastic. But Tyne went above and beyond."

In the days before John's death, Doug kept him busy talking about carpentry. He helped John clean out his workshop in the garage. He also helped his older brother finish the armoire he was building for Sam.

Doug says the last few days were tough on John physically.

"I, along with the doctors, never really thought he would make it to the date that he was shooting for," says Doug. "They were shocked that he made it to the date, but he was a very determined fella."

As community paramedics, Tyne Lunn and Amber Bagan had no formal role to play in John's death. Lunn paid a visit to John the day before his scheduled death.

"Well, you're going to be there, right?" John asked Lunn straight up.

"Yes, yes," she replied. "If you want me to be there, I'll be there."

Always the team, Lunn and Bagan went together.

"We showed up, and then there were the physicians, there was a pharmacist, and then two of the patient's family members. So it was quite a houseful."

= = =

FOR JOHN'S FINAL hours, he and Doug were joined by a third brother I'll call Peter, who drove in from Edmonton.

As Lunn, Bagan and the other members of the team gathered to witness John's assisted death, Doug approached Lunn.

"Would it be okay for the three brothers to have a shot of Fireball Whisky and say our goodbyes?" Doug asked Lunn. Fireball Cinnamon Whisky was the brothers' favourite alcoholic drink. Made by the Sazerac Company in New Orleans, it is a mixture of Canadian whisky, cinnamon flavouring and sweeteners.

Ten minutes later, the brothers signalled for everyone to gather in the living room.

"I went back into the room, and I chatted with John," Dr. Mildenberger recalls. "I had a little table that we could pull up next to his armchair. And I made sure he was still happy with the decision."

"The pharmacist said a brief goodbye," says Lunn. "Dr. Mildenberger's hands were shaking." Once John gave his final consent, Lunn and the others in the room said their goodbyes.

Lunn says it was over very quickly.

"As soon as John was asleep from the sedative, his brother's tears came," says Lunn. "Sitting next to Doug, I put my hand on his shoulder."

She says John died peacefully, sitting in his chair, his brothers each holding one of his hands. In a province to the east, other family members watched on Facebook, thanks to a smartphone. For a while afterwards, the brothers stayed close to John and cried softly.

"I didn't know how I was going to respond," says Lunn. "It's one thing to be supportive of it and everything. It was very peaceful, and I felt the most overwhelming sense of relief, because I knew, without a doubt, deep in his bones, that's what he wanted. He had so few things in his life that he controlled, and that he really got to orchestrate, and plan. That mattered so much to him."

Lunn was not completely lost in her own thoughts. She was also aware of how John's death was affecting the team.

"I recall hugging Dr. Mildenberger and Amber," says Lunn. "It was a nice moment to share compassion for my colleagues."

= = =

As of June 2019, a total of 13,946 people had had a medically assisted death in Canada since the enactment of federal legislation in 2016. That number is undoubtedly higher today. Men, women, mostly older adults, some younger.

What makes John's assisted death so special is that it took place far from the province where he lived most of his life. Except for the final few days, there were no family members present. Sam, John's closest friend, who provided the basement flat where the death took place, was too skittish to view the proceedings.

It's even harder to believe that this took place in a rural part of a province that John had called home for less than six months.

Every assisted death in Canada has its challenges. I can't imagine John's preferred death being possible without the team that cared for him.

Dr. Mildenberger says one member of the team or another was communicating nearly constantly with the pharmacy team to get John's medications filled, blister-packed and delivered. Home Care was doing assessments in between the days when the community paramedics were seeing him to make sure his symptoms were as under control as reasonably possible.

"It really took a whole village," says Dr. Mildenberger. "Because he didn't have his family there with him, we almost acted like that to try to help him. I can only be in one place at one time, and I have to start relying on everybody to help me out."

Tyne Lunn thinks John's story shows where healthcare is heading.

"Teamwork is important in healthcare because it's not realistic to expect a solo practitioner to do it all," she says. "A healthcare team is necessary because everybody has expertise, and understanding, and experience, and perspective in different things. When we cultivate and empower people to be in professional roles in which they are doing what they do best, and then we take that team, all those bests, and the full holistic sphere, and transplant that onto the focus of a patient's needs, we nail it."

In John's case, they certainly nailed it.

I'm giving the last word to John, or at least to his final words as Dr. Mildenberger remembers them.

"He thanked the whole room," Dr. Mildenberger recalls. "He said, 'Thanks for everybody's help for this.'"

(In 2021, a year after John elected to have MAID, the law was revised following a 2019 decision by the Superior Court of Québec. The court found the "reasonable foreseeability of natural death" eligibility criterion in the Criminal Code to be unconstitutional.)

CHAPTER THIRTEEN

CHAOS

When teamwork is a matter of life and death

T HE BEST TEAMS are put together with thought, reflection and great care. Sometimes, the team you need isn't apparent. Occasionally, when calamity ensues, a carefully developed team falls apart like the proverbial house of cards. When that happens, a new team can sometimes form out of the chaos and spin a miracle in real time.

= = =

ON OCTOBER 1, 2017, the Route 91 Harvest country music festival was drawing to a close and some 22,000 country music fans, blessed by balmy weather and clear skies on the third and final night, danced and sang across the fifteen-acre open-air venue located in the Las Vegas Village.

Headliner Jason Aldean was two lines into the song "When She Says Baby" when the first burst of gunfire cut through the crowd, at about 10:05 p.m. *Rolling Stone Country* reporter Mark

Gray had been covering the festival and was watching the show with friends just outside their ground-floor suite on the grounds of the Mandalay Bay Resort and Casino. It was the start of an ten-minute siege, planned for weeks and executed by a sixty-four-year-old man barricaded in two rooms on the thirty-second floor of the Mandalay Bay hotel.

"In the beginning, it sounded like two firecrackers going off," wrote Gray, who with friends initially took shelter in the suite before deciding to run out a back door. Concertgoers had pulled down a chain-link fence to let people escape through a parking lot.

"I looked up at Mandalay Bay and saw a light flickering, while shots were still ringing out," wrote Gray.

For roughly ten minutes, Stephen Paddock fired more than 1,000 rounds, the bulk into the panicked crowd about 335 metres away, then shot himself in the head with a small revolver as police closed in.

His final minutes were spent firing at two jet-fuel tanks about half a kilometre away on the edge of McCarran International Airport. Two of eight shots hit their mark, with one puncturing a tank, but the fuel did not ignite.

The twenty-four-weapon stockpile included automatic rifles with "bump stocks," a legal device that reduces recoil and allows for bullets to be fired with machine-gun speed.

The shooting stopped, wrote Gray, but the chaos continued. The smell of gunpowder was thick in the air.

"As I continued to run from the venue, I saw pickup trucks driving insanely fast with people yelling about hospitals ('Where's the fucking hospital?' someone shouted). I saw police and ambulances driving fast towards the festival grounds."

It was the worst mass shooting in US history. Fifty-eight people were killed. Thirty-one died on or near the festival grounds. Twenty-seven people would be pronounced dead at five area hospitals, most shortly after they were delivered to swamped emergency rooms by friends and strangers who had loaded the wounded into the backs of cars and beds of trucks; the last died about forty hours after the shooting started.

Sunrise Hospital received and provided care for sixteen people who would be counted among the dead—ten women and six men, ranging in age from twenty-one to sixty-one. They were just a fraction of the hundreds of people Sunrise would provide with emergency care. Many more arrived with their lives hanging in the balance. And many of them would be saved.

= = =

SUNRISE HOSPITAL & Medical Center sits on South Maryland Parkway, close to the Las Vegas Strip, in a part of town known as Winchester. The for-profit hospital is owned by Hospital Corporation of America and is operated by Sunrise Healthcare System. Built in 1958, Sunrise is a Level II trauma centre. That means the hospital is ready and able to care for just about any type of injury that comes its way.

During a typical twenty-four-hour period, Sunrise receives twenty trauma patients. On the night of the Las Vegas shooting, its staff saw and treated 199 patients in just six hours. That number includes 124 with gunshot wounds. Eventually, more than a hundred doctors and two hundred other staff would converge on Sunrise, including five chaplains.

Dr. Kevin Menes was the ER physician on duty at Sunrise that night. The forty-four-year-old MD is a powerfully built man in a compact, five-foot-eight-inch frame, with dark hair combed to the side and dark eyes that seem to notice everything.

Like me, Menes likes working nights.

"The action tends to come in on nights," says Menes. "I've been doing night shifts since residency. The sicker patients, the more acutely ill patients tend to come in at night. That's what I enjoy doing. That's why I became an emergency room doctor."

ER nurse Debbie Bowerman has worked at Sunrise for twenty-two years. She was also on duty that night.

"For Sunrise, it was actually a quiet night," Bowerman recalls. "It was really weird because Sundays can go either way. And it was pretty mellow."

Dr. Menes started his night shift at 8:00 p.m.

"When Menes came on, we were actually sitting around joking and laughing, which is something that we never get to do," says Bowerman.

Just over two hours later, an overhead page summoned Menes to Station One stat.

"The only time that a physician gets paged stat is when somebody is crumping [medical slang for dying]," says Bowerman. "He ran up there, and me being 'Miss Nosy' ran up behind him. That's when we heard over the radio that there was a mass casualty."

Within five to ten minutes after the first shots were fired, Menes and Bowerman got their first inkling of the disaster.

"Our EMS telemetry system went off, telling us to prepare for a mass casualty incident," Menes recalls. "There just happened to be a police officer who was there right next to the radio. I looked at him and I asked, 'Hey, is this real?' And he said, 'Yeah.' So I ran down to my car and grabbed my police radio."

Menes owns a police radio because, at the time, he was a tactical physician with the Las Vegas Metropolitan Police Department SWAT team. The implications of that and its connection to teamwork will soon become clear.

Menes turned his police radio on and started listening to the chatter. "Code red, at 169 . . . 179 . . . Patrol, 361 . . ." Gibberish to a person not steeped in law enforcement, like me, but not to Menes.

"And one of the first things that I heard one of the police officers say was 'automatic fire,'" he recalls. He had already heard that the shooting took place at a large outdoor concert. "I'm thinking worst-case scenario would be automatic rifle fire into a crowd of thousands of people," he says. "Knowing what the ballistics of a rifle round does, we're probably looking at hundreds to potentially thousands of victims. A very large-scale mass casualty incident."

A mass casualty incident (MCI) is defined as an "overwhelming event" in which there are more casualties seeking treatment than local resources can handle. Typical causes include shootings, earthquakes and tsunamis, mudslides, building collapses, train derailments and airplane disasters.

The September 11 attacks on the World Trade Center caused far more casualties than the Las Vegas shooting. Unfortunately, very few of the people who ultimately died in the Twin Towers survived to be taken to local hospitals.

The biggest MCIs are the ones that result in the largest number of injured survivors who require lifesaving. That's how the Las Vegas shooting became the largest MCI in American history.

Menes had worked on MCIs before, like the night a woman drove her car into several people walking along Las Vegas Boulevard. But neither Menes nor anyone else on duty that night had ever cared for 199 trauma victims in such a short interval of time.

"I told the secretary that we needed to get every operating room open," Menes recalls. "We needed to get every surgeon to the hospital, because that ends up being the choke point in taking care of penetrating traumas, right?"

ER doctors stabilize these patients. The magic really happens once they get to the operating room, where surgeons seal up bullet holes and stop the bleeding.

"We were going to do everything that we could to keep the patients alive while they were with us," says Menes.

Menes was ready. But he needed a team. Many of his colleagues worked with one another in smaller groups. None had assembled for an MCI like this.

Fellow ER physician Dr. Daniel Inglish told news outlet Azcentral that he was at home when he got a call summoning him to help out. It was thirty minutes after the first shots were fired.

"I rushed to the emergency department," he said. "I got here at approximately eleven thirty."

Trauma surgeon Dr. David MacIntyre set up the trauma bays. He gathered his surgical residents and assigned each to their own area. Four other trauma surgeons would eventually join him that night.

To Debbie Bowerman, Menes was the leader.

"He was giving direction to everybody," she says. "'We need housekeeping to bring down all the gurneys that are available and we need all wheelchairs.'"

The hospital called in every available off-duty surgeon, nurse, respiratory therapist and ER physician. Some took an hour or two to get there. The initial bunch of casualties arrived just fifteen minutes after the first shots were fired.

Dorita Sondereker, an ER and trauma nurse with thirty-nine years of experience under her belt, was Sunrise's administrative director of emergency and trauma services. That night, she was relaxing at home with her husband when the hospital's interim director of trauma informed her of the MCI. It was around 10:20 p.m. She called the ER.

"Whoever answered the phone was in hysterics," says Sondereker. "I can remember the shrillness of her voice, and . . . the worker answered, 'Oh you got to talk to the charge nurse.' I talked to her and she goes, 'Oh my God, you have to get here now, this is horrible, this is horrible.'"

She drove to the hospital, passing through the strip where the shooting had taken place.

"As I'm driving, I'm turning the radio on, and I hear seventy-five ambulances dispatched to the strip, and I know this is bad," she says. "I've never heard of seventy-five ambulances being dispatched."

Traffic slowed as she neared the hospital. It didn't take long for her to figure out why.

"I remember pickup trucks honking, pulling, cutting me off, and of course that's pissing me off, right?" she says.

Then she saw the glimpses of the injured and possibly dying inside each vehicle.

"I see body parts in the back," she says. "I see arms, legs, not understanding [yet] that's how people got moved to the hospital, [in] trucks and Ubers and Lyfts."

Dr. Menes prepared to meet them.

"Anybody who could push a gurney or push a wheelchair came down to the ER and waited out there in the ambulance bay," he recalls.

In a two-car collision, there might be five or six patients in need of trauma resuscitation and damage control surgery. The ER physician assesses each patient, figures out who goes first in priority and tags them accordingly. The idea is to distribute limited medical resources while providing immediate care for the patients until more help arrives. Triage tags were used in Napoleon's army, thanks to a French surgeon named Baron Dominique Jean Larrey.

The tags used today are colour-coded. Green tags are for patients with minor wounds who can wait the longest. Yellow tags are for patients with injuries to the arms or legs. They need surgery, but they too can wait. Red tags are for patients with severe internal injuries who can be saved if they are resuscitated immediately with IV fluids and (if necessary) blood transfusions. Grey tags mean the patient is alive but beyond hope. Black tags mean the patient is dead or very close to it.

The book on MCIs says you're not supposed to try to save black- and grey-tagged patients because the odds of success are too low and because trying to help them compromises the chances of saving patients who are more likely to survive.

Bowerman says Menes arranged the physical space in the ER into zones for each tag colour. He also invented one more category: orange tags, representing patients with life-threatening gunshot wounds in critical areas who had not yet crashed.

"As we were running back out to the ambulance area, Menes was prepping us on where he wanted things to go and how he wanted things to flow and what we were going to be doing," she says.

Station One was for patients with red tags, Station Two was for orange tags, and Station Three was for yellow tags. As they waited for the first patients to arrive, Bowerman stuck like glue to Menes.

"He was very calm," she says. "When I saw how important this was to him, when I saw that this was serious, then I knew that this was something that we could be overwhelmed with. I just was hoping that we could just take care of it all."

The ambulance bay at Sunrise is shaped in a half-circle. Menes, Bowerman, another nurse named Nate and some paramedics assigned to the ER waited at one end.

"It was eerie because there was dead silence," says Bowerman. "All of a sudden, you could hear the sirens in the background. And then they started getting closer and closer."

The first vehicle to arrive was a police cruiser with five trauma patients inside. That was just the start. Early that night, each arriving car had that many patients. It quickly got overwhelming.

"They called a disaster code, which means anybody in the hospital that's available, get down to the ER," says Bowerman.

Menes was first into the police cruisers, checking out patients.

"He would yell out for a gurney, or he would yell out for a wheelchair," she says. "Whichever the patient could go in, somebody would wheel it over, and then we would get them onto that piece of equipment, whichever one was deemed necessary for them."

There was no time to gather the kind of detailed information ER physicians like me depend on. Not even names. Menes used a marker to write notes directly on patients' flesh. He named them in alphabetical order of arrival.

"Debbie: Female, gunshot wound to the chest."

"Eddie: Male, gunshot wound to the abdomen."

"The first two hours all hell had broken loose," says Menes. "Almost everybody you're looking at is dying. There were multiple needles in each haystack, and if you didn't find all the needles and resuscitate them, they were going to die. I actually calculated that I had a little over ten seconds to triage these patients."

For each patient, ten seconds to decide if it was worth going full bore to try to save them or not. Ten seconds.

"Ten seconds to look at them, use my ballistic calculations and stuff that I had learned and make a decision on are these people going to die now or maybe die in the next twenty to thirty minutes if I don't do something," he says.

Menes figured he had to try some unorthodox procedures if he was going to save as many lives as possible.

"Right at that point, I knew that we were going to do things that were never proven or [that] go against pretty much every convention there is for running a mass casualty," he recalls. "If we were unsuccessful, then I would turn in my badge and resign. Once I made that decision, it wasn't hard to work from there."

Recognizing that ten seconds was not enough time to triage patients perfectly, Menes put some wiggle room into the tagging system.

"I sort of lumped those three categories [black, grey and red] into one, because I knew those grey tags could be saved, and we did save a huge majority of them."

Those marked with black tags came in with no pulse.

"Instead of pronouncing them dead, I figured that if I sent them into the ER and another doctor agreed with me, I could sleep comfortably the rest of my life knowing that I didn't doom somebody to die that could have been saved," he says.

Revising the tagging system was just the first rule Menes had to change amidst the chaos. The second was more problematic. After the first wave of gunshot victims were moved into the ER, the nurses needed Menes inside to help with resuscitative efforts.

That meant abandoning his perch at triage.

"The textbook says that the most senior-year physician should be triaging patients," says Menes. "It makes sense in the beginning of a surge because you're finding all of those needles in the haystack."

But even Menes could not be in two places at once. All along, he had shown Bowerman and the others how to assess incoming patients head to toe in ten seconds.

"His instructions were to just assess every patient that came in and see if they were vitally stable," she recalls. "Where are they shot? Did they have a tourniquet on? Anybody that had a shot to the torso . . . anybody who had controlled bleeding. He was giving us each possible scenario and was directing us which station they should go to."

Menes had been at triage fifteen minutes when he decided to delegate the task.

"At that point I had to hand over triage to Deb Bowerman," Menes recalls.

It's a moment Bowerman will never forget.

"We were outside and one of the nurses came out screaming 'Menes,'" she says. "And she said, 'They need you in Station One right now.' I'm thinking, 'He's out here with me, so he can't go inside.' He grabbed me by the shoulders and said, 'You've been watching what I was doing, right? I've got to go inside.' I said, 'You have to stay out here.' And he said, 'You got this, you can do this.' And then he ran inside, and I was like, 'Holy crap. He just left me.'"

Bowerman took over. By this point, most of the patients were arriving by ambulance, accompanied by paramedics. "They would fling open the [ambulance] doors," she says. "I don't really know how to explain it, but if the paramedics just looked at me in a certain way, I knew they had to get to Station One right away. There was one that came in that I threw open the doors and they said, 'Okay, she's critical. We can barely get a pressure on her.' I jumped on the gurney and did CPR down towards Station One. As we rounded the corner, I screamed out for Menes and he came out."

Menes says Bowerman did an exemplary job.

"Anytime you ask somebody something new for the first time, they're kind of shocked," he says. "But she wasn't afraid. She was able to sort the patients enough that, in the end, the numbers speak for themselves. That's a testament to what she did [and] to what everybody had done that night as a team."

Menes broke other rules that night. The trauma bay has several rooms separated by sliding doors or privacy curtains. That night, there were so many patients needing resuscitation that Menes and colleagues were wasting precious time running from one room to the next.

So Menes did something unorthodox. If several patients needed to be intubated at the same time, he got the nurses to arrange the stretchers in a circle, like spokes on a wheel, with each patient's head pointed towards the hub, and Menes. That reduced the distance he had to walk between patients to the shortest possible.

When there were more patients who needed intubation than there were ventilators, Menes pioneered the use of a technique that became standard during the worst days of COVID-19. He rigged the tubing so that two or more patients could be connected to a single ventilator.

Critically ill patients need a host of intravenous medications for pain relief and to sedate and paralyze them so they can be intubated. That includes powerful opioids, which are controlled substances. Ordinarily, these medications are dispensed one at a time and under a doctor's strict orders. To save precious time, Menes circumvented the usual system and gave nurses enough medications in syringes to keep in their pockets.

Dorita Sondereker says the thing she remembers most about Menes was how he helped nurses know when resuscitative efforts were likely to be futile.

"My nurses had to start doing CPR, and Kevin or other physicians had to say, 'Stop doing CPR, this patient's not going to make it,'" says Sondereker. "That's not our norm, right? It gives me shivers right now talking about it."

Debbie Bowerman remembers when Menes told her that night to stop doing CPR on a twenty-four-year-old woman.

"This one gets me every time," says Bowerman. "I was very angry at him because we couldn't try to save her. I know that I let my emotions get the better of me because I have a daughter who's about the same age and loves country music and very well could have been at that concert."

Meanwhile, in the trauma bays, Dr. MacIntyre stabilized patients arriving from triage. He used a crude system to decide how urgently they needed care. He asked their name; if they answered, he was free to move on. Those who couldn't respond were intubated and resuscitated with IV fluids.

MacIntyre grouped patients with gunshot wounds to the head in one area. Dr. Keith Blum, the neurosurgeon on call, raced through traffic to get to the hospital. He told Azcentral that he only had time to assess each patient briefly. Any flicker of purposeful reaction during a physical meant they got first dibs in the OR. Some of these patients survived, like a twenty-seven-year-old female who had been shot through the eye.

More and more off-duty doctors and other healthcare providers arrived. Menes says just about every one of them had the same look of shock, disbelief, horror and confusion on their face.

"I would grab them and tell them all the workarounds that we had been doing," he says. "And then I told them, 'You're a shark, get out there and find blood.'"

What he means is that he instructed them to identify patients with internal bleeding. His instructions brought clarity to his colleagues.

"You would see that look of shock melt away," he says. "That look that ER doctors get when they're ready to work would come over their face, and then they would go."

Menes and his colleagues wielded ventilators and IV drips to stabilize patients before handing them over to the surgeons for damage control operations. Menes says he was amazed by the turnout of professionals who weren't called in but volunteered to help.

"We ended up getting some EMS firefighters sticking around," he says. "We had a flight crew that had just dropped off a transfer patient from another hospital. They stuck around to help."

Menes says he worked flat-out until 5:00 a.m. He knew it was time to step aside when he could not read a CT scan report on a computer screen.

"I could not make the words out," he says. "I realized I was more dangerous to the patients than I was of any help. Fortunately, a lot of my colleagues had come in. I turned it over to them, knowing that they would do a great job."

Dorita Sondereker credits the entire team for stepping up. She singles out Dr. David MacIntyre, the trauma surgeon on call, and Dr. Kevin Menes.

"Dr. Kevin Menes was there at the beginning," she says. "He was phenomenal. He did a great job. . . . We were blessed . . . that Kevin was there, who started it all."

She says she had previously worked as a flight nurse with Dr. MacIntyre on medical flight evacuations.

"Dr. MacIntyre and I could read each other without speaking," she says. "We had it going so all of us could work as a group and we really didn't even have to talk. We just did it."

Paramedics who brought patients to Sunrise were very impressed.

"They said it looked like we had practised it before," says Menes. "They said it looked like a machine. It went as smooth as anything like that could have ever gone."

Debbie Bowerman feels proud that she did what Menes asked of her that night. I wondered how she and her colleagues felt as Menes broke one rule after another.

"You're taught in school that those things don't happen," she says. "Not changing your gloves in between patients. Well, who the heck has time to change their gloves in between over two hundred patients? Things like that."

I can think of some nurses who might have cited rules or simply refused to follow him.

"I have no problem speaking up to anybody," says Bowerman. "If I felt that it was something detrimental to a patient, then I would have stood up to him. There are extenuating circumstances to everything. And I believe that particular night was full of extenuating circumstances."

The Las Vegas Metropolitan Police Department would determine that of the more than 870 people who sustained documented physical injuries in the attack, roughly four hundred were injured by gunshot or shrapnel. One hundred and ninety-nine people were brought to Sunrise that night; sixteen died.

===

WHAT HAPPENED AT Sunrise that night was born of chaos, but it was no accident. The people at the hospital faced the worst MCI in American history and managed it superbly because a group of talented and dedicated individuals acted as a team.

And the team was guided by an inspired physician with an extraordinary ability to lead and bring out the very best in those working with him. That is one of several reasons why Dr. Kevin Menes was the right person in the right place at the right time.

One of the standout leadership moments that night was when Menes put his trust in Debbie Bowerman to triage patients so he could work on resuscitation. That level of faith in the team is unusual in medicine, where highly trained MDs tend to believe they alone can crack the case or manage the emergency.

"You can't be in all places at all times," says Menes. "Having people you can trust and the reverse—where your staff knows you're not going to bite their head off and that they can bring their problems to you while in the middle of resuscitating somebody— is important in turning chaos into order."

Menes learned to trust the team during his emergency residency in Detroit, where one night, a patient with multiple stab wounds was brought to the ER. The trauma team was summoned and assessed the patient.

"Everybody came to the bedside," Menes recalls. "The airway and the breathing were fine. There was maybe a slash to the chest, but equal breath sounds. No punctured lung, and the blood pressure was okay."

Trauma assessment concluded, Menes ordered CT scans of the chest and abdomen to look for internal bleeding, then went to check on his other patients. A while later, he returned to the trauma bay to find the patient had not gone for the CT scans. Instead, he found an ER technician doing an electrocardiogram.

"I asked why he was doing an ECG," Menes recalls.

"The patient is complaining of chest pain," said the technician.

Menes assumed that a patient with stab wounds to the chest would have pain caused by the stab wounds. That the ER tech was doing an ECG prompted Menes to ask the patient about the pain. Turns out he was feeling pressure in his chest, like he was having a heart attack—a completely separate issue from the stab wounds.

"The tech finished up the ECG and, sure enough, the patient had 'tombstones.'" Menes recalls.

The "tombstone" pattern is a shape formed by elevated lines on a section of the ECG tracing called the ST segment. The elevation indicates an acute heart attack caused by a coronary artery blockage. The feature gets its name because it resembles a tombstone, and because death is likely to ensue if the heart attack is not diagnosed and treated promptly.

"I could not believe it," Menes recalls. "This is a tech with far less medical training than I have."

Menes immediately paged the cardiologist on call, who arranged for the patient to have an angioplasty to unblock the coronary artery that had triggered the heart attack. The patient survived, thanks to the technician.

"He could have ended up with congestive heart failure," says Menes. "He could have had a cardiac arrest. That tech basically saved that guy's life. It's things like that where I learned that it isn't just about me in this job. It takes a bigger team. That was the kind of teamwork I tried to put together when I arrived in Las Vegas."

What Menes accomplished is a source of pride among ER colleagues. Dr. Trevor Jain, the emergency and disaster medicine physician at Queen Elizabeth Hospital in Charlottetown, likens what Menes did to what he did when he was seconded by the military for the Swissair disaster to design, set up and run the morgue as the pathology operations officer.

"If you let people do what they're trained to do, and grow into the role and encourage it, you as a leader, it's just going to make you look outstanding," says Jain. "It's not insecurity. A leader should never be insecure. They're just going to make you look phenomenal."

Menes says he learned from his attending physicians how to be helpful during critical situations. It's something he carried forward when he started working at Sunrise and got to work with a cohort of young ER physicians just starting out.

"We would jump into each other's resuscitations and try to assist," he says. "That's the teamwork that we had developed over all of those years. If somebody was having a difficult airway, you always felt this sense of a safety blanket that was there if you needed it."

Menes also learned during his residency to trust nursing colleagues like Debbie Bowerman because an attending ER physician once put her trust in him. As Menes explains it, the physician had a habit of lurking around whenever the residents would resuscitate a patient. To the others, it felt like she was getting ready to take over the resuscitation because she didn't trust them. Menes saw it differently.

"It wasn't that she hovered and would tell you what to do," he recalls. "She hovered and told you what to do because a lot of residents would take shortcuts. She would work up everything to the full extent every single time and just do it faster than everybody else."

Menes figured she was pushing him to do better, so he kept pushing himself to try harder to do things without her help.

One day, he was resuscitating two patients at the same time, going back and forth from one stretcher to the next.

"She opened the door to the resuscitation bay and saw me running both codes at the same time," Menes recalls. "I intubated one patient, switched places with the respiratory therapist, came back over and intubated the other patient."

He says his mentor looked at the job he was doing, turned around and walked away.

"I knew at that point I was ready to graduate," he says.

Menes learned that a good team leader trusts the team.

As a resident, Menes mastered his craft by learning the rules. As an attending physician, he learned when to break the rules, an essential skill during the Las Vegas shooting.

The kind of time pressure Menes and his team experienced that night reminds me of a conversation I had with Chesley "Sully"

Sullenberger. He's the retired Air Force fighter pilot and commercial airline pilot who in 2009 guided US Airways Flight 1549 to a water landing on the Hudson River in Manhattan. His actions that day saved all 155 passengers and crew on board.

Shortly after takeoff from LaGuardia Airport, the Airbus A320 Sullenberger and First Officer Jeffrey Skiles piloted struck a flock of Canada geese, knocking out both engines. Sullenberger says it took just 208 seconds (just under three and a half minutes) from bird strike until the belly of the plane touched the river.

Sullenberger says he had to rely on his co-pilot to understand intuitively and immediately the situation as it was developing. The other thing Sullenberger needed to do was to depart from careful preparations if he was to have any chance of saving the passengers, the crew and himself.

"Everything that we're taught about how to handle a more normal in-flight emergency is when there's more time," he says. "It really required us to improvise in this extreme emergency because we knew that we had time to do only the highest priority items and [had to] ignore everything else."

So Sullenberger ditched the rule book. Operating the plane as a glider, he brought it down as safely as he could while his co-pilot called out airspeed, altitude and direction. Menes did the same kind of rule-breaking when he went off-script on triage, empowered the nurses who worked with him, and rigged ventilators so two and even three patients could be resuscitated with one machine.

Menes learned a lot about teamwork during his residency in emergency medicine. But that's not the only professional training he has had. As noted earlier, Menes was a tactical physician with the Las Vegas Metropolitan Police Department SWAT team.

For seven years, Menes provided medical support to the SWAT team, working on a wildly diverse and interesting team operating outside of medicine. His partner was an armed officer who was also either a paramedic or an advanced emergency medical technician. They would be stationed alongside snipers who would watch from a distance, with powerful optics, as entry and assault personnel were tasked with breaching and entering buildings and other structures, often with explosives.

Menes estimates he assisted on hundreds of missions. These included "no-knock" warrants (issued by a judge, these warrants allow law enforcement to enter a property without immediate prior notification to those inside) as well as "call-outs," or missions in which there are either barricaded or armed suspects.

He learned a lot about teamwork on the SWAT team.

"What happens in the movies where one guy goes into a building, kills all the bad guys and saves the girl is not how things really happen in real life," he says. "Having a team effort and people who specialize in different things and are able to do their particular job at a very high level is how there's an overwhelming advantage for the SWAT team."

Menes remembers one time when a suspect had doused the building where he was hiding with a flammable substance and was threatening to set the place on fire. Menes and his partner were the primary medics at the scene, assisting firefighters and SWAT officers.

"We needed to de-escalate the situation and get this guy into custody, but not let him burn and blow up everything," says Menes. "The SWAT officers got the fire guys to suit up in their gear, and they protected them while firefighters hosed down the building and made it so wet that any accelerant wouldn't light."

Menes says the suspect eventually surrendered.

"Nobody got injured, nobody got burned, no one got blown up, and everybody worked together," says Menes. "There were other members of the team that ended up doing more of the heavy lifting, but together as a team [we] were able to solve that problem."

Menes says incidents like that taught him a lot about how to run a team in the ER, especially during an MCI.

"It's a different environment, but they still have the same sort of issues with responsibility," says Menes. "There's always a leader who says yes or no to the plan. The team leader makes the final call and takes a lot of responsibility if the plan works or not."

By listening to his police scanner on the night of the Las Vegas shooting, Menes deduced the kinds of guns and ammunition that the shooter had deployed and used that information to predict both the number of casualties and the types of gunshot wounds he'd be dealing with. His experiences as a volunteer MD on the SWAT team and with mass casualty incidents help explain his expertise. But his knowledge of ballistics comes from the fact that he's a gun owner.

"I own both handguns and rifles," he explains. "I own rifles because of what I did with the SWAT team. I needed to learn how to manipulate their weapons, make them safe or render them harmless. In a worst-case scenario, I might end up having to defend myself and the team, so I needed to know how to do that."

Many ER doctors hate guns and gun ownership because they must treat gunshot wounds and inform the family members of those who die. It's jarring for some (though not surprising to me, given the scale of gun ownership in the US) to learn that an ER physician who saves patients with gunshot wounds owns firearms.

"I believe that people do have the right to bear arms," he says. "I think that mentally ill people shouldn't be allowed to have firearms, but to take firearms away from people such as myself, where I can't defend my wife and my kids. . . . The response time of most police officers to a call is not immediate."

Kevin Menes has been preparing for a Las Vegas–style MCI for years. "You sort of plot that out, and you have a plan to handle the worst case," he says. "If something happens that's not as bad, then it wasn't as hard to handle."

Debbie Bowerman, who was at Menes's side for much of that night, says all that preparation paid off.

"There is no way on God's green earth that we could have pulled that off without teamwork," she says. "That night, nobody was better than anybody. Housekeeping was just as important as the trauma doctor because our floors were so puddled with blood that any of us that were riding in or the employees that were taking the wheelchairs or the gurney into the specific areas, they could have slipped and cracked their heads. They could have been a trauma themselves. That housekeeper who was there mopping the floor after every single gurney and patient went by was just as important as that ER doctor or that trauma surgeon that was putting in a chest tube, in my opinion."

=＝=

SINCE THE SHOOTING, Menes and Debbie Bowerman have given countless speeches to ER physicians and nurses across the United States. So has Dorita Sondereker.

Today, Menes does ER medicine in Texas. But he hasn't forgotten that night at Sunrise.

"I'm proud of what we did," he says. "I know that every patient that could have been saved that night, we saved them."

He says many of his former hospital colleagues have found comfort in the visits they've received from the patients they saved that night who have come back to thank them.

Bowerman still works in the ER at Sunrise. She likes to stand outside the ambulance doors and wonder what's coming next. Just like Menes.

"I learned so much from him as a nurse fresh out of school with zero experience," she says. "I would always watch him, and I would always listen to what he was asking. And I would always listen to the questions that he wanted to know."

Bowerman hasn't worked another night like the Las Vegas shooting.

"It was truly an incredible night," she says. "When you step back and think about how it all played out, the whole thing was just incredible."

An incredible display of teamwork creating order out of chaos.

THE POWER OF TEAMWORK

Summing up

DO YOU WORK on a team, or do you only think you do because you work with a group of individuals? That's what I asked you at the beginning of this book.

Now, you can follow the clues. Chances are, you work in a group and not a team if members keep their thoughts to themselves, especially during a crisis. You work in a group if your meetings are places where ideas—even good ones—go to die. You work in a group when people don't make suggestions for fear of looking foolish or having their ideas slapped down. When the hierarchy is so tight that every complaint and idea is seen as dissent.

You work in a group when personal status is so important that a shared sense of accomplishment is rare.

You work in a group when few if any members want to help you when you're in trouble. That's true during ordinary times, and it's true during a crisis.

I BELIEVE THE future inside and outside of healthcare is teamwork. As an ER physician, I've seen the benefits. When I work solo, I can function as the physician on duty. But my knowledge and skill in diagnosis and decision making are much better when I'm joined by a team of nurse practitioners and physician assistants. Even one addition makes a big difference. I notice more clinical findings when a teammate picks up on them first. More medical facts are available to my thinking process when a teammate prompts me to recall them.

As the host of a weekly radio show and a medical podcast, being on a team means we come up with more story ideas than any one of us would working alone. We're also able to take story ideas from a superficial treatment to something deeper and more satisfying.

I've gone from working alone to working on a team, and I don't want to go back to the way things were. I'm not alone.

Dr. Teodor Grantcharov, the surgeon who is spearheading the development of the OR Black Box, says teamwork makes him a better surgeon on days when he's not on top of his game. Michael Nolan, Renfrew County's paramedic chief and director of emergency services, says teamwork is bringing twenty-first-century healthcare to one of Canada's most austere and sparsely populated environments. In the aftermath of the worst mass casualty shooting in US history, Dr. Kevin Menes created a team on the fly that saved dozens of patients brought to Sunrise Hospital & Medical Center, in Las Vegas.

And the teamwork we're learning inside the hospital is also being taught to people who work on the outside. Friday Night at the ER, a game developed to teach hospital managers to cooperate has been played at Fortune 500 companies and by the CIA. Dr. Daniela Lamas, a physician who learned all about teamwork in the ICU at Brigham and Women's Hospital in Boston, brought that experience to the writers' room on a TV show in Hollywood.

Jennifer Brandel, a journalist and the CEO of Hearken, is taking the lessons given to medical students and applying them to news organizations.

Wherever you work, more teamwork means better results with greater efficiency. It means a better safety record and a higher profit margin. For the people you work with, it means higher morale and less burnout and attrition. It also means getting more juice and joy out of shared goals and responsibilities.

This book has detailed the steps you can take right now that can set the stage for greater teamwork. If you're a leader, make like Alexa Miller, who teaches Visual Thinking Strategies, and ask the three questions she asks first-year medical students when she takes them to the museum.

When you ask members of the team "What's going on in this picture?" you're encouraging them to speak up when they see something wrong or something else that needs to be stated. When you ask them "What makes you say that?" you're engaging their critical thinking skills by getting them to provide evidence for what they see. Asking the third question—"What more can we find?"—encourages them to look deeper for observations and opinions. Asking all three gives leaders access to the collective wisdom of the team.

A strong leader listens to everyone on the team and recognizes the talents of each individual, not just the high achievers. A strong leader helps create a shared goal and makes certain everyone on the team feels that they contributed to its achievement.

That is true whether the team is trying to win a championship or improve on last season's record. It's true whether you're putting on a theatrical production or performing transplant surgery.

Also true is the fact that you get members of a group to act more like a team on serious matters by first getting them to play together—whether by playing actual games or even playing music. Drumming, for example, teaches you to operate in rhythm with other members of the team. It also teaches you that it's okay to make a fool of yourself.

Improv teaches you to use "Yes, and" dialogue as a way of building on instead of blocking the ideas of teammates. It also teaches people that one of the secrets to teamwork is making those working alongside you look good.

Leaders embrace teamwork by gathering and listening to voices from outside the circle of a closed system. Hospitals such as Cleveland Clinic are learning lessons from ex–Navy SEALs like Brian Ferguson and former car mechanics like Carl Allamby. Journalists like Jennifer Brandel learn from artists like Alexa Miller.

Once slow to embrace teamwork, healthcare is starting to change. Hospital CEOs and managers are discovering that teamwork does not flourish in a leadership vacuum. Authority need not always go to the brightest and most honoured for their demonstrated expertise; it can also be given to those best able to foster teamwork. Domains with a rigid chain of command, like the military and law enforcement, need to find the sweet spot between maintaining command and control and encouraging initiative.

They can learn a thing or two from Dr. Trevor Jain, who organized a temporary mortuary in the wake of the Swissair 111 crash and helped identify the remains of all the victims. Jain's advice for teamwork is to trust each member, empower them to do their jobs, and back them to the hilt.

===

ELAINE BROMILEY, WHOM we met in the introduction, died on April 11, 2005, at the age of thirty-seven. If she were alive today, she'd be fifty-four. Her two children are now young adults. Martin Bromiley has moved on with his life. Today, he is happily remarried with a blended family.

"Elaine died and I can't change that," he says. "But what I can do is change the conditions for the future."

Bromiley does that, and he keeps Elaine's memory alive by telling her story to anesthesiologists and other healthcare providers both experienced and just starting out. As the man behind Clinical Human Factors Group, Bromiley has met with countless surgeons and physicians, nurses, researchers and hospital CEOs to advocate for a more systematic and diligent effort at patient safety.

In 2007, he appeared in *Just a Routine Operation*, a documentary film that re-enacts Elaine's story and teaches health professionals and students about the "can't intubate, can't ventilate" scenario. This film, which was produced by thinkpublic for the NHS Institute for Innovation and Improvement, has been watched by close to one million healthcare professionals and trainees.

Bromiley says he gets emails from doctors and from patients demonstrating that the film has saved lives.

And yet he has seen how hard it is to make the lessons stick. Bromiley says more copies than he can count of the film, the coroner's inquest verdict and the independent review by Professor Michael Harmer have been distributed to anesthesiologists. He says many doctors who hear Elaine's story say it would never happen to them. But when caught off guard in a teaching simulation, many still fail to recognize the "can't intubate, can't ventilate" scenario.

"More importantly, they've never been in that situation themselves for real," he says. "So the role of simulation is very beneficial in that it gets you to see yourself."

Bromiley is still a commercial airline pilot. What he wants is for doctors and other health professionals to do regular training on rare emergencies in an OR simulator, just as he does in the cockpit simulator.

"I've been flying the aircraft I fly for twenty-two years," he says. "I'm a training captain. I teach people this stuff. And yet I get the same training exercises given to me and I still make mistakes and I still see stuff I've not come across before. It's a very valuable way to understand how you react. You suddenly become so much more humble and you realize the benefit of the people around you."

What drives Bromiley to keep going is the realization that he or any member of his family may end up in hospital one day.

"I want to be able to say to the kids that their mom died but this is less likely to happen to a lot of other people as a result," he says.

He gains hope from talking with his stepdaughter, who is training to be a nurse. She speaks with him about what she sees first-hand.

"There's a lot of stuff that happens these days that is so much better than it was before. Now, that might be nothing to do with me, but it does feel like healthcare has moved a long way, although we know there's still problems. So that's what drives me. You can't change the past. But you can change the future."

= = =

IN MY PROFESSIONAL past, I was a solo act. I was that physician who didn't know how to ask for help and didn't take kindly to appearing as if I needed it, to the detriment of my own well-being and perhaps that of my patients.

A recent story tells you exactly where I am on the journey to becoming an advocate for teamwork.

I was on duty in the ER when an older man came in with shortness of breath and an irregular heartbeat. His lungs sounded wet, indicating heart failure. His kidneys were also failing, which caused an elevated level of potassium, which if high enough can literally stop the heart.

I ordered medications to stabilize his heartbeat and reduce his potassium level to a less dangerous level. And I started seeing other patients.

Suddenly, I heard a "stat" page to my patient's room. His blood pressure had dipped to a dangerously low level, and his heart was close to stopping. He was having what looked like epileptic seizures. My patient needed to be sedated with an anesthetic drug, intubated and placed on a ventilator. He needed invasive blood pressure monitoring and a central line to administer powerful intravenous drugs.

I ran to my patient's room, but I was beaten there by a much younger and in many ways wiser colleague, who had taken charge. This happened during COVID-19, which meant we had to assume my patient was infected with the coronavirus and intubate him in full personal protective equipment.

A large team of ER attending physicians, resident doctors, students, nurses and respiratory therapists had gathered just outside my patient's cubicle. Some were donning PPE and others were watching them carefully to make sure they did so safely. We had done lots of drills and simulations, and the team knew what to do.

By the time I got to the bedside in full PPE, my young colleague had assumed the role of leader, the thing that was missing in the OR when Elaine Bromiley could not be intubated and ventilated.

As soon as I arrived, my colleague's instinct was to have me take over. At another time, I would have, regardless of what I could see with my own two eyes. But instead of thinking about myself, I found myself thinking about the team. I saw a young yet astute leader who was communicating the plan to a room full of competent professionals and learners—some with vast experience and some just starting out.

And I knew exactly what to do.

"Why don't you lead the team, and I'll whisper my suggestions into your ear," I told her.

My colleague agreed. She told the team of our decision and carried on. A colleague of ours watched over a resident who intubated the patient. Since I knew the immediate history of my patient's potassium level, I narrowed my efforts to dealing with just that, and kept our leader informed.

Everyone on the team did their jobs superbly. We got the patient intubated, stabilized and into the ICU in record time. Everyone felt a shared sense of accomplishment.

During a quiet moment following the resuscitation, my colleague apologized for appearing to take over without asking me. I told her I could see she had things under control and that it would have been detrimental to the team to have changed leaders.

Instead of feeling embarrassed by the idea that I'd somehow failed as a leader, I felt relieved that I had such a great colleague to back me up. I felt energized that I had the situational awareness to size things up as they happened, and to decide to be a good follower. I felt elated to practise emergency medicine as part of a team.

Animals form teams by instinct. For humans, it's a choice. Inside and outside of healthcare, I think it's the best choice. It's only when you put it into practice that you'll realize just how much teamwork can be your superpower.

ACKNOWLEDGEMENTS

COVID-19 CHANGED SO much in all of our lives, mine included. The lockdowns during the first wave of the pandemic meant I did most of my broadcasting duties from home. I normally give a fair number of out-of-town speeches, but all of them were cancelled. As a result, I had much more free time than usual on my hands. That's when I started thinking about a topic for my next non-fiction book.

I did not set out to write *The Power of Teamwork*. I want to thank Brad Wilson, my editor at HarperCollins Canada, whose back-of-the-envelope idea formed the basis for the book. One of the great challenges for authors of non-fiction books is finding an intriguing topic for one's next effort. He mentioned *The Checklist Manifesto*, a book in which author and surgeon Dr. Atul Gawande argues that checklists in the OR could reduce human error in surgery just as they did in aviation and other high-risk industries. Reading between the lines of that bestseller, Brad saw teamwork as the great enabler of checklists.

317

He had one more thought: Checklists are just one of many safety ideas aviation has taught to medicine. He wondered whether healthcare has returned the favour and taught its lessons to aviation.

I had doubts that doctors had done much of anything to influence the culture of aviation or any other field outside of medicine. But then I met a cardiothoracic surgeon who put down his scalpel to become a commercial pilot.

I have my agent, Rick Broadhead, to thank for a solid piece of sleuthing that immediately supported Wilson's idea and got me excited. Rick sent me a newspaper clipping about a tabletop game named Friday Night at the ER, and how successful companies far outside of healthcare were using it to build teamwork.

The concept for the book really came into sharp focus when I met Alexa Miller at the 2019 dotMD conference in Galway, Ireland. She was the first "outsider" to medicine that I interviewed for this book. Her writings and her wise musings on the critical importance of team diagnosis told me that the book might have a message that medicine needs to hear if it wants to get better and safer for patients and health professionals.

Teamwork is good for medicine, and it's essential for writing books. I was determined to turn *The Power of Teamwork* into an exercise in team building, and I was not disappointed. Erin James-Abra, a talented writer and the nature and geography subject editor at *The Canadian Encyclopedia*, was one of the key researchers and story gatherers on my previous two books. With a preschool son named Jacoby plus a full-time job, she wasn't available to put in those demanding hours. However, I'm grateful that she had time to assemble a vast database of articles and book titles that got the process going.

I am eternally grateful to two incredibly hard-working women for helping develop the narrative arc of the book and for developing the content of many of its best chapters. Erin Byrnes is a producer and journalist whose articles have been published in Agence

France-Presse, Al Jazeera America, the *Eastern Door*, the *Globe and Mail*, the *National Post*, *New Internationalist*, *The Economist* and many more. Erin did most of the interviewing for the chapter on games and simulations. Through Erin, we got to meet TV writer and critical care specialist Dr. Daniela Lamas and Lindsay Somers, a paramedic and Canada's first intimacy coordinator.

Emily Mathieu is a former reporter for the *Toronto Star*, where she covered affordable and precarious housing; she was also a member of the investigations team, where she reported on mortgage fraud, the absence of standard sexual violence policies at colleges and universities, and lax standards within Toronto's taxi industry. Lately, she has been the fact checker on many of CBC's most edgy podcasts.

Emily interviewed Dorita Sondereker, one of the most memorable healthcare people who worked at Sunrise Hospital to help patients who were critically injured during the Las Vegas shooting. She did countless other interviews too, including car-mechanic-turned-physician Dr. Carl Allamby and ER physician and video director Dr. Max Montalvo.

Emily and Erin were my core teammates as the book began to take shape. They reviewed each chapter critically for style and for potential cuts. Without them, I would not have been able to get the word length to a manageable level.

Emily also helped me work through a unique problem in journalist ethics. Her fact-checking was greatly appreciated.

Brad Wilson was an essential sounding board on that issue and countless others. I appreciated his support for the book and his ability to help me cut through the noise and solve the inevitable problems that crop up. His empathy for readers provides an underpinning of advice that is essential to successful trade books.

I want to thank Linda Pruessen both for her steadfast copyediting and for her very helpful ideas on chapter subheadings.

Noelle Zitzer did a wonderful job shepherding the book through the production process.

I want to thank my colleagues at *White Coat, Black Art* for offering support and encouragement while I was working on the book.

I am most grateful to the many experts who shared their wisdom on teamwork. I want to thank Dr. Ronan Kavanagh, a clinical rheumatologist and director of the dotMD conference, for putting me in touch with Alexa Miller, who is one of the lynchpins of the book. She explained rather patiently the method of VTS and the purpose behind it. She went above and beyond the call of duty by sharing a large bibliography of supportive papers and by introducing me to countless experts, many of whom appear in this book. Other experts I wish to single out for their help and support include Dr. Niall Downey, Dr. Teodor Grantcharov and Chief Michael Nolan.

I could not have written this book without the support of my family. Early on during the pandemic, my partner, Tamara, and I started taking evening walks in the neighbourhood. Almost every walk was filled with discussions about the latest interview for the book. Tamara's enthusiastic interest helped sustain me through the long process of research and writing. Our children, Kaille and Alex, loved learning the lessons about teamwork I shared with them.

They gave me time and space to write this book. That it happened during a pandemic and during a major family crisis was proof that when it comes to writing a book about teamwork, it takes a team to sustain you.

Finally, I want to thank Martin Bromiley for sharing painful memories of what happened to his wife, Elaine. Her tragic story serves as the frame of the book and offers a lesson all of us can and should learn about the lifesaving value of teamwork.

INDEX